# THE
# GREAT
# PRETENDERS

# THE

# GREAT

# PRETENDERS

*The True Stories behind Famous*

*Historical Mysteries*

JAN BONDESON

W. W. NORTON & COMPANY

NEW YORK | LONDON

For information about permission to reproduce selections from
this book, write to Permissions, W. W. Norton & Company, Inc.,
500 Fifth Avenue, New York, NY 10110

Manufacturing by The Haddon Craftsmen, Inc.
Book design by Jo Anne Metsch
Production manager: Amanda Morrison

Library of Congress Cataloging-in-Publication Data

Bondeson, Jan.
  The great pretenders : the true stories behind famous historical mysteries / Jan
Bondeson.— 1st ed.
       p. cm.
Includes bibliographical references.
  **ISBN 0-393-01969-1**
  1. History—Miscellanea. 2. Impostors and imposture. 3. History—Errors, inven-
tions, etc. 4. History—Historiography. I. Title.
  D10 .B58 2004
  001.9'5—dc22                                                      2003022813

W. W. Norton & Company, Inc.
500 Fifth Avenue, New York, N.Y. 10110
www.wwnorton.com

W. W. Norton & Company Ltd.
Castle House, 75/76 Wells Street, London W1T 3QT

1 2 3 4 5 6 7 8 9 0

# Contents

# Introduction

HISTORICAL MYSTERIES HAVE a perpetual fascination. We all like to read books presenting new theories about the identity of the Man in the Iron Mask, or of Jack the Ripper, in the hope of discovering some new fact or a worthwhile new hypothesis to prove or disprove. A characteristic of the most famous historical mysteries is that they present vast amounts of contradictory evidence, giving rise to a multitude of theories, but at the same time rendering it unlikely that a permanent, universally accepted solution will ever be found.

This book is devoted to the most durable kinds of nineteenth-century historical mysteries, namely questions of disputed identity. With time, some of these have taken on the status of national enigmas. Generations of French scholars have pondered the fate of the Lost Dauphin, the son of Louis XVI and Marie Antoinette. Imprisoned in the Temple tower in Paris by the revolutionaries, the little prince was reported to have died in 1795, after both his parents had been guillotined. But rumors said that a substitution of children had been made and that the dauphin had been saved by the royalists. There were later more than one hundred pretenders claiming to be the Lost Dauphin. The corresponding German national mystery is that of Kaspar Hauser, the Child of Europe. This sixteen-year-old boy appeared in Nuremberg in 1828 after spending his entire youth in a subterranean dungeon. Since such extreme measures had been taken to hide Kaspar away from the rest of humanity, it was speculated that he must be someone very important. Immense effort has been put into researching every aspect of Kaspar's short and tragic life, and the majority of twentieth-century scholars have agreed he was the prince of Baden, kidnapped from his cot in 1812 by an unscrupulous noblewoman. Immortalized by the novel of Jakob Wassermann and the brilliant film by Werner Herzog, the figure of Kaspar Hauser has taken on a life of its own in modern culture.

Other countries also have their national enigmas. In Russia, historians pondered whether Tsar Alexander I, the conqueror of Napoleon, lived on for several decades as a pious hermit in Siberia after faking his death in 1825. In Britain, there have been persistent rumors that King George III had married in secret and that his later marriage to Queen Charlotte was bigamous and the entire royal family bastards with no right to the throne. Indeed, George III's children from this alleged first marriage, and their descendants, would be the rightful heirs to the crown. There was also much debate about the Tichborne mystery: a wealthy young baronet was lost at sea in 1855, but twelve years later a man claiming to be he turned up in Australia. Although a commoner in every sense of the word, and more than twice as heavy as the lost Sir Roger Tichborne, the claimant kept the courts busy for years. His many adherents were certain he was the real Sir Roger, but he was finally imprisoned as an impostor and perjurer. And what about the Great Druce-Portland mystery: did one of the wealthiest dukes in Britain lead a double life as the keeper of a furniture shop in London? Throughout the nineteenth and twentieth centuries, scholars and enthusiasts have tirelessly tried to solve these mysteries. Archives have been trawled, old letters deciphered, and yellowed newspapers read in the hope that somewhere a vital clue would be found that would solve one of these riddles.

This book will re-assess some of these famous historical mysteries. Using both historical and medical arguments, including findings from modern DNA technology, I will attempt to expose the hard facts about these extraordinary historical legends after the accumulation of 150 or 200 years' worth of romantic fantasy, and to analyze the mysteries that often remain. And what factors have helped some of these mysteries of disputed identity to develop into national enigmas, over which duels have been fought, political parties founded, and thousands of books and articles written? Is it just the actions of clever and persistent impostors, or are deeper undercurrents of folklore and psychology at work? What is it about these tales of lost heirs, secret marriages, and immortal monarchs that has turned them into immortal mysteries that engage the minds of millions?

# THE
# GREAT
# PRETENDERS

# 1

---

## *The Lost Dauphin*

PRINCE LOUIS CHARLES, the second son of King Louis XVI of France and Queen Marie Antoinette, was born on March 27, 1785. When describing his early youth, sentimental historians have called him the happiest of little princes, and it is true that there did not appear to be much sadness in his life. He was a pretty, clever little boy with blue eyes and long blond curls, high-spirited and easily amused. His proud parents doted on him and often attended his lessons or watched him play. Louis Charles was particularly devoted to his mother and made a habit of bringing her flowers from a little garden he tended himself. In 1789, his elder brother Louis Joseph died of consumption, and Louis Charles became the dauphin, the heir to the throne. At about this time, Marie Antoinette described him in a letter: he was a strong, healthy lad, with a gay and lighthearted temperament. Unconscious of his own importance, he was more pleased to inherit his brother's dog than to become heir to the crown of France.

Later that year of 1789, the dauphin's life was to change forever.

Two engravings of the undoubted Louis Charles, the right-hand one
after a portrait by Kucharsky in 1792, the left-hand one
probably a composite from other portraits.

The Paris fishwives marched on Versailles, and the royal family was
taken back to Paris, surrounded by a howling mob. In the Tuileries,
the king and queen were little more than captives, valuable pawns
for the revolutionaries to have in hand. In June 1791, the brave
Swedish nobleman Axel von Fersen arranged for the royal family to
escape the increasingly hostile Parisian environment. They were
smuggled out of the Tuileries into a carriage, in the hope that they
would reach the headquarters of the royalist general marquis de
Bouillé. In the town of Varennes, close to the royalist troops, they
were arrested by the national guards. A stalwart royalist, the duke de
Choiseul, cleared the streets with a troop of forty hussars and
offered to escort the king to safety, but the vacillating Louis XVI
refused to be rescued, or even to save his children, on the grounds
that the blood of some of his subjects might be shed. This was a
decision he would bitterly regret. The outcome of the flight to
Varennes was that the royal family was forced back into their
carriage and escorted back to Paris, a long and grueling journey,

surrounded by a furious mob. The angry sansculottes spat in the king's face, tore the queen's dress, and frightened the little dauphin out of his wits. As a result of this failed attempt to escape, the royal family was imprisoned in the Temple tower in Paris.[1]

The Temple tower in Paris.

## IN THE TEMPLE

THE TEMPLE HAD originally been the property of the Knights Templar, its great tower looming over the Parisian houses since the thirteenth century. It was a massive square building, about 150 feet high and with walls nine feet thick. The queen was imprisoned in a room on the third floor of the Temple tower, along with her daughter Marie Thérèse. The king's sister Madame Elizabeth was in the adjoining room. A third small chamber was shared by M. and Mme. Tison, an elderly couple employed as servants, but whose real duties were to spy on the royal prisoners. The king occupied a suite of rooms on the second floor, along with the servant Cléry. On the fourth floor was a gallery where the prisoners were permitted to walk to get fresh air; a partition separated the area allowed to the king from that allotted to his female relatives. The dauphin slept in the king's room on the second floor. There is a story that once, when a workman was reinforcing one of the doors, the king demonstrated the tools to the dauphin, showing him how to use them. The workman commented that when the king was released, he could say that he had helped build his own prison. The king sighed deeply, questioning how much longer he would be incarcerated by his own people. The dauphin, who understood what was happening to his parents, was distraught.

The queen resented the way her family had been treated, and hoped the Austrian and Prussian armies that had invaded revolutionary France would come to their rescue. On September 2, it became known in Paris that Verdun had fallen and that the invaders were marching for Paris. The result was widespread rioting. The queen's lady-in-waiting, Princess de Lamballe, was seized in the Paris streets and butchered by the mob; her entrails were fed to dogs, and the frenzied sansculottes cut out her heart, cooked it, and ate it. They then mounted her head on a pike, took it to a barber's shop to have the hair dressed, and marched to the Temple to show it to Marie Antoinette.

The revolutionaries were well aware that there might be attempts to save the royal family, and they kept improving the security. Bolted

and padlocked double doors prevented access to the spiral stairc
in one of the turrets, and the outer door of the Temple tower was kept
bolted and guarded by two sentinels. A high wall was built around the
tower, and guarded day and night. Outside this wall was the Temple
garrison of at least two hundred soldiers, some of whom were guarding the sole exit leading to the Rue de Temple. At night, guards slept
in the antechambers of the king and queen. The ground floor of the
great tower was an assembly room for the revolutionaries who administered the Temple; thus, if there were sounds of a fight, reinforce-
ments would be readily available. A successful plan for the escape of
any member of the royal family would need to involve well-organized
outside help. Several royalists in Paris conspired to save the king, foremost among them being the adventurer Baron de Batz, who kept
thinking up dashing schemes à la the Scarlet Pimpernel, although
with less skill and determination in executing them. The king and
queen also had a firm friend in England: Charlotte Atkyns, a former
actress who spent much money on harebrained plots concocted by a
gang of French villains who pretended to be royalists, but who were
in reality just swindling her out of her money.[2]

The king and queen still hoped that the Austrian and Prussian troops
would save them, but the French armies prevailed in several battles. In
September 1792, France was declared a republic; the jailers told the
prisoners in the Temple that they were now just the citizen Capet and
his wife. The next step was to put the king on trial for treason. As he
was taken off to the National Convention in December 1792, the
dauphin was given over to his mother and moved up to her chamber
on the third floor of the Temple tower. On January 20, 1793, the
dauphin saw his father for the last time. The king, outwardly calm and
collected, made him promise that he would never try to avenge his
father's death. The following morning, the king was taken away for execution. Later the same day, Marie Antoinette told Louis Charles that
his father was dead and that he was now King Louis XVII of France.

As a result of the execution of the king, several countries, Britain
and Russia among them, joined the ranks of the enemies of revolu-

Louis XVI is torn from his family and taken to the guillotine.
This dramatic scene was a popular theme for popular prints
after the Restoration of the Bourbon monarchy.

tionary France. In addition, one of the leading French military commanders, General Dumouriez, changed sides and became a royalist.
In the Vendée region, there was a full-scale royalist uprising. But the
revolutionary leaders fought back hard on all fronts. In April 1793, the
Committee of Public Safety was set up, with far-reaching powers in
raising new armies and fighting France's internal and external enemies. Moderate elements were gradually removed from the circles of
power and extremists promoted to take their places. Jacques René
Hébert, editor of the populist newspaper *Le Père Duchesne*, was the
worst of the lot; he openly advocated that the widow Capet and her
foul progeny be exterminated once and for all. Anaxagoras
Chaumette, procurator of the Paris Commune, fully shared his opinion that France should be cleansed of the royals. Infighting was fierce

between the different phalanges of revolutionaries, for this was the time of the Terror, when thousands of people were guillotined. The Commune, forever on the lookout for attempts to save the royals from the Temple, redoubled its precautions: there was a system with trusted officers, the so-called commissaries of the Temple, who were on duty in shifts to take responsibility for the prisoners. They inspected the premises each day, making sure the royal captives were safely locked up and strictly guarded.

In early May 1793, Louis Charles complained of a headache, an intermittent fever, and a stitch in his side that prevented him from laughing. The queen's entreaties that he should be seen by a doctor were ignored for several days, but finally the prison doctor Thierry was called in. Although the treatment prescribed was largely placebo by the standards of modern medicine, Louis Charles recovered completely within a few weeks. The following month, he had an accident at play when straddling a stick he was pretending to ride. With difficulty, the queen again managed to obtain medical attention for her son. The hernia specialist Dr. Pipelet prescribed a bandage that soon cured him. Louis Charles then developed an abdominal complaint, and Dr. Thierry suspected worms. Anti-verminous enemas were resorted to, with considerable success: the patient passed a prodigious quantity of worms and again appeared to be cured. The doctors came back to see him once or twice, but did not prescribe any medicine, and there is no record that Louis Charles complained of feeling ill.

## THE JAILER SIMON AND HIS PUPIL

ON THE NIGHT of July 3, 1793, a troop of six guards burst into the queen's room and tore Louis Charles away from his mother. He was moved down into Louis XVI's old room on the second floor, where he was received by his new tutor, the cobbler Antoine Simon. After half a lifetime of obscurity, this individual had become known to the ruling terrorists as a loyal republican. The plan of Chaumette and Hébert was to separate Louis Charles from his family and to make him lose all ideas of privilege. Simon could not offer his pupil much in the way of regular education, being himself completely illiterate. Instead, he did his best to transform little Capet, as he was called, into a proper little sansculotte: through imitating his tutor, Louis Charles was taught to swear like a trooper, to sing revolutionary songs, and to acquire the manners of a Paris guttersnipe. Simon and his friends were overjoyed when he referred to his mother and aunt as "those damned whores." Marie Thérèse later wrote that one of her prevailing memories from this time was to hear her brother singing, accompanied by Simon, "the songs of La Carmagnole, the Marseillaise, and a thousand other horrible compositions of the same kind."[3]

Royalist historians have made Simon into a monster who tortured Louis Charles. He was certainly a stupid, uneducated boor, who liked to bully his pupil and have him wait on him at table. From time to time, he beat the boy when he had been naughty or when Simon himself wanted an outlet for his aggressions. But there is good evidence that with time Simon and his wife actually grew fond of the royal child left in their care. To help him forget his mother, he was given a large dog named Castor, a birdcage with canaries, and a pigeon coop. He had a billiards table, and Simon also liked to play checkers with him. Simon lessened the harshness of the regime, and there was a constant stream of visitors. Little Capet was given a good deal of freedom, even being allowed to play with the daughter of the Temple washerwoman in the garden outside the tower. He was well fed and decently clothed and bathed. The aim was thus clearly to convert him into a willing tool for the authorities, and not to kill or harm him.

Part of the scheme of Chaumette and Hébert was to turn Louis Charles against his mother. When Simon reported that he had more than once seen his pupil "indulging in a boyhood pastime detrimental to his health and morals," Hébert hatched a diabolical plot. He made Louis Charles confess that it was in fact his mother who had taught him to masturbate, and that when he had shared her bed, they repeatedly committed incest. Hébert also questioned the nature of the swelling of the

The little prince is beaten by his brutal jailer Simon. A plate from
M. Mühlbach, *Marie Antoinette and Her Son* (New York, 1867).

boy's testicle some months earlier: was this not a result of venereal disease, transmitted to him by his own mother? They tried to persuade Dr.
Pipelet to agree to this, but the doctor indignantly refused. Instead, they
forced Louis Charles to sign a certificate accusing his mother and aunt
of incest. It is curious that his signature at the bottom of this heinous
document is large and scrawled, very unlike the tidy writing in his school-
books, probably because he had been drugged, or made drunk, before
being coerced to sign it. This certificate was added to the list of accusations against the queen when she was put on trial for treason. When his
sister and aunt were confronted with these scandalous lies, little Capet
was rude and insinuating, particularly toward Madame Elizabeth, whom
he accused of having shown him how to masturbate. His sister Marie
Thérèse, a girl of fifteen, was tormented for three hours; while she was
subjected to the most vile insinuations, her brother was as merry as ever,

swinging his legs and frequently mixing in the conversation to contradict her. When the queen was confronted with her son's accusations, she replied that nature could only recoil from such incredible fabrications. On October 16, 1793, Marie Antoinette was guillotined; the same day, her eight-year-old son was laughing heartily with Simon and his cronies, playing billiards, and drinking wine. He was never told about the death of his mother.

For several months to come, Louis Charles lived on with Simon and his wife in the Temple tower. The cobbler had been praised by Chaumette and Hébert for his part in turning the boy against his mother, and he probably thought he might expect further fame and fortune if he could persuade his pupil to level additional accusations against Madame Elizabeth. Accordingly, little Capet divulged that she had a system of delivering secret messages, and that he suspected her of minting false coins in her prison. This time, there was much less interest in his stories, and Simon became aware that things were changing. In early January 1794, he was suddenly sacked from his post. He had to move out of the tower with great haste, although being allowed to live in lodgings within the Temple for two weeks; the important thing was apparently to get him away from his pupil. Simon later told his friends that little Capet had been sad to see him go, since he had been looking forward to becoming Simon's apprentice and learning to make shoes. In spite of himself, the boorish cobbler was also sad to see his pupil for the last time; he even told two of the guards that he would have liked to adopt the boy, if this had been allowed. His last official act was performed on January 19, when he delivered the keys of the prison rooms to four commissaries, who signed a certificate stating that he handed over the prisoner Capet in good health.

## · IMMURED ALIVE

WE NOW REACH the most enigmatic part of the mystery of the Lost Dauphin. During his stay with Simon, Louis Charles had been seen by many people: friends and drinking companions of Simon, guards and commissioners who made their rounds, and people who wanted to view him as a curiosity. But by mid-January all this was to change. One of the rooms on the second floor, probably the one formerly used as the king's dining room, was made into a dungeon with a grille and a hatch on its stout, double-padlocked door to allow the guards to deliver food to the prisoner without undoing the locks. The window was covered and secured with iron bars, leaving the prisoner in almost constant darkness in the damp, inhospitable room. Up on the third floor, Marie-Thérèse felt convinced her brother had been taken away, since she could no longer hear him singing and shouting in the company of his mentor. In fact, after the hustle and bustle of Simon and his wife's moving out, the tower was as still as death.

For January 1794, and for several months afterward, there are no records regarding the child imprisoned in the Temple tower. One can only speculate what the lonely prisoner felt in his dismal dungeon. One of the guards later testified that the Temple Child (as I will call him from now on) was mostly lying in his bed, which was swarming with all kinds of vermin. A particularly chilling detail is that the room was also infested with rats, and that the boy used to leave some remains of his meals on the table so that he could get some sleep while the animals fought for the food. Every evening, the commissaries of the Temple came around, opened the grille, and screamed, "Capet, are you asleep? Child of a race of vipers, get up!" Sometimes, they could hear a feeble response, as if the prisoner were laboriously getting out of his bed and stumbling through the darkness; at other times, when they looked in through the grille, they could only just see the silhouette of the boy lying in his bed.

Late July 1794 brought further political upheavals. Robespierre's reign of terror was ended, and he was guillotined along with more than seventy of his adherents. Hébert, Chaumette, and Simon had already perished on the guillotine. General Paul Barras, one of the leading members of the National Convention, heard a rumor that little Capet and his sister had been rescued, and decided to investigate. At the

Temple, he was assured that the rumor was untrue and that the prison cells containing the tyrant's two children were well guarded, but he nevertheless wanted to see them. Once the dungeon was opened by the jailers, Barras noticed the vile smell emanating from the heaps of waste and excreta in the corners. The Temple Child was lying in a small cradle. He was awake and did not seem startled, although these must have been his first visitors for many months. Barras was curious why the boy preferred the cradle to his bed; the boy replied that he suffered less where he was now. When asked where he was hurting, he pointed to his head and knees. He was dressed in a waistcoat and a pair of gray pants that seemed much too small for him. Barras had them cut open only to see how swollen and livid the wretched child's knees were. The skin was scabious and unwholesome looking, and the child's entire body was crawling with vermin. When pulled out of the cradle, the Temple Child was unable to stand up.

The general ordered that the room be cleaned and the sick boy given medical attention. Appalled by the state of the dungeon, he instructed that the boy be allowed to get some fresh air and permitted to meet with his sister.[4] Barras nominated a certain Christophe Laurent to act as the guardian of the two royal children, but neither this man nor the guards and commissaries of the Temple complied with the general's orders for the Temple Child to receive medical attention and be reunited with Marie Thérèse. Laurent and his assistant Gomin at least had the decency to see to it that the prisoner was bathed and his hair cut. His vermin-infested clothes were disposed of, and the room was thoroughly cleaned.

Again several months went by, until in December three members of the Committee of General Security inspected the Temple tower; one of them, Jean Baptiste Harmand, left important notes of his observations. As they went into the room of the Temple Child, they observed him to be clean and well dressed. Harmand asked him a number of questions, but the child did not reply. Harmand then offered the silent prisoner games, cakes, a dog, and a companion his own age, in the vain hope of getting him to utter a single word. This has led to speculations that he was a deaf-mute substitute, although it is notable that the Temple Child was actually able to follow Harmand's instructions to stand, an indication that there was nothing wrong with his hearing. Harmand's description of the child tallies well with that of Barras: he was feeble, chronically ill, and had large swellings on the knees and on one wrist. There was a discrepancy between the child's long, thin extremities and his narrow thorax and hunched shoulders.[5]

Then follows yet another lengthy hiatus, where we have very little accurate information about the Temple Child. One of the commissaries of the Temple was allowed to enter the dungeon in early 1795, on the express condition that he not try to speak to the prisoner. The bedridden invalid could barely rise to a sitting position, his articulation was but a breath, and his face was covered with ulcers and scabs. The commissary found him the most piteous specimen of humanity he had ever seen.[6] In early May 1795, the two jailers Gomin and Lasne (Laurent had left in March of the same year) informed the Committee of General Security that the child Capet was now dangerously ill. The committee consented to call in a doctor, given that the child was not to be examined without the jailers' presence. The distinguished surgeon Pierre Joseph Desault went to see the Temple Child. He realized that the boy was dying, but did his best to alleviate his sufferings, prescribing infusions of hops and a massage of the swollen, livid joints with alkali. He returned to the Temple several times, touched by the gratitude of the feeble little prisoner, who once held him by the coat sleeve, saying, "Please do not leave me among these wicked men!" There are reports that Desault told his friends and family that he had seen a dying, idiot child; he did not specify whether he recognized the prisoner as the dauphin. His niece later testified that Desault had told his wife that he had immediately grasped that the Temple Child was not the little prince he had several times seen before the royal family was imprisoned. But Desault was afraid of the reaction of the revolutionaries—rightly so, according to some, since he himself died on June 1. His family and some of his colleagues and pupils were convinced that he had been poisoned, but there was at the time a cholera epidemic at the hospital where he worked, and two junior doctors also succumbed.[7] There is no trace of any report made by Desault to the Committee of General Security; if there once was one, which is likely, it has been destroyed.

## DEATH AND BURIAL OF THE TEMPLE CHILD

AFTER THE DEATH of Dr. Desault, the Temple Child was without medical attention for about a week, before Dr. Philippe Jean Pelletan was appointed in his place. Pelletan was the surgeon in chief at the Hôpital d'Humanité and a lecturer on anatomy at the medical school. According to one source, he was an active revolutionary, who acted as a spy when seeing patients in various prisons.[8] Pelletan first saw the Temple Child on June 6. The prison room was now clean and tidy, and the child decently clothed, with Gomin and Lasne in attendance. Pelletan found that the prisoner's abdomen was swollen and that he suffered from a chronic diarrhea. The child was frightened by the great noise made when the prison door was bolted and locked, and Pelletan recommended that this be stopped in the name of humanity; the bedridden, enfeebled child was certainly not going to escape. He prescribed tonics, white bread, and nourishing food. It was clear to Pelletan that the child was the victim of a wasting internal disease of long duration. A surgeon himself, he asked for the help of the physician Dumangin. A few days later, on June 8, the child fainted, and the two doctors realized that he would not live long. His pulse was weak and the diarrhea incessant. They prescribed broth, medicinal enemas, and an analgesic preparation, and wrote an urgent message to the committee that Capet's son was seriously ill and needed a nurse to attend him.[9] But before any further action could be taken, the condition of the child deteriorated further, and he died in Lasne's arms at 3 P.M. that same day.

Gomin and Lasne had clearly received instructions to keep the death of the Temple Child a secret, since their first action was to seize the turnkey Gourlet, who had inadvertently seen the dead body and who could apparently not be trusted to keep this to himself, and to shut him up in one of the cells. Gomin himself carried a letter to the committee, announcing the death and asking for instructions, and Lasne kept ordering medicines and broth to be delivered to the outer door of the prisoner's cell, to give the impression that the child was still alive. When Pelletan arrived at 4:30 P.M. to see the dead body, Lasne told him that in order to maintain absolute secrecy, the doctor himself was now a prisoner. Pelletan meekly obliged, since he had earlier been solemnly warned not to divulge anything about what he might see and hear in the Temple. Later Gomin returned, saying that he had received orders that the next day two other doctors be found to dissect the body of little Capet and ascertain the cause of death. Pelletan was released, after once more being sworn to absolute secrecy. In the meantime, the two jailers continued to deceive the Temple staff by having medicines and meals delivered at the doors of the prison room, as if the child were still alive.

The following day, at 11:30 A.M., Pelletan and Dumangin returned for the autopsy, along with their colleagues Lassus and Jeanroy. Gomin and Lasne were asked whether the corpse was that of the child of Louis Capet, and they replied in the affirmative. The doctors then set about their handiwork. The body was beginning to putrefy, and the windows were opened to get rid of some of the stench. As an anatomist, Pelletan was used to performing dissections, and he did most of the work, the other three doctors standing by the window to escape the noxious fumes. When their attention was elsewhere, Pelletan took the opportunity to steal the child's heart, which he wrapped in his handkerchief and put in his pocket. The child's head had been shaved, and the turnkey Damont was allowed to collect some of the locks of hair as souvenirs.

The corpse of the Temple Child was deformed and emaciated, and the face pinched and pallid. The belly was hugely distended by the gas-filled intestinal tract. The autopsy report tells that there were two skin tumors, one on the inner side of the right knee, the other on the left wrist; both were filled with a thick, foul-smelling fluid. However, the description of these "tumors" makes it evident that they were nothing of the sort; rather, they were synovial cysts, resulting from the chronic infection of the joints in question. The synovial cyst of the knee contained nearly two ounces of a grayish, purulent matter. The intestines, swollen with gas and adherent, were covered with a great quantity of tubercles; similar tubercles were observed on the stomach, mesenterium, and diaphragm. Otherwise, the inner organs appeared healthy. The lungs adhered to the pleural sac throughout their surface. Pelletan was surprised that he did not find any tubercles in the lung tissue itself, although there were some about the trachea and esophagus. Pelletan's diagnosis was that the child had suffered from "a scrofulous tendency, which had long been in existence." This would imply, in present-day medical terminology, generalized tuberculosis, and Pelletan's diagnosis was no doubt correct. There had clearly been a tuberculous pleuritis, which explains the adherence of the lungs to the pleural lining, and an advanced intestinal tuberculosis with peritonitis, causing the child's death.[10]

Pelletan then put back the entrails, roughly stitched up the cadaver, and pulled the skin flaps over the sawed skull. A large bandage was put around the corpse's head, over the shaven pate, to hold them in place. The officers on duty, and several soldiers and turnkeys, were allowed to see the mangled body late in the evening; they signed the official declaration of death to signify that they had recognized the corpse as that of the son of Capet.[11] The day after, on June 10, the body of the Temple Child was put in a coffin hastily purchased by a man named Voisin, who was in charge of the funeral. In the evening, the coffin was nailed up outside the prison, lifted onto a stretcher, and carried off to the Sainte-Marguerite cemetery. The official account says that it was dumped into the common grave for the poor, which was little more than an open trench. Some earth was shoveled onto it, without either ritual or prayer. A sentry was posted at the grave, another at the gate of the cemetery. In spite of these precautions, there emerged some odd stories indicating that the coffin did not long remain undisturbed. A gardener named Charpentier later testified that on June 13 he was part of a working party sent to dig a grave at another Paris graveyard, the Clamart cemetery. A carriage appeared with a coffin in it, as well as three members of the local revolutionary committee. The coffin was buried, and the workmen were ordered to take care that no trace of the grave remained. One of the revolutionaries gave a coarse laugh and said, "Little Capet will have a long journey to make to rejoin his family!" Another story was told by the gravedigger at the Sainte-Marguerite cemetery, a man named Bertrancourt. He said that he had sneaked out later, dug up Louis XVII's coffin from the common pit, and reburied it near the church wall. Other witnesses, including Voisin and Lasne, claimed that the coffin had never been put in the common pit at all, but in a special, unmarked grave.[12]

## FALSE DAUPHINS

IN 1796, a mysterious teenage boy was tramping around the French countryside. He told various people that he was of high birth, the son of a prince or duke, and he certainly did not look like any ordinary vagabond. Very attractive, with fair hair and blue eyes just like the dauphin's, he had fine manners and a winning charm. Ladies of all ages swooned for him. At the town of Châlons, he was imprisoned as a vagabond. When asked to give his name, he said he was the son of the late Marquis de Longueville. At this time, there was much speculation in the French countryside that Louis XVII had been rescued; it did not take long for inquisitive people to wonder whether this mysterious boy might actually be the martyr king of the Temple. With winning modesty, he admitted that this was indeed the case. He soon had a large following, and people traveled long distances to see him hold court in his prison cell. The warders acted as his servants, wealthy supporters gave or lent him money, and his lady friends showered him with expensive presents. The young scoundrel basked in the glory of all this admiration and played the part of Louis XVII with considerable talent. There is a story that he was once visited by a former guard from the Temple. The pretender loudly announced, "Here is a gentleman who knows me, and who will say so if he has the courage!" The man hesitated, but the pretender reminded him of an incident when his shuttlecock had gotten caught in a bell rope, and the former guard bowed low, saying that he was indeed in the presence of the son of the unfortunate king.

Disaster struck in early 1799, when René Hervagault, a tailor from Saint-Lô in Normandy, announced that the pretender was none other than his son Jean Marie, who had run away from home some years earlier. The pretender admitted this and was eventually sent off to Normandy to rejoin his family. He was soon up to his old tricks, however, and was sentenced to two years in prison for swindling. While behind bars, he read a popular novel by the author Regnault-Warin, entitled *Le cimetière de la Madeleine*, a fictional account of the escape of Louis XVII from the Temple, which would literally become a handbook for prospective false dauphins. Returning to his old hunting grounds, young Hervagault was received by his supporters with open arms. Helped by Regnault-Warin's novel, he told them a spicy story about how he had been smuggled out of the Temple in a wicker basket. The king of England advised him to go to Rome to visit the pope. Not content with merely crowning him king of France, Pius VI had also branded him on the leg with a red-hot iron. If anyone showed signs of doubting this yarn, Hervagault would pull up his trouser leg, to reveal the imprint of the shield and lilies of France! But although his band of supporters included several noblemen and one former bishop, Hervagault was soon in trouble again, since the authorities had had enough of his activities. One account tells that the wily police minister Joseph Fouché suggested to Napoleon Bonaparte that he recognize young Hervagault as Louis XVII. The pretender should then be captured and forced to acknowledge Napoleon as his true successor, after which he would become disposable. Napoleon did not follow this plan, however, and Hervagault was imprisoned in the notorious

Bicêtre prison in Paris. After further escapades, he served a second term in this prison, finally dying there in 1812. On his deathbed, he swore an oath on the Bible, in front of the attending priest, that he was really the dauphin.[13]

The second pretender of importance arrived at the seaport of Saint-Malo in 1815. He was an ugly, scruffy-looking fellow, his face was disfigured by scars, and he had lost many teeth. When arrested for drunkenness and vagrancy, he first said he was a New Orleans baker named Charles de Navarre, then blurted out that he was really "Daufin-Bourbon!" and demanded to be taken to the Tuileries in Paris. Although the man looked rather like a dirty, drunken tramp, the magistrates decided to keep him in prison pending the investigation of his claim. Charles de Navarre received visitors in the prison and soon became a local celebrity. Amazingly, given that he was such an unprepossessing character, his court of followers grew steadily. They reasoned that the dauphin's forced education with the loathsome Simon might well have degraded his intellect and sentiments; his prolonged residence among beggars and criminals in the United States could have done the rest. Charles de Navarre's adherents were badgering the duchess of Angoulême to make her acknowledge the pretender as her brother. The duchess, apparently not convinced that Louis XVII was really dead, sent two noblemen to meet him and even prepared a set of questions for him to answer. When Charles de Navarre was finally on trial for swindling in 1818, there was some debate about his true identity. Was he Mathurin Bruneau, the orphaned son of a village cobbler, the son of a woman named Phélippeaux, or even Hervagault himself, miraculously escaped from prison? But Bruneau, as most people have called this mystery man, ruined his own case by behaving like a madman in court, screaming insults and threatening the judges. He was imprisoned for seven years, and died in a madhouse in 1822.[14]

After the July revolution in 1830, the Bourbons were ousted in favor of King Louis Philippe, from the house of Orléans. A haughty, verbose manifesto objecting to the election of Louis Philippe came from Baron Richemont, one of the resident false dauphins in Paris.

Two false dauphins: the coarse-featured Mathurin Bruneau
and the dapper Baron Richemont.

This man had enjoyed a long and varied career as a swindler and petty crook before starting his career as a pretender in 1828, after careful preparations. Issuing bombastic proclamations and impressing people with his knowledge of court life at Versailles, he soon made a name for himself among those who wanted to believe that Louis XVII was still alive. He had been rescued from the Temple tower by a quack doctor named Ojardias, he said, and the rescue had been planned by none less than Josephine de Beauharnais, later to become Napoleon's first empress. As his court of supporters grew, Richemont became increasingly audacious; he claimed that he was both Hervagault and Bruneau, having been miraculously rescued from prison no fewer than three times. After he had printed libels against the usurper Louis Philippe and advocated his assassination, he was arrested as an impostor and put on trial in 1834. This trial was Richemont's finest hour. He defended himself with vigor and confounded the foolish prosecution witnesses. One of them swore he was Hervagault, another that he was Bruneau; a female police spy fell on her knees and declared he was her true monarch, Louis XVII! But it soon became apparent that

Richemont had been using twenty or thirty different names and noble titles during his lengthy career as a con artist, and that he was probably none other than a Paris crook named Herbert. Sentenced to twelve years in prison, he managed to escape in 1835. Still maintaining his claim, he lived on in relative obscurity until 1853.[15]

———

DURING THE TRIAL of Baron Richemont in 1834, another pretender made a bold appeal: he knew that Richemont was an impostor—because he himself was Charles Louis, the son of Louis XVI and Marie Antoinette! With his usual coolness, Richemont remarked that any person laying claim to a name should at least know that name: the dauphin had been baptized Louis Charles, not Charles Louis. The newcomer had to retreat in confusion, but would later be back with a vengeance; among the 101 false dauphins, he remains the one recognized as the main claimant. This mystery man first showed up in Berlin in 1809, at the age of twenty-four, giving his name as Carl Wilhelm Naundorff.[16] He worked as a clockmaker, being quite successful in his trade and something of an inventor. He also invented tales about himself, however, hinting that he was of high birth. In 1824, when he was on trial in Germany for forging money, Naundorff gave wildly conflicting accounts of himself, one of which being that he was a Frenchman of high birth, named Ludwig Burbong. When asked to speak French, he said he had forgotten it. Naundorff was sentenced to three years in prison. Some of his French followers later insisted that a dreadful miscarriage of justice had been committed: as the king of France, their hero had the right to mint his own money!

After spending some years in Germany, no doubt reading up on the part he was to play, Naundorff came to Paris in 1833, with a small court of supporters. It speaks highly of the man's sheer audacity that he thought he might have a chance of convincing anyone he was Louis XVII after an absence of not less than thirty-eight years, particularly since he spoke French very badly, with a heavy German accent. But Naundorff went from strength to strength. Several old servants of the royal family recognized him as the Lost Dauphin, as did a bishop and Louis XVII's former minister of justice. Naundorff's plausible manner and intimate knowledge of court life at Versailles in the 1780s won him many friends, and he certainly looked every inch a Bourbon. His band of followers grew steadily, many of them recruited from the dwindling court of his rival Richemont. Naundorff explained his bad French by claiming that his long stay in Germany and the many sad memories from his youth in the Temple tower had made him forget it. But the first language learned by any person is the one most firmly

Naundorff, the most persistent of the pretenders.
A plate from *The King Who Never Reigned* (London, 1908).

imprinted in his or her memory, and Louis XVII spoke only French from 1785 until 1795. Moreover, Naundorff had no good explanation why it had taken him so long to establish his claim. His main tactics were to bombard the duchess of Angoulême with letters. The early communications were full of tender endearments, urging her to embrace her long-lost brother. After she had publicly denounced him as an impostor, the letters became angry and threatening. Naundorff even had the audacity to summon the duke and duchess before the civil court of the Seine, demanding to prove his identity. This plan backfired, however, since the police had learned about his former career in Germany as a forger and suspected arsonist. Naundorff was expelled from France and forbidden to use the Bourbon name.

In 1835, Naundorff moved to London, where he set about writing his memoirs. He had some amazing stories to tell. In November 1794, he had been rescued from the Temple, a dumb child named Tardif taking his place. In June 1795, there had been a second substitution, an invalid child named Gonnehaut taking the place of Tardif and dying four days later. Naundorff/the dauphin, who was hiding in the attics of the Temple tower, was smuggled out in the latter's coffin. Naundorff presumed that Louis XVII's coffin was taken to the cemetery in a carriage, but, as we know, it was in fact carried by four soldiers, rendering a rescue very difficult. In Naundorff's autobiography, further kidnappings, escapes, and shipwrecks followed, before the pope branded him with the insignia of the Holy Ghost.[17] His memoirs being actively suppressed in France, they failed to cause much stir.

Naundorff then tried to build a novel explosive device, which he called the Bourbon bomb. In May 1841, his workshop caught fire. Naundorff plunged into the flames to save the bomb, but it exploded, burning him badly. In March 1842, the bomb factory was again burned to the ground, and the inhabitants of this densely populated area were at the point of rioting, enraged by the accident-prone adventurer's careless handling of his explosives. Without any customers for his bomb, Naundorff soon fell into dire financial straits; in 1843, he was an inmate of the Horsemonger Lane debtor's prison, owing £5,000 to various creditors. But the Dutch ministry of war bought the design for the Bourbon bomb in 1845, and Naundorff went to Delft to continue his research into explosives. He soon fell ill, however, and expired on August 10, 1845. His death certificate was signed using the name of King Louis XVII of France, and the obliging Dutch government later allowed his sons legally to assume the name de Bourbon.

The Naundorffists continued to believe in his claim and detested Louis XVIII as the nemesis of Naundorff's hopes. Ex-empress Josephine of France had tried to convince Tsar Alexander I of Russia that Louis XVII was still alive, they claimed; not long afterward, she was allegedly poisoned. The murder of the duke de Berry, who they claimed had found out that Louis XVII was still alive, was also attributed to the king's hired assassins. Another bête noire of the Naundorffists was Marie Thérèse, the sole royal survivor of the Temple tower, who had denounced their hero as a brazen swindler. But the Naundorffists claimed that Louis XVIII had kidnapped the real Marie Thérèse and replaced her with a look-alike impostor! The reason for this kidnapping was, of course, that Marie Thérèse knew that her brother was still alive and that Louis XVIII wanted to hide her away to secure his throne. This explained, to the satisfaction of the Naundorffists, why the substituted duchess of Angoulême was so unimpressed by their hero. To prove their case, they quoted a story circulating in Germany about a mysterious couple known only as the Count and the Countess, who had lived in near-complete seclusion at the castle of Eishausen for many years. The "Countess" could sometimes be seen to walk in her garden, watched by the "Count" standing in a window and holding a pistol. This sad "Countess" of Eishausen was the real Marie Thérèse.[18] The Naundorffists also made much of the discrepancy between the good looks of the youthful Marie Thérèse and the somewhat forbidding countenance of the middle-aged duchess of Angoulême.

During the Third Republic, the Naundorffists strengthened their position and actually became a force to be reckoned with in French politics. There were, at the time, Bourbon legitimist, Orléanist, Bonapartist, and Naundorffist deputies in the French parliament, ensuring vigorous debates when the question arose of who had the legitimate right to the throne. In 1874, Naundorff's sons petitioned that their father be recognized as Louis XVII, but they lost their case. Infighting between Naundorff's grandsons lowered the movement's esteem during the 1910s, and the outbreak of World War I dealt an even tougher blow. Some French politicians spread rumors that the Germans planned to recognize the Naundorffs as the true heirs of Louis XVII and then to make them surrender the throne to one of Kaiser Wilhelm's sons. The Naundorffs kept a low profile between the wars, and some of them hit hard times; one died in a Paris poorhouse in 1944, and another was employed in a circus. In 1954, a great-grandson of Naundorff's, appealed the 1874 verdict, but the result was not what he wanted. Amid widespread newspaper publicity, the circus manager who claimed to be king of France was much laughed at. The verdict was again that Naundorff was a cheat and impostor, who had no right to the throne.

———

THERE HAVE BEEN false dauphins all over the world. Their number exceeds one hundred, and some of them have had very curious yarns to tell. England had its own pretender, Augustus Meves, who claimed that his alleged father, a London tradesman, discovered that his own son greatly resembled the imprisoned dauphin, took him over to Paris, and effected a substitution of children. On learning that her Augustus was now a state prisoner in Paris, the irate Mrs. Meves, who did not share her husband's reverence for royalty, also went to Paris and single-handedly rescued her son, this time substituting her charwoman's deaf and dumb child.[19] Naundorff met Meves in London, and they had a pleasant conversation about their experiences in the Temple tower.

America had at least five false dauphins. The tombstone of the mystery man Louis Leroy, who came to New York in 1797, is decorated with a royal crown. Another pretender, Pierre Brousseau, of

Chicago, is said to have received a pension from the duchess of Angoulême. There have also been rumors that the famous naturalist John James Audubon was none else than the Lost Dauphin. Audubon himself was never a pretender, but several later writers have imagined that some cryptic writings of his referred to his true origin.[20] Far better known is the missionary Eleazar Williams, who was at large as a pretender for many years. His claim had a serious drawback, however: he was half Native American and had difficulties explaining his darker skin color to sneering rationalists. At length, he became so fed up with the ridicule that he withdrew to a log cabin near Hogansburg, New York, living there until his death in 1858. His obvious demerits as a pretender have not prevented the audacious lady historian Elizabeth E. Evans from wholeheartedly accepting his claim.[21]

There have been reports of Louis XVII's ending up as a sailor in Buenos Aires, a plantation owner in the Seychelles, a Trappist monk in Spain, or a mystery man in Siberia. A French general has proposed that the assassin Louvel, who murdered the duke de Berry in 1820, was none other than Louis XVII, who killed the usurper duke in a fit of frenzy. Saved from the Temple tower, he instead perished on the guillotine. Even more preposterous is the suggestion that Louis XVII became a transvestite, masquerading as the Versailles gentlewoman Jenny Savalette de Lange, who was discovered to have been a man after her death in 1858.[22] It is also told that an old French antiquary immersed himself in the riddle of the Lost Dauphin, carefully sifting the evidence for several decades before emerging from his study to announce that the mystery was solved: he himself was Louis XVII, and he had the evidence to prove it!

## WAS LOUIS XVII RESCUED?

THE RIDDLE OF the Lost Dauphin can be simplified as follows. A young prince is imprisoned along with his family. He is last seen by his mother, sister, and aunt in October 1793. At that time, he is in reasonably good health. During Simon's reign as jailer, he is observed by many people, who would have noticed a substitution of children. Any attempt to explain an escape during this period would require the positing of a huge conspiracy, involving people who had no interest at all in saving the prince. In January 1794, he is virtually walled in alive in a dungeon, without any obvious explanation why such extreme and barbarous measures were taken. There is reasonably strong medical evidence that the child taken out of the dungeon just before his death in 1795 was the same chronically ill, invalid child seen by Barras, Harmand, and Desault. In any event, an escape or rescue from the fortified, strongly guarded prison cell during any time from January 1794 until the child's death in June 1795 would have been a most unlikely occurrence. The mystery would thus be reduced to the question whether the prince put into the dungeon in January 1794 was the same wreck of a child who died eighteen months later.

There might be several reasons for a substitution of children. The one touted by every false dauphin is that the real Louis XVII had been rescued. As for the Temple Child, it was presumed either that the clever royalists brought with them a substitute child that looked very much like Louis XVII or that the revolutionaries found the dungeon empty and decided to put an invalid child in there to make sure the escape was kept secret.

But the proponents of this escape theory have some virtually insurmountable obstacles to overcome. First, a successful escape from the Temple would have been a crushing blow for revolutionary France and a great moral victory for its enemies. Had Louis XVII reached Britain or Austria, the martyr king, saved from his oppressors in Paris, would have become a rallying point for every French royalist. He would also have been a most valuable asset for the alliance of European powers opposing France; far from hiding him away or sending him to the pope to be branded on the leg, as the false dauphins suggested, they would have made the most of him as a propaganda tool. But no person, either in France or abroad, even attempted to take political advantage of Louis XVII's being rescued.

Second, the stories of heroic royalists saving Louis XVII from the Temple certainly do not ring true. The most fanciful ones told of a series of substitutions: a double for Louis XVII, then a deaf-mute child, and finally a chronically ill child that was soon to die. The Temple tower was a high-security penitentiary, where the little prisoner was guarded twenty-four hours a day by hostile revolutionaries armed to the teeth. A single escape would seem most unlikely and a series of substitutions of children, along the lines suggested by Naundorff and others, virtually impossible.

Any conspiracy to rescue Louis XVII would have had to be large and well organized and to have had access to swift and reliable means to smuggle him away from Paris. But it would have been very difficult to organize such an elaborate plan in Paris during the Terror, a time when royalists and aristocrats were hunted like wild animals and when every citizen was a potential police informer. It is odd that, if such a conspiracy existed, none of its members ever claimed credit for rescuing Louis XVII. Surely, the leaders of such a rescue attempt would have become the heroes of the royalist cause, able to claim rewards from the wealthy French émigrés in London. Moreover, it is reasonable to suppose that the menial participants in such a purported conspiracy would have emerged from their hiding places after the Bourbon Restoration in 1814 to claim their rewards, but again there is no contemporary evidence of any individuals' coming forward.

A trump card for the believers in the escape of Louis XVII is that in later life Madame Simon actually testified that she had observed the substitution of children.[23] After her husband had been guillotined, she sank low in the slums of Paris. In 1796, she was admitted to a hospital that bore the depressing name Hôpital des Incurables. For many years, she gave no hint that she had any particular knowledge of the fate of Louis XVII. But in 1810, after the nuns had been allowed to return to the hospital, she started talking. Like many other people who had been involved in various misdeeds during the revolution, she was eager to exonerate herself. She claimed that she had dearly loved her little Bourbon, as she called him, and that she had treated him like her own child. When this pack of lies had been accepted by her audience, she improved her story: the Simons had actually helped rescue Louis XVII, by smuggling another child into the prison, hidden inside a large pasteboard horse, and then took the little king out inside a basket of dirty linen. When in an expansive mood, the audacious old woman even added that in 1802 Louis XVII had actually visited her in the hospital, to thank her for her help in the heroic rescue.

In 1816, Madame Simon's gossip came to the attention of the police. They bullied and scolded her severely; as a result, she signed a document disavowing her disclosures completely. Having recovered from her fright and returned to her friends in the hospital, she then resumed her old ways, telling her story about the rescue of Louis XVII to all and sundry. But, as we know, the Simons were known as Hébert and Chaumette's underlings and informers: would any person really try to recruit these people to a conspiracy to rescue the little king? And how could they effect the substitution of children with such ease, when every object large enough to contain a child that was taken in and out of the prison was closely searched by the guards on duty? Madame Simon also had a strong motive for making up such a story: as the wife of the notorious Simon, she would not have had a high standing with the nuns and fellow patients, but by inventing her tale of the rescue of Louis XVII she became something of a local celebrity and was much better treated than she otherwise would have been.

A crushing argument against the rescue and survival of Louis XVII is that none of the pretenders passes muster. In particular, Naundorff fails miserably on several counts; it is amazing that he could ever attain such a following, before or after death. Bruneau was a vulgar oaf, Richemont a crook and a con man; some of the others, like Augustus Meves and Eleazar Williams, were wholly ludicrous. Personally, I have always had an inclination in favor of young Hervagault, who had some advantages not shared by the others. He was the first of many pretenders and made his claim before Regnault-Warin's novel was published. He looked like Louis XVII and had manners suggesting a privileged upbringing, far from that of the son of a provincial tailor. He appeared to be around thirteen years old, just as Louis XVII would have been, but according to his certificate of birth, Jean Marie Hervagault should have been eighteen at the time. The very timely arrival of old Hervagault to claim his errant son has also given rise to suspicion: was he the pawn of a conspiracy against the claimant? But, if so, why did the pretender admit he was young Hervagault, instead of denouncing the tailor and trying to muster his army of followers in his defense? Psychology delivers another crushing argument against Hervagault. Could a thirteen-year-old boy, who had been kept imprisoned for several years under the most dismal circumstances and who had lost both his parents to the bloodthirsty rabble threatening his own life, have behaved with such frivolity? His story of the escape from the Temple tower is clearly impossible, since he claimed to have been smuggled out in a linen basket with help from a royalist sick nurse (which the Temple Child never had). He dated his escape to May 1795, a time when the Temple Child was a bedridden invalid, already marked by death; Hervagault himself was healthy and able-bodied.

An alternative escape theory is that a conspiracy of revolutionaries themselves took Louis XVII away to some safe place in the country, for use as a pawn in the struggle for power. The kidnappers may have substituted another child, or the governing revolutionaries could have put a child in the dungeon to cover up the fact that Louis XVII had been kidnapped. Then it may be that the kidnappers were tracked down and killed by the police, or that they perished in the huge struggle for power in 1794. They might have left Louis XVII with simple country people, who perhaps did not even suspect the identity of the child. With his kidnappers out of the way, no one would have known where the little king was, and he would have grown up with his foster parents like an ordinary child. Tormented by the recollections of his lost youth and the horrors of the Temple, he might have decided to suppress these memories and try to lead an ordinary life. There emerged some theories along these lines, one of them suggesting that Louis XVII was taken to Switzerland, where he resided among common people. The more audacious historians have claimed that this

Swiss Louis XVII was once imprisoned in Germany, where he came into contact with the swindler Naundorff, who stole his documents and decided to impersonate Louis XVII himself. This would also explain Naundorff's great success in duping various French worthies in the early 1830s.[24] But this theory, as well as others involving various plebeian characters pointed out as Louis XVII late in life, or after several generations, suffers from a chronic lack of solid evidence.

## WAS THERE A SUBSTITUTION OF CHILDREN?

HAVING EXAMINED THE evidence, or rather the lack of it, that Louis XVII left the Temple alive, we must turn to the alternative hypothesis that there was a substitution of children because of the death of Louis XVII in the Temple in January 1794. One of the mainstays of this theory is the sudden and unexplained decision to isolate the Temple Child in mid-January. There is no obvious reason for such high-security imprisonment. The risk of a royalist conspiracy to save Louis XVII was actually lower in early 1794 than it had been earlier. It has been suggested that the revolutionaries had decided to deliberately murder Louis XVII through mistreatment and neglect. But surely, had they wanted to dispose of the little king in a permanent way, they could easily have murdered him, openly or in secret. Furthermore, as we know, Louis XVII had great value as a political pawn in possible future negotiations with the country's enemies.

The proponents of a substitution of children have queried why Simon was suddenly sacked in early January 1794. Was it because he could not be trusted to be sworn into the conspiracy to kill Louis XVII and substitute another child? Three servants who knew Louis Charles were also sacked between October 1793 and January 1794. Was this because someone wanted to get rid of every person who would have the ability to see through the deception? It is striking that on January 19 Marie Thérèse recorded that she heard a great noise from the downstairs prison rooms. She thought it was her brother being moved out of his cell and another prisoner being put into it. Historians have presumed that she actually heard the Simons leaving the tower, as they did that very day. But a prisoner held in the same cell in a prison for a long time learns to tell apart the different sounds in the prison. Had she not actually heard the door of Louis Charles's cell being opened, a scuffle of some sort, and then silence? This silence, continuing for many months, is in itself another mystery. Throughout Simon's tenure as jailer, Louis Charles had tormented his female relatives with his shouting and singing. There is no doubt, moreover, that he had learned to express himself forcefully in a vulgar tongue. Was it really credible that the "little sansculotte" would not object in any way when taken away from the Simons, to whom he had grown attached, and isolated in a dungeon? The real Louis Charles wept for two days when taken from his mother. Was it not an even greater trauma to be imprisoned in complete isolation? Louis Charles had never been alone before. Any child, if not drugged or greatly enfeebled by a wasting disease, would have pounded on the door and rattled the bars to try to get out of the prison cell, and screamed and shouted for help. But Marie Thérèse never heard a sound.

If we choose to believe Barras and Harmand when they claimed that they had tried to procure medical attention for the Temple Child, it amazes us that Laurent chose to ignore their recommendations entirely, although it must have been apparent to him that the child was severely ill. It is also notable that when medical help was at length sent for, the prison doctors who had treated Louis Charles back in 1793 were not called in. Another very peculiar circumstance is the official identification of the Temple Child as Louis XVII. There is no doubt that this identification took place at 11:30 at night, in a dark prison room, after the child had been dissected and then stitched up again. Not only must there have been effects of putrefaction (the child had been dead thirty hours), but the features were altered by the sawing of the skull and the division of the skin into several flaps. Moreover, the child's head was shaven, and a great bandage put around the jaws, partially covering the head. We do not know how the individuals identifying the Temple Child as Louis XVII had been chosen, and what incentives they were given to identify the mangled body on the autopsy table as the child of Capet. No effort was made to seek out people who had seen Louis Charles in the Temple just a few years earlier, like the servant Tison, the cook Meunier, and the doorkeeper Baron. The person who knew Louis XVII best of all, his sister Marie Thérèse, was never allowed to see the Temple Child, either living or dead.

———

IN JUNE 1801, a certain General d'Andigné was a political prisoner in the Temple. As he and some other prisoners were digging in a flowerbed near the Temple wall, they found the skeleton of a child that had been buried in quicklime. The general turned to the prison governor, a man named Fauconnier, who had come out to view the skeleton, and said that surely this must be the remains of Louis XVII. The governor looked embarrassed at the general's question, but quietly affirmed that this was indeed the case. Fauconnier had come to the Temple in 1797, but it may well be that he had heard the details from the turnkey Gourlet, a man known as a gossip, whose actions back in 1795 indicate that he may have known more than he wished to tell about the identity of the Temple Child. General d'Andigné was an honorable military man and a firm royalist, who had no motive for making this story up. It has been objected that this could have been any skeleton, but it appeared to be of a child of about the right age, and had been buried the right length of time, to fit in with what we know of Louis XVII. It must also be noted that this child had been clandestinely buried without a coffin in a rigorously guarded prison; Louis XVII would have been the only fitting child prisoner. I have discovered evidence that the general actually returned to the Temple grounds after the Restoration. He *and others* still remembered where they had seen the skeleton back in 1801, but, to their dismay, a house had recently been built on this very spot. The general proposed to the duchess of Angoulême that the house be pulled down and the skeleton of the martyr king dug up, but she was so distraught at his suggestion that he did not press the point further.[25]

General d'Andigné's story is the mainstay of the hypothesis that

Louis XVII died and was buried in the Temple grounds, and that it was a substitute child that died in June 1795. It has support from some other sources. M. Senar, secretary to the committee in early 1794, wrote a cryptic note that it had been decided that Louis XVII was to be gotten rid of. The conspirators had killed him and clandestinely buried his body near a tower; it was not Louis XVII but the corpse of another child that had been cut open by the doctors. Senar did not specify at which stage of Louis XVII's captivity he had been murdered. In June 1795, there was a rumor in Paris that Louis XVII was dead and that he had been buried at the foot of the Temple tower. This rumor was reported by the royalist Frotté, by the Paris lawyer M. Guérinau, and by Austrian and Spanish diplomats. At about the same time, one of the deputies in the National Convention hinted that he had dangerous information regarding Louis XVII's death, but he never spoke out about this matter. An obscure book from 1816 again refers to this matter, adding that a turnkey (Gourlet?) had said that the real Louis XVII had been secretly buried in the grounds of the Temple.[26]

––––––

THE HISTORIAN LOUIS HASTIER proposed that the real Louis XVII died of disease in the first days of January 1794, and that a substitute was smuggled into the Temple just after the Simons had left on January 19.[27] He tried to support his theory by scrutinizing the records of the washerwoman of the Temple; he found that fewer socks were delivered in early January than during the rest of the weeks covered by her lists. The reason for this, he suggested, must be that at this time there was no child in the Temple to wear them. But other historians have pointed out that although the number of socks decreased, shirts were still delivered; they have also emphasized the fallibility of drawing far-reaching conclusions from such flimsy evidence.[28] I would fully agree with them in this respect. Furthermore, the reason that fewer socks were needed may well have been the decrepitude of the Temple Child; a bedridden invalid does not need to change his socks as often as an active child. Hastier also tried to implicate several of the Temple staff in a conspiracy to cover up the death of Louis XVII, but his evidence has been severely criticized by other scholars. It is at this point that the chain of evidence for a substitution is at its weakest. If Louis XVII died from disease, why replace him with a dying invalid child? This would merely have led to the recurrence of the same problem once the substitute expired. Nor is there any solid evidence that Louis XVII was seriously ill at the end of 1793.

The historian Joseph Turquan advanced a slightly different hypothesis, namely that Louis XVII was murdered on January 19 and buried by the Temple wall, and that an invalid child was put in the dungeon to make France's enemies believe that Louis XVII was still alive.[29] The drawback to this theory is that there was no motive for the revolutionary government to kill Louis XVII, since he was a valuable pawn in the political game. A more intriguing line of thought is that a coterie of extremists carried out the murder in secret. The bloodthirsty extremists Hébert and Chaumette would be the obvious suspects as the leaders of such a conspiracy. They openly advocated the complete extermination of the royal family and had no shortage of desperate, fanatical adherents, to whom it would have been a mark of honor to eliminate the son of Louis XVI and the hated Marie Antoinette. The difficulty lies in explaining how these men were able to enter the rigorously guarded Temple tower, effect the substitution, and get clean away. But did they get away? It is recorded that not only Hébert and Chaumette perished on the guillotine a few months later but so did the steward of the Temple, Simon himself, and three of the four men signing the certificate that Simon had delivered the son of Capet in good health. If these men were part of a conspiracy to secretly murder Louis XVII, they took their secret with them.

## THE RATIONALISTS STRIKE BACK

THE HISTORIANS CLAIMING that Louis XVII and the Temple Child were one and the same person have rightly objected that the evidence

summarized above is all circumstantial. There is no clear-cut proof of
any conspiracy to substitute another child for Louis XVII. Such a conspiracy would have had to involve many people, some of whom, like
Laurent, Gomin, and Lasne, survived revolution, war, and upheaval.
Yet none of them spoke out at a time when there were great incentives
for doing so. And if Laurent had been a key player in the conspiracy,
with a great secret to guard, would he really have applied to have an
assistant? And if Gomin and Lasne had been involved, why would
they, toward the end of the life of the Temple Child, have carried the
prisoner up to the fourth-floor gallery of the Temple tower? Here he
could have been seen from the outside, and there would have been a
risk of people's finding out he was not the real Louis XVII.

No person who actually saw the Temple Child alerted the authorities, saying he was not Louis XVII. On the contrary, ten people signed
the certificate saying that the child that died in the Temple tower was
really the son of Capet. Some of these specified that they had seen
Louis Charles in the Tuileries five or six years earlier. In particular, it
is important to note that Dr. Pelletan, who saw the child on several
occasions, does not appear to have had the slightest doubt that his
patient was Louis XVII. When interviewed in 1816, the doctor added
a heartrending anecdote: the ailing prisoner motioned to him to talk
more quietly, since otherwise his sister might overhear the conversation, and it would cause her grief if she knew that her darling brother
was sick. The turnkey Damont added that he had previously seen
Louis Charles in the Tuileries when acting as a national guardsman,
and his colleague Gourlet attested that he had known him since he
came to the Temple in August 1792. The commissary Darlot later
signed an affidavit that he had clearly recognized the corpse as that
of Louis XVII, whom he had several times seen in the Tuileries gardens. The architect Bellanger saw the Temple Child during Gomin's
time as jailer and had no difficulty in recognizing the prisoner as Louis
Charles, whom he had seen at Versailles many years earlier.[30]

A mainstay in the arguments of the rationalist historians is the testimony of Gomin and Lasne.[31] Both men lived to a ripe old age and

became minor celebrities through their association with the mystery. When the historian Alcide de Beauchesne interviewed them, they did their best to impress on him that, far from being brutal, bloodthirsty revolutionaries, they had been royalists at heart and the tender, caring friends of Louis XVII. Gomin was a master at telling—or inventing—pathetic stories of how he had helped and comforted the royal prisoner. Gomin used to give him flowers, and the child's gratitude was touching. When the feeble Temple Child wanted someone to read to him or to play cards or checkers, his friend Gomin was always there. Once, when Gomin helped the Temple Child downstairs after an airing in the Temple tower gallery, the child clutched a handful of flowers, a present for his mother just as in happier days. Gomin and de Beauchesne also milked every last drop of sentiment from another pathetic scene: the child once begged Gomin that he be allowed to see his dear mother one last time, but was denied by his friend the jailer, who knew that Marie Antoinette was long since dead. Gomin even had the audacity to tell de Beauchesne that he had openly defied the commissaries of the Temple when they had threatened his dear friend the prisoner, or made insulting remarks mocking the church. Lasne, who depicted himself as another stalwart friend of the ailing prisoner, said he used to sing the old songs of the royal guards to amuse the boy, Gomin accompanying him on the violin. He added that he had several times seen Louis Charles in the Tuileries gardens and that he had no doubt it was really he who had died in the Temple.

Most relevant archival sources on the mystery of the Lost Dauphin are held by the national archives in Paris. Because of the size and somewhat erratic organization of these archives, persistent scholars were able to discover important primary material there well into the mid-1900s. The intense partisanship of Naundorff, and the wish to believe that Louis XVII was really saved, led some people to forge documents and letters to aid the cause of the pretender.[32] Elderly academics worked for years and decades in dusty archives, threading the labyrinth of France's national mystery, hoping one day to find a clue to what had really happened. By selectively choosing which people to believe, and which documents to regard as authentic, some of these scholars erected the most fantastic theories about heroic escapes, substitutions of deaf-mute children, and the ubiquitous pope approaching with his red-hot branding iron, only to have these houses of cards torn down, with glee, by the sneering skeptics.

An immense secondary literature on the mystery of the Lost Dauphin existed already in the late 1800s, and debates raged even concerning the most trivial and peripheral details of the Temple drama. A perennial problem for the Louis XVII historian is the tendency of many witnesses to change their testimony to ingratiate themselves with the person questioning them. This is particularly apparent with Gomin and Lasne, whose unctuous anecdotes have been quoted above. Both these men were cunning liars who knew what their audience wanted to hear from them. Should the historian believe Gomin when he told Marie Thérèse that her brother was greatly enfeebled and on the way to imbecility, or the same witness when he told de Beauchesne that they used to read classical texts together? In the trial against Richemont in 1834, where he was a witness, Lasne said that he had every day discussed philosophical subjects with the Temple Child; in the trial against Naundorff six years later, he curtly stated that he had only once heard the miserable prisoner speak.[33] The abundance of contradictory evidence, both primary and secondary, has led some historians to presume that the real truth will never be found out from this mass of lies, forgeries, and impostures. Others have, not entirely unreasonably, concluded that since there is no clear-cut, incontrovertible evidence that the Temple Child was anyone else but Louis XVII, one should have no doubts about his identity.

## MEDICAL EVIDENCE

THE OBVIOUS ASPECT of medical evidence in any case of disputed identity is the analysis of distinguishing physical marks. For example, if Louis XVII had lost his thumb and Naundorff had all ten fingers intact, then they could not be the same person. Unfortunately, Louis XVII had few distinguishing marks—just a scar from the bite of a rabbit, and smallpox inoculation marks on both arms. This was enough to confound more than one of the false dauphins, however. Louis XVII's old nurse, Madame de Rambaud, asked to see Naundorff's inoculation scar; she then burst into tears and embraced him, becoming one of his most fanatical followers. It is a pity she did not examine both arms, since Naundorff was inoculated on only one arm! The dauphin's mark from the rabbit bite was on the left base of the jaw, but the pretender Bruneau's rabbit had bitten him on the cheek, and Naundorff's scar was on the upper lip. A German police document from 1825 adds that at this time Naundorff had dark brown hair. Naundorff was also quite badly pockmarked, but with his usual readiness to invent fantastic stories, he found an explanation for this defect. When he returned from Rome after being crowned and branded by the pope, his ship was captured by the French, and three sinister masked men tortured him by pushing an instrument bristling with sharp needles into his face.[34]

The same method is applicable also in the case of a suspected substitution of children: we know that Louis XVII had blue eyes, and if it could be conclusively established that those of the Temple Child were brown, then they could not be the same person. Again there are difficulties due to uncertain and contradictory evidence, but a few points are worth noting. First, what is probably the only genuine drawing of the Temple Child, by the artist Morier, depicts a rather sinister-looking, dark-haired child, older than Louis XVII. Another curious portrait alleged to depict the Temple Child agrees well with this drawing.[35] Some of the descriptions of the Temple Child hint that he was quite tall for a boy aged ten, but Louis Charles was just three feet two inches tall in March 1793, according to a note made by Marie Antoinette. Although it is true that children grow in spurts, it is not reasonable to assume that he grew a great deal when fed a meager diet and imprisoned in solitary confinement. It is a great pity Pelletan and his colleagues did not measure the corpse of the Temple Child. The

The Temple Child. A portrait reproduced by
G. Lenôtre, *The Dauphin* (London, 1921)

only hint comes from the man Voisin, who later stated that he found
the Temple Child a tall boy for his age, and purchased a coffin that
was four and a half, or even five, feet long.[36] Finally, there is the question of the hair samples from the Temple Child, kept by the commissary Damont. In 1817, he wanted to give these to the royal family, and
was received by the duke de Gramont, captain of the bodyguard. The
nobleman rejected these hair samples in no uncertain terms, since
they were much darker than the hair of Louis Charles, whom the
duke had seen many times.[37]

THE SECOND PART of the medical evidence concerns the search for the skeleton of the Temple Child. The majority of writers have chosen to believe that the remains of the Temple Child were interred at the Sainte-Marguerite cemetery, at a site known only to the gravedigger Bertrancourt. When the Bourbons returned to France in 1814, Louis XVIII immediately ordered a search for the remains of Louis XVI and Marie Antoinette, whose bones were transferred to the Saint-Denis crypt. No similar effort was made to locate the remains of Louis XVII, and it was actually Gabrielle Bertrancourt, the gravedigger's widow, who approached the king rather than the other way around. In an audience granted her in January 1816, she told the king about her husband's story that he had salvaged the remains of Louis XVII and

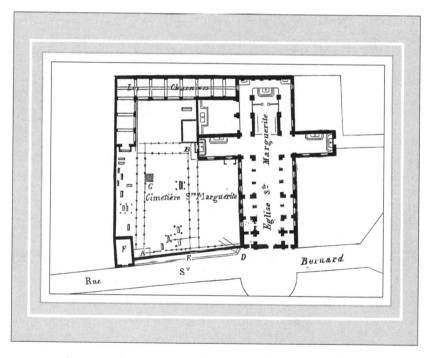

A nineteenth-century plan of the Sainte-Marguerite cemetery;
the presumed place of burial of the dauphin is marked with an A.

reburied them in a safe place. After lengthy deliberations, plans were made to excavate the site indicated by Madame Bertrancourt, but they were unexpectedly stopped. The reason given was that one could not be absolutely certain about the site of burial, but the truth very likely was that Louis XVIII still had doubts whether his nephew was really the invalid child who died in the Temple. Two false dauphins were at large demanding his crown, and the king probably feared the gossip that would result if the excavation found nothing. The next year, a Professor Simien-Despréaux again suggested an excavation of the grave site. He knew Dr. Pelletan, who had told him that he hoped he would recognize both the skull he had sawed through to expose the brain and the cloth he had used to wrap the head. Simien-Despréaux also thought the tumors on the knees of the Temple child might well have corroded the bones, leaving traces that could be seen on the skeleton. But the king and his ministers again were adamant that the site not be excavated; when the professor offered to do it on his own behalf, he was bluntly told that his assistance was not needed.

In 1846, Abbé Haumet, the priest in charge of Sainte-Marguerite, decided to have a shed built by the chapel door. It may well be that he had actually ordered the work clandestinely to find the remains of the dauphin, since he certainly was aware of Bertrancourt's story. Only three feet underneath the surface, a five-foot lead coffin was found. The priest was surprised to see that it was a lead coffin, because he knew that the dauphin had been buried in a pinewood coffin. He was even more surprised to see the size of the coffin, which seemed designed for an adolescent rather than for a child. At any rate, the coffin was taken to the presbytery and opened in the presence of a Dr. Milcent. Inside was a skeleton whose skull had been sawed open during an autopsy, and both Haumet and Milcent felt certain these were the bones of Louis XVII. Some other doctors were consulted, and they agreed that the bones were from a male child or adolescent who had suffered from some kind of infection affecting one thigh bone and one leg bone. But the size of the arm and leg bones, and the development of the teeth, seemed to point to a boy of at least fifteen years of age. There was a discrepancy between the long arms and legs and the narrow thorax, and doubters hinted it could not even be proven that the bones were from one and the same cadaver, particularly as the skeleton was far from complete; many bones were missing, including a large part of the spinal column. Still, there was an uncanny resemblance between these characteristics and Harmand's description of the ailing Temple Child: the long arms and legs, the chronic infection of the knees, the hunched back, and the narrow chest. Haumet had the bones put in an oaken box inscribed L. XVII, which was reburied at the same site.

For almost fifty years, the debate whether these bones were really those of Louis XVII grumbled on in both the historical and the medical press. In 1894, another exhumation was organized, with five specialist doctors standing by to give their opinions. This time, the doctors were more critical. Dr. Felix de Backer examined the jaws and teeth and found that all milk teeth were gone and that the wisdom teeth were actually at their last stage of development; this would point toward the skull's belonging to a boy who was at least fifteen or sixteen years old. The anthropologist Dr. Manouvrier estimated the individual's height, on the basis of the length of the bones, and calculated an interval of between five feet one inch and five feet four inches, again suggesting a child much taller than the dauphin.[38] The advocates of the notion of a substitution of children have argued that the state of the bones proves that the Temple Child was much older and taller than the dauphin. But it is unrealistic to expect that the guardians at the Temple would have accepted, without inquiry, that their prisoner suddenly grew a foot in height. The final death blow for this theory comes from Dr. Pelletan's autopsy report; he wrote that he sawed the skull at the level of the orbits. But the skull reproduced by Dr. de Backer had been sawed through much higher up. It is known that the Sainte-Marguerite cemetery was very busy in the years around 1800; corpses from several hospitals were buried there, many of which had been autopsied by the medical students. It is not unlikely that the lead coffin just contained a jumble of body parts from different subjects, carried off from the medical school when the students were finished with them.

This raises the question of where the Temple Child was really buried. The answer is probably that the child's remains went into the common pit. Either Bertrancourt's story was an invention, or he dug up the wrong coffin; the former is the more likely, given the many discrepancies involved. For example, Bertrancourt told his wife he had dug the coffin up the same day; he told a friend he had waited three days before doing so. The historian Georges Lenôtre and others have presumed that Bertrancourt was right, and that if the 1846 working party had continued to dig after finding the unrelated lead coffin just three feet below earth, it would have found the bones of the Temple Child deeper down. But in 1970 and 1979 a third excavation was performed under the direction of the historian Michel Fleury, with three

The skull exhumed from the Sainte-Marguerite cemetery:
note that it is sawed through far above the orbits.

doctors standing by to examine the bones. Although the 1894 bones were again brought to light, nothing of interest was found during an ambitious search of the area indicated by Bertrancourt.[39]

In 1943, the historian André Castelot decided to use another method of analysis, namely trichoscopy, or microscopic examination of the hair. He knew that hair samples had been preserved from the real dauphin, from the Temple Child (at autopsy), from the 1846 skeleton, and from Naundorff. Castelot did what he could to verify that the hair samples in question were authentic, and then eagerly awaited the results from the laboratory of the leading trichoscopist Dr. Locard. Encouragingly, two samples from the dauphin showed the same phenomenon, the median channel of the hair being excentered. Neither the hair taken from the 1846 skeleton nor that from the Temple Child shared this characteristic. Castelot concluded that an exchange of children had been made. Amazingly, Naundorff's hair also had an excentered median channel. Greatly taken aback by this unexpected finding, Castelot wrote an article claiming that a great injustice had been done—Naundorff was really Louis XVII. Later, he became suspicious that some individual might actually have substituted some of the dauphin's hair for Naundorff's for the purpose of deceiving him. Naundorff's body was exhumed in 1950, and Castelot managed to secure some undisputed hair samples from it; his suspicion turned out to be well founded, since this hair had nothing abnormal about its median channel.[40] Present-day forensic science has little use for trichoscopy, and the method has been dismissed as uncertain. Castelot's findings are further undermined by the inherent uncertainty concerning the origin of the hair samples: it has been said that if all the hair from Louis XVII kept in museums or private collections is genuine, it can be used to make one of the flamboyant wigs fashionable at the time of his great-grandfather Louis XIV.

———

ONE OTHER ASPECT of the mystery is susceptible to analysis by scientific means, namely the history of the illness of the undoubted Louis

Charles, compared with that of the Temple Child.[41] We know that in May 1793 the previously healthy Louis Charles suffered an acute infectious illness, with fever, headache, a pain in the side that prevented him from laughing, and a feeling of suffocation when he was lying down. He was ill for fourteen days, but then recovered completely. The most likely diagnosis is either a pleuritis (infection of the pleural sac outside the lung) or a pleuro-pneumonia (pneumonia also involving the pleural sac). These forms of infection can be caused by several different bacteria and viruses; the favorable outcome in the case of Louis Charles speaks against a fulminant bacterial infection. There are two ways to go from here. One is to assume that Louis Charles suffered a non-specific pleuritis or pleuro-pneumonia. This leaves no indication that he was infected with tuberculosis prior to early 1794, and renders the acceptance of Louis XVII as the Temple Child very unlikely indeed. The second way is to assume that the illness in May 1793 was a tuberculous pleuritis, the first sign of the disease that was later to take his life. Nothing in the case history directly contradicts this assumption, nor is there any hard evidence to prove it. It has been suggested that the treatment prescribed by Dr. Thierry was supposed to have a specific antituberculous effect, but this is untrue; the same drugs would have been used in any acute febrile illness.

Some rationalist historians have attempted to add further evidence that Louis XVII showed signs of generalized tuberculosis prior to 1794. We know that in June 1793 Louis Charles ruptured himself when playing, but recovered under the care of Dr. Pipelet. However, another medical man consulted at the time, the surgeon Soupé, described a hard swelling in one of the boy's testicles, and it has been presumed that this was a tuberculous orchido-epididymitis, an infection of the testicle.[42] But if the hypothesis that Louis Charles had a tuberculous pleuritis in May 1793 is accepted, this must have been his first attack of pleuritis. This would indicate that he was infected with tuberculosis in early 1793, since the first attack of pleuritis typically occurs three to six months after infection. Tuberculous orchido-epididymitis in children is very rare and always occurs late in disease, when there is also involvement of the renal tract; thus it is well-nigh impossible that Louis XVII suffered such an infection of the testicle. Furthermore, this kind of tuberculous infection lingers for months, if not years, if left untreated; Louis XVII recovered in a matter of weeks.[43] Thus there is little doubt that Louis Charles really suffered a hernia, as correctly diagnosed by the specialist Dr. Pipelet.

For the period when Simon was the guardian of Louis Charles, there is almost no information about the boy's health. Some anecdotes hint that his health was reasonably good: in October, he was roaring with laughter at a joke; in mid-December, he was active playing with his caged birds; and as late as December 27, a doctor visiting Simon's wife saw nothing wrong with the boy's health. On the contrary side, some English spies reported that at this very time Louis XVII was getting weaker and that he suffered from diarrhea. There is also the account of the artist Morier, who visited the Temple during Simon's reign as guardian and found Louis XVII sad and melancholy; the pure lines of his features were altered, and his back was beginning to stoop. It should be noted, however, that one of the four commissaries who signed the certificate that Simon delivered Louis Charles into their hands *in good health* was actually a doctor; from professional pride, if nothing else, he would certainly have objected to this phrasing had he noticed anything untoward about the little prisoner's condition.

For it to be at all conceivable that the Temple Child was the same person as Louis Charles, we must accept that his tuberculosis spread with such lightning speed that the boy, who was in reasonable health in late 1793, became an invalid just seven months later and died of tuberculosis, a shadow of his former self, in another eleven months. From the autopsy report, it is clear that the Temple Child had widespread, severe tuberculosis, affecting the skeleton and the intestinal tract, and probably other organs as well. We have considerable knowledge about the natural history of untreated tuberculosis, and the time it takes from infection until various organ systems are affected.[44] Normally, it takes at least a year, and sometimes as long as three years, before the first signs of skeletal tuberculosis are seen; as we know, the Temple Child had manifest tuberculous arthritis when seen by Barras in July 1794. Moreover, it is not typical for a child to develop such severe intestinal tuberculosis within a mere two years from the time of infection. It is known, however, that the resistance to infection is affected by nutrition and other external factors. The solitary prisoner of the Temple tower, shivering in his damp room and too enfeebled to eat his food, was clearly predisposed to a rapid spreading of the disease. It is a pity that Pelletan's autopsy report is not more detailed. It would have been valuable if the doctors had taken the time to examine the joints and bones more carefully, particularly since one of the Temple Child's main complaints was chronic arthritis involving the knees and other joints, but they did not do so. Furthermore, it was observed during the lifetime of the Temple Child that his back was badly hunched, but Pelletan does not appear to have examined this part of his anatomy. In the absence of such clinical data, it can only be concluded that, though unlikely, it is not impossible that if Louis XVII was infected with tuberculosis in early 1793, his life could have been ended by the rapid spreading of this disease just thirty months later.

## THE HEART OF THE TEMPLE CHILD

AS WE KNOW, Dr. Pelletan wrapped the heart of the Temple Child in his handkerchief after the autopsy in 1795 and carried it back to his house in the Rue de Touraine. He put it in a crystal vase filled with alcohol, which he hid behind the books on the top shelf in his library. When looking at the vase eight or ten years later, he found it empty of fluid and the heart completely desiccated. Pelletan added it to a collection of dried anatomical specimens that he kept in his desk. Since he did not want to be accused of being a closet royalist, he did not show it to any person, apart from his pupil Dr. Tillus. For several years, Pelletan thought little of the heart, until one day he noticed that it was missing. He knew that Tillus was the only person aware of its existence and decided to track down his former pupil, who had left him some years earlier to get married. When Pelletan found Tillus's house in 1810, the doctor's widow told him that her husband had recently died of tuberculosis. When challenged, she produced a purse containing the dauphin's heart. The relieved Dr. Pelletan immediately recognized "the object he had seen and touched more than a thousand times" and triumphantly brought it back home. In 1814, when the Bourbon monarchy was restored, the doctor thought the time had come to restore the heart of Louis XVII to the royal family. No doubt, he hoped there would be a reward in this for himself as a loyal servant of the monarchy. But as we know, Louis XVIII was very cautious in any question relating to the lost Dauphin, quite possibly because he suspected that the child autopsied by Pelletan was not the real Louis XVII. Moreover, Pelletan's envious hospital colleagues had accused him of Bonapartist sympathies, and this led Louis XVIII and his courtiers to have serious doubts about the doctor's motives and the authenticity of the relic he offered them.

After Louis XVIII had been succeeded by King Charles X, Dr. Pelletan resumed his attempts to return the heart to the Bourbon family. Monseigneur de Quelen, the archbishop of Paris, agreed to act as an intermediary, and in 1828 he took care of the heart and deposited it in his library until he could persuade the king to accept it. In July 1830, disaster struck. There were full-scale riots in Paris, and the mob stormed and pillaged the archbishop's residence. A printing worker named M. Lescroart entered the library, where he saw a wooden box containing the crystal goblet with the heart, and a bundle of papers from Pelletan vouching for its authenticity. Lescroart took the wooden box, but one of the rioters grabbed it; when Lescroart tried to defend his loot, the other man struck it with his saber, shattering both the wooden box and the crystal goblet into little pieces. To avoid becoming the recipient of another saber cut, Lescroart skulked off with the bundle of papers. Reading these a few days later, he was aghast to learn what a singular relic he had come so close to taking away. Pelletan had died in 1828, but his son Dr. Philippe Gabriel Pel-

Dr. Pelletan, the custodian of the heart. An engraving
from *The King Who Never Reigned* (London, 1908).

letan was active at the same address, and the printing worker contacted him. Lescroart and young Pelletan went back to what remained
of the archbishop's palace, hoping to find the heart among the debris.
In the cabinet, they found first the remains of the shattered goblet and
then, as they were about to give up the search, a piece of sable cloth
containing the heart itself.

Young Dr. Pelletan put the heart into another crystal goblet, along
with the fragments of the original one. The heart had no further
adventures until his death in 1879, when it was passed on to Pelletan's
wife's cousin, the architect Prosper Deschamps. He tried to persuade

one of the exiled Bourbons, the comte de Chambord, to accept it, but this nobleman wanted better evidence of its authenticity. In 1887, Deschamps died and bequeathed the heart to Edouard Dumont, his wife's son from an earlier marriage. In 1895, Dumont and a friend, the

The heart of the Temple Child in its urn, as it can be seen today.
A photograph from the collection of M. Philippe Delorme,
reproduced with permission.

royalist historian Maurice Pascal, offered the heart to the main Bourbon claimant to the French throne, Don Carlos, the duke of Madrid.
After all, it was the one hundredth anniversary of the death of Louis
XVII, and they thought it very appropriate that the heart should rejoin
the other relics of the Bourbon family. Don Carlos agreed to receive
it, and Pascal took the heart with him to Venice and handed it over to
him. A few weeks later, it was put in the Bourbon shrine at the castle
of Frohsdorf in Austria, together with the bonnet Marie Antoinette
had worn on the day of her execution, and her bloodstained scarf. The
heart was to stay there for almost half a century, until Princess Massimo, daughter of Don Carlos, took it back to Italy in 1942. This was
a wise precaution on her part, since Frohsdorf was pillaged by the
Soviet troops in 1945; nobody knows what use they would have made
of the 150-year-old heart of a prince. In 1975, two of Princess Massimo's daughters presented the heart to the duke de Bauffremont,
president of the memorial to the kings and queens of France at the
Basilique Saint-Denis just outside Paris, where it joined a large collection of relics from various kings, queens, and princes of the old
Bourbon dynasty.[45]

## THE MYSTERY SOLVED?

IN 1995 steps were taken to use DNA technology to solve the mystery of the Lost Dauphin. The Dutch scholar J. H. Petries and the
Paris professor Philippe A. Boiry knew that Naundorff's tomb in Delft
had been opened in 1950, to find out whether he had been poisoned
with arsenic, as the Naundorffists alleged (he had not). The right
humerus bone was still in storage in Holland, as were hair samples
taken at the time of Naundorff's death in 1845 and at the exhumation
in 1950. The two scholars also managed to trace hair samples from
Marie Antoinette and from two of her sisters. Two living descendants
of two of Marie Antoinette's aunts, in the female line, each consented
to deliver a blood specimen and a hair sample. The plan was to use

analysis of mitochondrial DNA to test the hypothesis that Naundorff was the son of Marie Antoinette. The mitochondria are subcellular organelles that play an important role in the generation of cellular energy. They contain their own DNA, which is always inherited in the female line, since the mitochondria are transferred through the egg, not the sperm. Mitochondrial DNA is present in high copy numbers because of the abundance of mitochondria, and it has the added advantage to be more likely than chromosomal DNA to survive for prolonged periods of time. Mitochondrial DNA has two regions on its so-called D-loop that vary considerably between individuals who do not share the same matrilineal descent; it is possible to analyze sequences from these regions in cases of disputed identity. If Naundorff were really Louis XVII, his mitochondrial DNA would be identical with that of Marie Antionette and her aunts. Petries and Boiry secured the cooperation of a genetics laboratory at the University of Louvain, Belgium, and another one in Nantes, France. Naundorff's descendants welcomed the study and gave official sanction for the use of their forebear's remains.

The hair samples from Marie Antoinette's aunts were from a rosary that had belonged to Empress Maria Theresia, kept in the convent of Klagenfurt. Those from Marie Antoinette herself came from a private collection in Cannes, and from a document kept in the library of the University of Nijmegen. The scientists found that the samples from Marie Antoinette and her two sisters coincided. Mitochondrial DNA from Naundorff's humerus showed several sequences not matching those from Marie Antoinette, her two sisters, and the two living relatives. Thus the scientists concluded that it was very unlikely that Naundorff was the son of Marie Antoinette.[46] Boiry, himself a Naundorffist, strongly disagreed, and so did the present-day pretender, Prince Charles Louis Edmond de Bourbon, alias King Charles XII of France. They demanded that Naundorff's bones be exhumed once more, so that undoubted skeletal remains could be analyzed, but their suggestion, which would have carried greater weight had it been made before the analysis was done, was not acted upon.[47]

In 1998, the historian Philippe Delorme suggested that in order to prove that Louis XVII really died in the Temple tower, the heart of the Temple Child should have its mitochondrial DNA compared with the samples from Habsburg descendants discussed above. In spite of the heart's marvelous odyssey, Delorme was convinced of its genuineness, and he was able to persuade the custodians of the Basilique Saint-Denis to deliver it for analysis. It was carefully studied by an anatomist and declared to be the heart of a child between five and twelve years of age, 2.4 x 1.2 x 0.8 inches, and completely desiccated and hard as rock. About 0.8 inches of the aorta remained. Pieces of heart muscle and aorta were taken for analysis and the heart replaced in the royal reliquary.

If it had turned out that the heart's mitochondrial DNA did not match that of Marie Antoinette and her sisters, there would, of course, have been joy among the historians who believed a substitution of children had occurred. The rationalist historians, however, would have found it easy to explain this away by casting doubt on the authenticity of the heart. To begin with, Dr. Pelletan might have lied about taking the heart, making up this story to ingratiate himself with the Bourbons and to avoid accusations of having had revolutionary sympathies. Second, the heart might easily have been exchanged when "lost and found" in 1810 or 1830. After all, one desiccated heart looks very much like another.

But the result of the analysis was that the DNA of the heart matched that of Marie Antoinette and her sisters, and it was concluded that Louis XVII had really died in the Temple.[48] The rationalists heaved a collective sigh of relief, and the news that the mystery of the Lost Dauphin had been solved by science after more than two hundred years reached the front pages of newspapers all over the world.

———

WHAT THE DNA ANALYSIS proves is that the heart comes from a child related, in the female line, to Empress Maria Theresia, mother of Marie Antoinette. She had no fewer than sixteen children, eleven of them daughters. Many of Marie Antoinette's sisters married into various royal or noble families and had numerous offspring. It was a not infrequent custom among European royalty to keep and preserve the hearts of the deceased; this was often done in the course of embalming. Could the heart of the Temple Child have been swapped for that of one of these Habsburg descendants at some time?[49] First, is it possible that Dr. Pelletan somehow got hold of an alternative royal heart? This is very unlikely. After all, if he had wanted to deceive the Bourbons, he could easily have obtained a suitable heart from his medical practice and given it out to be that of the Temple Child. There is no record that Pelletan had access to any repository where royal relics were kept. His story of how the heart was taken by Dr. Tillus is another hiatus, but it has the appearance of truth, and Pelletan clearly had no doubt the heart he recovered was the right one.

The most important hiatus in the heart's odyssey occurs in 1830, when it was lost during the sacking of the archbishop's palace. A vital clue concerning this comes from one of the 1890s articles about the heart. When describing the library of the archbishop of Paris, the article clearly states that, during its short sojourn in the collection of this prelate, the heart of the Temple Child was kept next to that of the dauphin's elder brother, Louis Joseph. In a letter, Pelletan himself refers to the archbishop's interest in these two royal hearts and to his plan to deposit them at the Val-de-Grâce.[50] Here was a heart from another child of Marie Antoinette, a heart of the right size and with the same mitochondrial DNA. We do not know how the heart of Louis Joseph had been prepared during autopsy; it may well have been bathed in alcohol and allowed to dry out. It was then put into an inner shrine of lead, within a more ornate shrine of gilt silver. It is not known with certainty whether the lead shrine was filled with alcohol or with some decoction of aromatic herbs. The embalming protocols for certain other French royals suggest a quite elaborate protocol, in which the dried heart was put into a glass vessel containing a complicated decoction of herbs and spices.[51] In a ceremony held on June 12, 1789, the shrine containing Louis Joseph's heart joined a collection of forty-seven royal hearts in the Val-de-Grâce chapel. But in 1793 the Paris mob broke into this chapel, threw the hearts about the place, and stole the gold and silver from their urns. With their customary lack of reverence for royalty, the people threw the hearts into a wheelbarrow and dumped them into a large fire that was burning in the Place de Grève. But in 1817, a secretary named Legoy appeared before the local mayor, explaining that he had been at the Val-de-Grâce in 1793 and saved the heart of Louis Joseph from the vandals. According to one version, the mayor contacted Louis XVIII, and the heart was deposed at the Basilique Saint-Denis. But when Philippe Boiry made inquiries in 1999, it turned out that the heart of Louis Joseph was not at the Basilique Saint-Denis, nor was there any evidence that it had ever been there.[52] This adds credibility to the account that the heart was in the archbishop's library in 1830. Boiry also made another interesting discovery, namely that two independent accounts stated that during the pillage of the archbishop's palace the urn containing the heart of Louis XVII had actually been stolen and thrown into the Seine. Tantalizingly, one story said that the heart thus disposed of was kept in a lead bottle (Louis Joseph's?); the other, that it was kept in a vase (the Temple Child's).[53]

A third alternative that needs to be ruled out is that the heart was replaced with that of some descendant of Maria Theresia sometime between 1895 and 1975, while it was kept at Frohsdorf. An argument against this is that, in general, the appearance of the heart agrees well with the 1894 descriptions. Some puzzling discrepancies have been pointed out, however. In 1894, the heart was specifically stated to be around 8 centimeters (3.4 inches) in length, 2 centimeters longer than the heart examined in 1999. A comparison between the 1895 plate of the heart in its crystal goblet and a photograph of the heart taken in 1999 clearly shows this discrepancy in size. But a dried anatomical specimen like this does not shrink with age. Furthermore, the 1894 description states that the left ventricle was flattened and deformed; in 1999, it was large and dilated. Is it possible that the heart of the Temple Child was swapped for that of a Habsburg descendant during its residence at Frohsdorf? We know that the urn must have been opened at least once, since the fragments of the original urn had disappeared. It is also known that other Bourbon and Habsburg hearts were kept at Frohsdorf. The historian Laure de La Chapelle has discovered a curious letter written by a French Jesuit priest, mentioning that a heart said to have been that of Louis XVII was at Frohsdorf in 1885.[54] This cannot have been the heart of the Temple Child, since, as we know, it was not accepted by Don Carlos until 1895. There is a distinct possibility that it was the heart of Louis Joseph. There was a tradition at Frohsdorf that the dauphin's heart had once been kept by the duchess of Angoulême, the sister of Louis XVII. From her, it had passed on to the comte de Chambord, and from him to the Frohsdorf collection of relics. This curious tradition, repeated by the Princess Massimo as late as 1975, would indicate that in the late nineteenth century, there were two dauphin's hearts at Frohsdorf: the one kept by the duchess of Angoulême and the comte de Chambord, and referred to by the priest in his 1885 letter, and the one handed over to Don Carlos in 1895. The discrepancy in size mentioned above might actually suggest that it was not the heart of the twelve-year-old Louis Charles, but that of the nine-year-old Louis Joseph, that was taken for DNA analysis. The crystal goblet has the inscription "Louis. Le coeur du Dauphin y est conservé," which would have fit either heart.

## THE FINAL VERDICT

THE RIDDLE OF the Lost Dauphin has all the hallmarks of a true historical mystery. The fate of Louis XVII is a singularly sad and tragic one. Throughout the ages, many people have passionately wanted a happy ending to the story, with the little martyr king escaping, but massive historical and medical evidence speaks against Louis XVII's leaving the Temple tower alive. The case for a substitution of children in January 1794 is far stronger. It has support from contemporary sources and would explain the immurement of the Temple Child as well as many other puzzling circumstances. But the sheer amount of conflicting evidence has rendered it almost impossible for any historian to decide this question. Depending on which witnesses one chooses to believe, one can build a convincing case for a substitution of children because of the death of Louis XVII, and then an equally convincing case that Louis XVII and the Temple Child were one and the same person. Nor, it must be said, is the medical evidence entirely decisive. There are some intriguing hints that the Temple Child was taller and older than Louis XVII, with darker hair. On the other hand, the arguments advanced by many writers that the findings from the skeleton in the Sainte-Marguerite cemetery favor the theory of a substitution of children are not valid, since these bones were not those of the Temple Child. Except for the shortcomings of Dr. Pelletan's autopsy report, it might well have been possible to solve the mystery by means of a critical analysis of the Temple Child's tuberculous illness. Still, the uncommonly rapid progress of the disease renders it unlikely, though not impossible, that Louis XVII and the Temple Child were the same person.

The study of mitochondrial DNA proves that the heart analyzed is from a matrilineal descendant of Marie Antoinette's mother. The theory of a substitution of children must be wrong unless one presumes that there was also a substitution of hearts. Again, this is unlikely, though not impossible. There is no reason to think that such a substitution was done deliberately. Dr. Pelletan was an honorable man, and wholly convinced of the value of the singular relic he had carried away. The guardians of the Frohsdorf reliquary were elderly, conservative aristocrats, for whom the dauphin's heart had an almost religious significance; for them, it would have been the utmost sacrilege to substitute the heart of Louis XVII for another. Still, the possibility that the heart of the then elder dauphin Louis Joseph was at the archbishop's palace in 1830 and the puzzling reports of the two hearts at

Frohsdorf in the 1880s raise the question whether the heart of the Temple Child might have been mixed up with that of Louis Joseph by accident. But Philippe Delorme does not doubt in the slightest that the heart analyzed was that taken away by Pelletan, and he rightly points out that the arguments to the contrary reviewed above are all circumstantial. He also emphasizes that in the eighteenth century, the hearts of many French royals were prepared with a decoction of herbs and spices before being deposited at the Val-de-Grâce; if it were to be proven that this was done to the heart of Louis Joseph, the arguments for a substitution of hearts would lose much of their weight. But the protocol for the embalming is nowhere to be found, and this has led to speculation that a less elaborate protocol might have been used.

———

THE AMOUNT OF new material that has come to light since 2000 would indicate the mystery of the Lost Dauphin is still alive and well, although the search is now on for evidence in favor of a substitution of hearts, rather than a substitution of children.

# 2

## The Mystery of Kaspar Hauser

He came as one who uninvited comes,
Secure of welcome, to a kinsman's hearth;
And rather as an inmate than a guest
He went, unbidden. Whither? No one knew,
Nor whence he came. An unsolved problem he,
Like Gaspar Hauser, or the Iron Mask.

— E. R. LYTTON BULWER, *King Poppy*

ON MAY 26, 1828, the Nuremberg shoemaker Georg Weickmann was standing outside his house in the Unschlittplatz, a square just south of the river Pegnitz. It was a holiday, and not many people were about in the street of this ancient town.[1] Out of idle curiosity, Weickmann watched a sixteen- or seventeen-year-old boy come trudging unsteadily down the hill toward his house. He was stocky and had broad shoulders and a healthy complexion; his face was rather vacuous looking, and his blue eyes had a vacant stare. He was dressed in odd-looking peasant clothes and a pair of boots that seemed intended for a much younger child. Seeing the shoemaker, the boy bawled out, in a thick dialect that was not the local one, "Hi there, lad!" and then "New Gate Street!" Despite his strange appearance and somewhat uncouth greeting, Weickmann offered to show the lost stranger the way to this street.[2] When they had crossed the river, the boy pulled out a large sealed envelope and handed it to Weickmann. Seeing that it was addressed to "The Captain of the Fourth Squadron of the Schmolischer Regiment," the shoemaker told the boy that they had

Kaspar is taken into Nuremberg. From a contemporary engraving.

better go to the guardroom at the New Gate itself. The boy then said, "Guard! Guard! New Gate must have been recently built," but the shoemaker replied that this was by no means the case, since it was in fact very ancient. As they were approaching the imposing old stone gate, Weichmann asked where the boy had come from, and he replied, "Regensburg." Weichmann inquired about the news from this town, but the boy appeared to know very little. When they entered the guardroom, the boy respectfully doffed his hat and handed over his letter. The corporal on duty told him where the captain lived and gave him directions how to get there. Weichmann had had enough of good deeds for one day and went back home.

The mysterious boy had no difficulty following the instructions given. He turned up outside the captain's house, showed his letter, and told the captain's servant Merk that he wanted to enlist as a trooper just as his father had once done.[3] He wept and said that he did not

The best-known illustration of Kaspar Hauser,
as he was dressed when discovered in Nuremberg.

know where he came from, except that he had been forced to travel day and night. He had been taught to read and write, he said, and had crossed a frontier every day to get to school. When he was shown the horses in the captain's stable, he seemed delighted and said, in his thick country dialect, "There were five of those where I was before!" Another servant gave the boy meat and beer, from which he recoiled in disgust, but he drank water greedily and ate some bread that was given him. Footsore and exhausted, he then fell asleep in the straw of the stable. At eight o'clock the same day, Captain von Wessenig returned home and was told of the strange visitor. The boy awoke from his deep sleep when the captain entered the stable, and came toward him smiling with delight. He seemed fascinated by the officer's gold-braided uniform and took hold of his scabbard, saying, "I want to be such a one!" When asked his name, he replied, "I do not know, Your Honor," and politely removed his hat, adding that his foster father had ordered him always to take his hat off and say "Your Honor" to his betters. Merk then handed over the letter, and the captain read the following remarkable communication, neatly written in German script:

Honored Sir,

I here send you a boy who wishes to serve his King truly. He was brought to me on October 7, 1812. I am a poor laborer with ten children of my own; I have enough to do just to keep alive. His mother asked me to bring up the boy. I asked her no questions, nor have I given notice to the police that I have taken care of the boy. . . . I raised him as a Christian, and since 1812 I have never let him go a step away from the house, so no one knows where he has been brought up, and he himself does not know the name of my house, nor of the place; you might ask him, but he can't tell you. I have taught him to read and to write and he can write just as well as I can. When you ask him what he wants to become he will say a Trooper like his father was. If he had parents (which he has not) he would have been a scholar; just show him any thing and he can do it.

I only took him as far as the Neumarkt; from thence he went himself. . . . Honored Sir, you may question him, but he does not know where I live. I brought him away in the middle of the night; he can't find his way back. Truly yours—I will not give my name since I might be punished.

And he has not a single Kreutzer by him, as I have none myself. So if you do not want to keep him, just beat him away or hang him up in the chimney.

This letter, whose callous ending forms an unappealing contrast to the unctuous sentiments expressed earlier, was inscribed, "From the Bavarian frontier; place not named, 1828." With it was a brief note, written with the same ink and most likely by the same hand, but in Latin characters:

> The boy is baptized; his name is Kaspar; his other name you must give him. I ask you to bring him up. His father was a trooper. When he is seventeen, send him to Nuremberg to the Schmolischer Regiment; that is where his father was. I beg you to bring him up until he is seventeen. He was born on April 23, 1812. I am a poor girl; I cannot keep the boy; his father is dead.[4]

The Captain had no idea what to do with this extraordinary recruit, but a police officer thought that the boy should be taken into custody. At the police station, Sergeant Wüst gruffly ordered the boy to state his name and place of residence. He promptly sat down and wrote Kaspar Hauser in a clear and legible hand, but when pressed to state where he came from, he replied, "I dare not say. . . . Because I do not know." All other questions he answered, in his thick country dialect, "I don't know" or "I want to be a trooper as my father was." When given a coin, he was delighted like a small child and cried "Ross! Ross!" making gestures indicating that he wanted to hang the coin on a toy horse. When another policeman threatened that he would be put in a thick forest alone if he did not state his origins, Kaspar wept bitterly and pleaded, "Not the forest, not the forest!" Since he could (or would) not give any coherent account of himself, Kaspar was imprisoned as a vagabond in the Luginsland tower. To reach his prison cell, he had to climb a flight of ninety-two steps. The police examined Kaspar's shabby clothes closely in order to find clues where he came from. His boots were unremarkable, except that they were very worn and seemed far too small for him. His trousers were reinforced between the legs like riding breeches. Kaspar's jacket had originally been fashioned as a tailcoat, as the collar showed; it had later been inexpertly stitched together. Both the jacket and the handkerchief had the initial K sewn into them. Kaspar's pockets were found to contain a rosary, an old worn-out key, a prayer book, and some Catholic religious tracts printed in Prague, Salzburg, and Burghausen, one of them as early as 1770. The most extraordinary finding was a folded paper containing a small quantity of gold dust.

The turnkey of the Luginsland tower, a man named Hiltel, was amazed by the strange behavior of his young prisoner. Now Kaspar seemed unable to walk or to understand what was said to him. He would touch no food except water and black bread. When a few drops of beer or coffee were put into the water, he vomited and developed headaches; when some meat was hidden in his loaf of bread, he smelled it immediately and shied away in disgust. Kaspar was very timorous and wept copiously at the slightest provocation. When Hiltel's two-year-old son approached him, he backed off saying, "No hit me!" When he saw a shiny object, he reached for it like a child; when it was pulled away from his reach, he wept. When someone put a lighted candle in front of him, he reached for the flame and burned his fingers. When facing a mirror, he reached for his own reflection and then wanted to walk around the mirror to find the person he thought was hiding there. The turnkey watched him closely and could detect no hint of deception. Hiltel gradually became greatly impressed with the natural innocence of his strange prisoner, and had he not already had many children of his own, he would gladly have adopted the foundling himself. Two doctors, Preu and Osterhausen, came to examine Kaspar; both left written documentation of their findings.[5]

The boy seemed about sixteen or seventeen years old, strong and well nourished. His facial expression was apathetic and animal-like. His hands and feet were very soft and entirely without calluses; the feet still had blisters all over them.

Hiltel's conviction that Kaspar was neither a criminal nor an impostor gradually changed the opinion of the Nuremberg police; the foundling kept his room in the tower, but was now treated more like an abandoned, neglected child. Rumors started to fly about this strange "wild boy" in the tower, and crowds of burghers came to see him. Some of them were kind people who gave him toys and coins. He also received a wooden horse that delighted him more than any other present. Other visitors were vulgar curiosity seekers who threatened him with a naked sword to see whether he would flinch, or who clandestinely adulterated his simple diet to observe the disastrous vomiting and diarrhea that would follow. All were amazed that this sturdy, sixteen-year-old lad behaved like a small child. His walk was very tottering and his manner childish in the extreme. Kaspar thought his wooden horses were alive and tried to feed them bread and water; when the turnkey hammered a nail into one of them, he was inconsolable. As his vocabulary gradually seemed to increase, the visitors congratulated themselves that they were teaching him to speak. He spoke of himself in the third person, but was soon able to make himself understood reasonably well. One day, Kaspar had a very important visitor: Judge Anselm von Feuerbach, the president of the court of appeals.[6] The judge had taken care to come early, before the usual throng of curiosity seekers, since he wanted to see this strange boy for himself. As the judge entered his room together with a military officer, Kaspar ran up to them trustingly, much impressed with the officer's bright uniform. Feuerbach showed him a large dirty coin and a small shiny one, and Kaspar preferred to take the smaller coin, although the judge tried to persuade him the larger one was worth more. Feuerbach at once took a great liking to him: Kaspar was virtuous and obedient, and almost obsessively neat and tidy with his clothes and belongings. His memory was remarkable, as was his thirst for knowledge.

Finally, the day came when Kaspar was able to tell all he remembered about his previous life.[7] He said that before having been taken to Nuremberg, he had always been imprisoned in a cell six or seven feet long, four feet wide and five feet high. Its two small windows were boarded up, leaving Kaspar in constant darkness. He could neither stand up nor lie down properly in this narrow dungeon, but had spent his life in a seated position. Every morning, when he awoke from his slumber, he would find a loaf of black bread and a pitcher of water by his side. Sometimes, the water had a bitter taste and he fell asleep after drinking it; when he awoke, he found that his clothes had been changed and his nails cut. In his cell, Kaspar had always been content. All day long, he had been patiently playing with his three toys—two wooden horses and a wooden dog—decorating them with red and

Kaspar Hauser in his dungeon. From a contemporary engraving.
The image is a fanciful one: note the bed, the open window,
and the dungeon's roomy proportions.

blue ribbons. He was dressed in a shirt and a pair of leather pants with no backside; next to him was a hole into which he could relieve himself. Kaspar knew nothing of night and day or the passing of seasons; indeed, he lacked any sense of time. He never heard a sound either from humans or from animals, not even thunder. But one day, a stool with a sheet of paper was put over his knees, and an arm reached into the pitch-dark dungeon, put a pencil in his hand, and guided it over the paper until Kaspar could write his name. When asked whether he had wondered where this arm came from, the pathetic boy replied, "Why should I? I had no idea there were other people in the world!" Later, he was taught to speak, or rather to repeat a few simple sentences, like "I want to become a trooper, as my father was." A few days after this rudimentary education had been completed, Kaspar was dragged out of the cell and taught to walk a few steps by himself, before being deserted within the gates of Nuremberg with the letter in his hand.

Nobody seems to have doubted a word of this fantastic story: policemen, doctors, and the great Judge von Feuerbach himself were all outraged at this unparalleled cruelty, and the name of Kaspar Hauser was on the lips of every burgher in Nuremberg. Kaspar was formally adopted by the town, and a sum of money was donated for his upkeep and education. The mayor of Nuremberg, named Binder, issued a proclamation in which he urged every citizen in possession of a human heart to report to the Nuremberg police office even the most remote clue or suspicion concerning this inhuman crime.[8] In particular, the disappearance of a child two or four years old twelve or fourteen years earlier was to be viewed with the greatest suspicion. But although this proclamation was disseminated widely, and every German newspaper and quite a few foreign ones had long articles about Kaspar's strange fate, not a single shred of evidence was brought forth. Anselm von Feuerbach spent much time pondering the mystery: if such great effort had been devoted to hiding Kaspar away from the rest of humanity, he must be someone quite important, possibly of royal birth. Feuerbach was disgusted by the sneering, hateful sentences of the two letters Kaspar had brought with him, and the vile irony of the name given to him: "Hauser" could be taken to mean someone who is always kept indoors. He also noted the further irony of the title of one of the religious tracts in Kaspar's pocket, "The Art of Replacing Lost Years and Time Misspent."


## KASPAR AND HIS TUTOR DAUMER

AMONG THE NUREMBERG people who took an interest in Kaspar was Georg Friedrich Daumer, a young schoolmaster who had retired at the early age of twenty-seven because of faulty eyesight.[9] He devoted his time mostly to pseudo-historical scholarship. One of his pet ideas was that the religion of the ancient Jews involved human sacrifice, and that every firstborn child was either burned alive or slaughtered in cannibalistic rituals. Daumer also believed that these same Jews had made their exodus from Egypt by a more formidable route than other historians had presumed: they had wandered across the entire continent of Asia and then on to Alaska (the Bering Strait had been frozen when they crossed, but thawed just in time to engulf the pursuing army of the pharaoh). He dabbled in spiritualism, homeopathy, and other contemporary forms of quackery. Although many people in Nuremberg thought Daumer eccentric, and some believed him to be far from sane, there was no objection to his becoming Kaspar's guardian and tutor.[10] Daumer was living in a house in Nuremberg with his mother and sister, and Kaspar became his permanent lodger there. Together with a homeopathic doctor named Paul Sigmund Preu, Daumer performed a series of experiments with Kaspar, dosing him with various homeopathic medicines and observing the resulting diarrhea, belching, and vomiting. Kaspar appeared to react even to the most diluted solutions of their drugs, thus proving the theories of Preu's mentor Samuel Hahnemann, the founder of homeopathy. Moreover, the strange boy had the most marvelous magnetic powers. Needles and other iron objects attracted him, and he could lead

Daumer to needles or scissors that had been hidden away. This proved, to the eccentric schoolmaster's satisfaction, some theories of his about "tellurian magnetism." Daumer also claimed that Kaspar could see in complete darkness and that his hearing and sense of smell were preternaturally acute. The two quacks watched for even the slightest symptom of sickness in their young "guinea pig" and treated him with homeopathic drugs for every cough or sneeze.[11]

But Georg Friedrich Daumer was not just a buffoon. A kind, tenderhearted man, he was clearly fascinated by this strange boy, whom he believed to be the victim of a most heinous crime, and took good care to educate him. Daumer saw Kaspar as a rare example of a "natural" human being, because the lengthy incarceration in the dungeon had preserved him from the corrupting effects of society. If so, Kaspar was a living refutation of the doctrine of original sin. Meek and gentle, he would not return insults or even blows, and he wept bitterly when seeing an animal killed or a child punished. Kaspar did not even hate the brutal jailer who had kept him in the dungeon, but Daumer records that once, when seeing the night sky filled with stars for the first time, he was lost in wonder how beautiful it all was, and lamented that he had been kept in isolation for so long. Kaspar responded well to Daumer's patience and kindness and soon made such rapid progress in reading, writing, and other subjects that many people thought that he must have remarkable mental gifts. This added fuel to the persistent rumors that he must be someone of very high birth.[12] Although weak and timorous in other respects, Kaspar was an excellent rider: after rudimentary lessons, he could ride even willful and difficult horses.[13] Feuerbach records that Daumer ascribed Kaspar's excellent seat in the saddle to the numbing effect of sitting on a hard floor for many years.

But after having spent about a year with Daumer, Kaspar began to change. Although Daumer never doubted any of his story, and remained attached to him as a friend and tutor, he regretted that his pupil's "nature had lost much of its original purity, and a highly regrettable tendency to untruthfulness and dissimulation had manifested itself."[14] Kaspar sometimes played truant from his lessons and liked to ramble or ride in the fields near Nuremberg. Daumer attributed this change to Kaspar's diet: eating meat products had dulled his homeopathic and magnetic talents, and gradually changed the wonder child of Nuremberg into an ordinary boy. On the morning of October 17, 1829, a quarrel broke out after Kaspar had obstinately denied playing truant, although Daumer had verified that he had been seen outside the city walls. Later that same day, Daumer's maidservant found a pool of blood on the stairs and followed a trail of blood into the cellar, where Kaspar was found in a half-unconscious condition, with a bleeding wound on his forehead.[15] When brought up into the house, he suffered a seizure that was so powerful that it took three men to hold him down; afterward, he remained unconscious for almost forty-eight hours. In his delirium, he repeated the words "Not kill me! Why does Man kill me? I also want to live! I never did you harm! . . . I ride down to Fürth, not to Erlangen in the Wallfisch!"[16] When he had recovered, Kaspar told Daumer that earlier the same day he had visited the house of the homeopathist Dr. Preu, who had offered him a walnut. Kaspar was uncertain whether this kind of food would agree with his delicate stomach, but the doctor, always keen to make experiments, nevertheless persuaded him to accept one quarter of the nut. Poor Kaspar immediately felt sick and, on returning to Daumer's house, had to excuse himself from his lessons. At 11:45, he went to the outhouse, and sat there for a long time, when he suddenly heard a noise from outside. He stuck his head out of the door to see who it was, but froze in fear when he saw a masked stranger dressed in black, with shiny boots and gloves. The man said, "You must die before you leave Nuremberg!" and struck him a violent blow on the head with a fearful-looking cleaver. Kaspar fell unconscious to the ground. After coming to, he dashed into the cellar to hide, leaving a trail of blood from the gaping wound on his forehead. Kaspar later said that although he could not see the man's face, he recognized him as his old jailer. There was a great hue and cry after the assassin, but no person answering his description was found. All the police could come up

Kaspar is assaulted in Daumer's house.
Another fanciful engraving.

with was two reports of a man roughly matching Kaspar's description exiting Daumer's house, and later washing his hands in a trough. A woman was adamant, however, that no one but a beggar had been to Daumer's house at the time Kaspar was wounded.

After the attempt on Kaspar's life, interest in him returned, and there was much speculation that he must be someone of high birth after all. Feuerbach speculated that the reason for the murderous attack was that the newspapers had reported that Kaspar was writing his autobiography, and that the mastermind behind the plot against him had decided he had to be silenced. To prevent any further assassination attempts, two police constables were commanded to stand guard over Kaspar day and night. At this stage, Daumer had had enough of his duties as Kaspar's guardian. He complained that his weak physique and failing health did not qualify him as the tutor, or rather bodyguard, for someone who was a target for assassination. Kaspar had to move out of Daumer's house, to live with Herr Biberbach, a wealthy merchant who declared himself willing to take charge of the foundling.[17] All accounts agree that Kaspar's situation in Biberbach's house was not a happy one. Kaspar's guardian Baron von Tucher complained to Feuerbach that the two police constables were up to much mischief with the Biberbachs' maid servants and that the pure-hearted Kaspar suffered much from being the constant company of such brutes. Moreover, Frau Biberbach, whom von Tucher describes as a very nervous, easily excitable lady, did not exert a beneficial influence. Daumer insinuated that this wicked, sensual woman had wanted to make Kaspar her "plaything," but that the chaste foundling resisted her advances.[18] Whatever the truth of this accusation, made many years later and not corroborated by any contemporary source, it is clear that Frau Biberbach nourished a strong dislike for Kaspar. She claimed that he lied freely and threw violent temper tantrums when found out. Once, when reproached for untruthfulness, he was sent sulking to his room. Suddenly, a pistol shot rang out. The two police constables came running in and found Kaspar lying on the floor, again bleeding from a head wound. The foundling explained that he had stood on a stool to take a book down from a high shelf, but slipped and grasped a loaded pistol that hung on the wall. This pistol was one of a pair that some misguided individual had given to the accident-prone foundling, as a last-line defense against the stranger in black.[19] After this incident, the Biberbachs had had enough, and Kaspar was taken in by Baron von Tucher. In his house, Kaspar was monitored more closely and kept busy with his studies. His proud guardian could soon report to Feuerbach that Kaspar's earlier tendencies to lying and vanity had abated and that he was eager to learn and quite intelligent. Von Tucher was very pleased with his progress and hoped that Kaspar would get apprenticed to a Nuremberg bookbinder, to become a useful member of society. But a more sinister player in this drama had other plans.

## LORD STANHOPE INTERVENES

PHILIP HENRY, the fourth earl of Stanhope, was born in 1781, into a family both distinguished and notorious.[20] He was the nephew of Prime Minister William Pitt, but his father was eccentric and his elder sister, Lady Hester Stanhope, even more so: she lived in Lebanon in the style of an oriental despot. Philip Henry studied at the University of Erlangen, and remained a Germanophile for the rest of his life. From 1806 until 1818, he was a member of Parliament, but spent much time traveling on the Continent. It is by no means unlikely that he served as an unofficial spy for the British government; the guise of a wealthy, traveling gentleman gave him ample opportunity to meet various German and Italian rulers, whose political activities were of importance for the grand alliance against Napoleon. In 1816, he inherited the earldom and took his seat in the House of Lords. A handsome, aristocratic man, he looked every inch an English gentleman and lived in affluence as befitting a wealthy grand seigneur. Little is known about how he financed his extravagances, however, for he never held any paid positions and the family fortune was not that great. It may well be that he kept his part-time job as an upper-class superspy; it is also likely that he served as a secret political agent for various German princes. In 1829, just at the time Kaspar Hauser was wounded, Stanhope was actually in Nuremberg. He heard all about the mysterious foundling and became intensely interested in him. Stanhope's daughter later wrote that her father was a very kind, impetuous, enthusiastic man, much given to sentimental friendships. He tried his best to meet Kaspar, but there was such a crowd of policemen, doctors, and busybodies that he failed to receive an audience with the wounded celebrity.[21] Two years later, when Kaspar was living quietly with von Tucher, Lord Stanhope returned. Many people were favorably impressed by his illustrious family and noble title and by his wealth and lavish spending, but the puritanical Baron von Tucher disliked him. Stanhope showed a great affection for the foundling and avidly learned every detail of his pathetic life story. He

Lord Stanhope. From a contemporary print.

showered Kaspar with expensive presents and gave him 500 gulden as a life annuity and 100 gulden as pocket money. The two were soon addressing each other by their first names, and spent much time together. Lord Stanhope declared himself convinced that Kaspar must be someone of very high birth, and pledged to restore him to his rightful position in society. This reawoke Kaspar's vanity, and he began to speak of how he would treat his subjects once he was a prince. Disgusted by the earl's sentimental ideas and his corrupting influence on Kaspar, von Tucher resigned his guardianship, which was promptly taken over by Lord Stanhope himself. Anselm von Feuerbach was completely won over by the earl, and expressed his delight that Stanhope would adopt poor Kaspar and take him back to merry old England, where the foundling would grow up surrounded by wealth and privilege and safe from the sinister forces that threatened his life.

In his search for Kaspar's true origins, Lord Stanhope was highly impressed with some experiments made with the foundling after he had appeared to understand some words in the Hungarian language. He fell down in convulsions when the name Pusonbya (the town of Pressburg) was mentioned, and when he heard the name Bartakowick (the maiden name of the Countess Maytheny), he screamed, "That is my mother!" There was also a wild story from a Catholic priest, who denounced a preacher named Wirth and a governess named Danbonne as the kidnappers of Kaspar Hauser; they had stolen him from the family of a countess living near Pest. A Frenchwoman named Anna Dalbonne, who had been a governess in Hungary, fell into a fainting fit when she heard this story, and later died in a madhouse. The impetuous Lord Stanhope decided that Kaspar should be taken to Hungary, since the sight of various castles and towns, and the constant exposure to the Magyar tongue, would be the surest way to jog his memory. The earl paid all the expenses for Kaspar and his traveling companion, the police lieutenant Josef Hickel. But in spite of Stanhope's wealth and Hickel's diligence, the journey was a complete failure. Kaspar recognized no building or monument and appeared to have lost whatever knowledge of Hungarian he might once have possessed.[22] A Hungarian nobleman who had met Kaspar in Munich later told Stanhope that he and his son had often had a good laugh when they recollected the strange boy and his histrionic

Probably the most accurate image of Kaspar.
A lithograph by J. N. Hoff from a
portrait painted in 1830.

behavior. The earl later wrote that, from this time onward, he began to nourish doubts about Kaspar's character and veracity.[23]

As soon as Lord Stanhope had become Kaspar's guardian, he seemed gradually to lose his interest in the strange boy; this grew even more evident after the disastrous trip to Hungary. There was never any question of his actually adopting Kaspar, or even taking him back to England. Instead, Lord Stanhope left Ansbach in January 1832 and devoted himself to his usual mysterious activities, traveling around Europe and visiting various magnates. Kaspar was lodged with an Ansbach schoolmaster named Johann Meyer. This individual was a small-minded, stern disciplinarian, not noted for kindness to his pupils. A strong mutual antipathy soon developed between him and Kaspar. It is certain that Meyer was spying on Kaspar, and probable that he was instructed by Lord Stanhope to do so. In particular, Meyer was eager to get his hands on a diary Kaspar was writing, but although he bullied and threatened his pupil, and even clandestinely searched his belongings, Kaspar managed to hide it.[24] Kaspar was never allowed out of doors unaccompanied, and his amusements were few: religious education with Pastor Fuhrmann, a kindly parson who liked Kaspar very much, and occasional visits to Feuerbach's house and to various parties arranged by the Ansbach burghers. Meyer force-fed him a stiff daily dose of history, Latin, and mathematics. It is not surprising that Kaspar learned little from this pedantic tyrant, or that Meyer wrote long letters to Lord Stanhope lamenting his pupil's lack of industry. Meyer's greatest complaint was that Kaspar tended to be untruthful, particularly when he wanted excuses to leave the house where his life was made so miserable. But as Daumer had previously noted, most of Kaspar's lies were childish inventions rather than deliberate false-hoods. In late 1832, Feuerbach arranged for Kaspar to be apprenticed to his own court as a junior clerk. Although Meyer objected that this work was too taxing for his pupil's sluggish brain, Kaspar appears to have executed his duties relatively conscientiously.

But Feuerbach also had another project. He had never ceased pondering the mystery of Kaspar Hauser, and earlier the same year he had published a book about the case, which he called an instance of soul murder: Kaspar's youth had been stolen away from him in this most obscure and enigmatic crime.[25] Feuerbach thought Kaspar must be a legitimate, not an illegitimate, child, in view of the great care taken to keep his birth secret. The radical means used to hide Kaspar from the rest of humanity, and the extraordinary power and means available to those responsible for this unheard-of crime, indicated that he must be of very high birth. Feuerbach advanced no speculation what his origins might be, but he hinted that the solution of the mystery would lie behind "certain golden castle gates"; privately, he was convinced Kaspar was the lost crown prince of Baden. But Feuerbach died suddenly in May 1833, and Kaspar lost his best friend. Meyer's bullying grew increasingly confident, and he openly voiced the opinion that Kaspar was nothing but a liar and a fraud and that he had faked the attempt on his life to gain sympathy and attention.

## THE DEATH OF KASPAR HAUSER

ON SATURDAY, December 14, 1833, Kaspar Hauser went to his religion lessons with Pastor Fuhrmann at 8 A.M. The parson wanted Kaspar's help in fabricating a cardboard box, but Kaspar saw that the unworldly clergyman had purchased paper that was too thin for this to be at all feasible. He himself went out to purchase better-quality paper and then began working with alacrity. At 9 A.M., he went to his clerical work in the chancery, before having luncheon with Meyer at 12:30. Such was his enthusiasm for the cardboard box, however, that Kaspar returned to the parson's house at 12:45 and kept working diligently until the pastor told him, at 2:27 P.M., that he was going to church. A few minutes later, Kaspar reluctantly left his handiwork and walked with the parson for a few blocks. He appeared cheerful and vigorous, saying that he was now going to call on Miss Lilla von Stichaner, whom he had met at one of Feuerbach's dinner parties, to help her make a fire screen, something he had promised to do the preceding Wednesday. He then left the parson, following the proper way to reach Miss von Stichaner's house. But then something must have happened that made Kaspar change his plans.[26]

Just before 3 P.M., two people saw Kaspar walking toward the Hofgarten park. Shortly thereafter, the wife and daughter of another Ansbach parson saw him walking in the park. The weather was very cold and windy, and Kaspar was alone. The workman Joseph Leich later saw Kaspar walking in the park together with a strange man; he was amazed that they were outdoors in this abominable weather, particularly because Kaspar wore no overcoat. He described the man as being six feet tall, in his forties, with a dark beard and mustache, and wearing a blue coat and a round black hat. A cooper named Pfaffenberger had first seen Kaspar walking alone at about 2:30 and noted that he appeared cheerful; he then met Leich at 3 P.M. and heard about Kaspar's meeting with the stranger in the Hofgarten. It later turned out that seven other witnesses, one of them a police constable and one a schoolmaster, had seen a stranger fitting this description lurking about in the main square or in the Hofgarten. A farmer said there must have been a fight, since he had seen a man with a bloodstained hand walk out of the gardens. At 3:30 P.M., the bell rang at Meyer's house. When the door was opened, Kaspar Hauser burst into the house. Grimacing spastically, he gestured first toward the left side of his chest, then toward the street. Still without a word, he then grasped the schoolmaster's hand and pulled him in the direction of the Hofgarten. Meyer saw that Kaspar was bleeding slightly from the chest and asked him whether he had suffered an accident in the park. Kaspar nodded and, gasping for breath, finally blurted out, "Went to the Hofgarten—Man had knife—Gave me pouch—Stabbed—Ran as fast as I could—Pouch is still there!" The schoolmaster asked him what he was doing in the park in the first place, in this foul weather, and Kaspar replied, "Man came to the chancery in the morning—Message I should be in the Hofgarten at two-thirty for something to be shown to me!" He then collapsed, and Meyer dragged him home, where he was put to bed.

Having gathered his wits after these dramatic events, Meyer put his narrow mind to work. He strongly suspected that the foundling had faked another attack on himself to gain attention and compassion. After all, the injury did not look serious. Meyer told Kaspar about his suspicions and upbraided him for this stupid prank. As the boy lay groaning with pain on the couch, Meyer threatened him with a sound birching. Although bullied for more than an hour, Kaspar did not change his story, and the furious schoolmaster finally stomped off to fetch a doctor. A certain Dr. Heidenreich came to the schoolmaster's

Kaspar Hauser is murdered. From a lithograph by Walde.

house and examined Kaspar. Probably influenced by Meyer's opinion that the wound was not dangerous, he thrust his finger into the open stab wound in Kaspar's chest to find out how deep it was. Even at this time, there was some awareness that it was not particularly wise for a doctor to use his own finger to probe a wound in this way, but Heidenreich was not exactly a leading light of the medical profession. To his amazement, the wound was very deep, and it must have given him a nasty shock when his finger practically touched Kaspar's still beating heart. The shaken Heidenreich declared that Kaspar's life was certainly in danger; aghast at this information, the schoolmaster belatedly ran off to the police station to report the crime. A constable went to the place where Kaspar said he had been stabbed, near the memorial to a poet named Uz. He found a small purse there, with a piece of paper inside, but no trace of the perpetrator of the crime or any other worthwhile clue.[27] This piece of paper had the following cryptic writing on it, words that have puzzled historians ever since:

> To be delivered.
> Hauser will be able to tell you exactly who I am, and whence I come,
> but to save him the trouble I will do it myself:
> I come from————
> At the Bavarian frontier,
> By the river————
> I will even tell you my name—M.L.Ö.

Later the same day, another local doctor, Horlacher, was consulted; he confidently stated that the injury was very trifling and that Kaspar would soon recover. Relieved to hear this, Meyer told his friends that the wound was really just a scratch and that the poor boy was merely suffering from a touch of jaundice as a result of the nervous shock.[28] When formally questioned by the police, Kaspar said that he had been approached outside the chancery by an individual looking like a workman, who had invited him to come to the Hofgarten to see some specimens of clay. Although clay specimens are not particularly interesting objects, and although the weather was cold and wet, Kaspar had obediently gone to the appointed meeting place, but found no one there. After waiting for a while, he walked toward the Uz memorial. Suddenly, a man came up to him, holding out a purse and saying, "I give you this purse as a present." Kaspar took the purse from him, and the man immediately stabbed him in the chest with a stiletto. The police constable showed him the purse, and Kaspar recognized it as the one he had dropped. Kaspar said the man who stabbed him was not the ordinary-looking "workman" he had met that same morning; the assassin had been bigger, with a ruddy face and a black beard and a mustache. He was wearing a black hat and possibly an overcoat. This remarkable story had several inconsistencies, one of which was picked up by the police: if Kaspar feared for his life, why had he skulked off on his own to a desolate part of town, and why had he not run away when a stranger accosted him? Kaspar feebly replied that, now that he had a foster father (the still absent Lord Stanhope), he had imagined he no longer had anything to fear. It also turned out that Kaspar had already seen the clay specimens and that he must have known that none were available on the day in question. No gardener or workman from the Hofgarten had been dispatched to see him. Several people had observed him running quickly from the park toward Meyer's house, but he had not cried out for help. After a few days, it became only too apparent that Dr. Horlacher's confidence was sadly misplaced; Kaspar was very ill, with a high temperature, weakness, and jaundice. As he lay writhing with pain on his bed, the bungling doctors could do little but stand and watch. Meyer was busy trying to persuade the police officials that Kaspar had stabbed himself; he did so within earshot of the wretched boy, who said, "Ach Gott, having to depart life in this way, in despair and dishonor!" Kaspar Hauser died in the evening of December 17, 1833.

Since Kaspar's death was considered suspect, an autopsy was ordered. Four doctors joined forces in this endeavor: the forensic physician Albert and the practitioners Koppen, Horlacher, and Heidenreich. Three of the doctors left independent accounts of the autopsy and opinions about the origins of Kaspar's wound.[29] This would have been beneficial had these doctors been reasonably competent, even by the standards of the time, but it turned out that poor Kaspar was as badly served by the medical profession after his death as he had been during his lifetime. It was found that the stab wound had cut through the pericardium and slightly wounded the apex of the heart, before perforating the left lobe of the liver and the walls of the stomach. A wound like this might well have been fatal in itself, but there are several contemporary accounts of military men stabbed in duels and battles who survived more serious injuries, with little or no assistance from the medical profession. In Kaspar's case, the cause of death is likely to have been bacterial pericarditis and pleuritis resulting from Dr. Heidenreich's polluted finger entering the previously clean knife wound, since the doctors noted that the pericardium was covered by large pseudomembranes and that there was a copious, foul-smelling pleural exsudate. Apart from some signs of peritonitis from the injury to the stomach, Kaspar's inner organs were normal, except that the liver was enlarged. Albert thought this phenomenon was a result of the twelve years Kaspar had spent in the dungeon, since he knew that the Jews used to lock their geese up in a small room so that their livers would become bigger! Heidenreich found that Kaspar's skull was particularly thick and that the brain was small and less convoluted than normal, but Albert's autopsy report, signed also by Horlacher and Koppen, mentions nothing abnormal about Kaspar's brain. It turns out, however, that Heidenreich was a phrenologist, who believed that the lumps and bumps on the head, and the overall structure of the brain, gave good clues to the character of the individual in question. His preconceived theory was, of course, that the twelve years Kaspar had spent in the dungeon had debasing effects on his brain structure, making his brain "animal-like" in appearance.

After surveying these dismal opinions from the four doctors, the reader will not be surprised that their opinions on the question of murder or suicide were wildly divergent. The whimsical Dr. Heidenreich was unable to deduce much from the autopsy findings, except a general impression that such a formidable stab wound could hardly be the result of a suicide. He also rightly pointed out that earlier that fateful day no person had thought Kaspar particularly depressed or dejected. Daumer wrote that, in a letter to Feuerbach's son, Heidenreich had declared himself convinced that Kaspar had been murdered, but he had been too fearful of controversy to make this statement in his official report.[30] In contrast, Dr. Horlacher found it likely that Kaspar had stabbed himself, but failed to give reasons other than that he thought Kaspar was left-handed and thus able to deliver such a stab wound to the chest. This disregarded affidavits from Pastor Fuhrmann and Baron von Tucher that Kaspar was definitely right-handed. The foolish Horlacher boldly claimed that suicides often appear very cheerful on the day they decide to end their lives. There is good evidence that this practitioner was much influenced by Meyer and that he actually helped the schoolmaster's amateur detective work to find evidence that Kaspar had killed himself.[31] Dr. Albert, the only one of the doctors who had any forensic experience, found the direction of the wound canal inconsistent with a suicide. He also knew that suicides usually bared their chest, and very seldom stabbed themselves through four layers of thick clothing as Kaspar was presumed to have done. On both these points, modern forensic science agrees with this otherwise obtuse German doctor.[32] Suicide by self-stabbing in the chest or abdomen is quite a rare phenomenon. It is a both painful and uncertain method of suicide; most people's knowledge of anatomy is wholly inadequate to making a lethal hit. If a dead body is found with a stab wound to the chest, forensic scientists have ways to differentiate murder from suicide. A suicide often has "hesitation marks," where unsuccessful attempts have been made to penetrate the chest wall; there were none on the chest of Kaspar Hauser. It is also known that a vertical entry line of the stab wound in the chest, as in the case of Kaspar Hauser, would indicate murder. In particular, it is very rare that clothes are stabbed through in a suicide; the few cases that have been reported often concern quite desperate individuals: raving lunatics, addicts high on crack cocaine, or frenzied Japanese swordsmen.[33] Even Meyer freely admitted that, far from being attracted by knives, Kaspar had always been very timorous and particularly afraid of handling sharp objects. Frau Biberbach added that Kaspar had always been cowardly and frightened of the slightest injury and especially the sight of blood.[34]

There was a general hue and cry after the presumed assassin, but to no avail. King Ludwig of Bavaria offered a large reward, and Lord Stanhope added to it, but no one was ever arrested.[35] This latter fact weighed heavily when the court was preparing its final verdict on Kaspar's death; it was argued that, had there been a murderer, the efficient Bavarian police would certainly have caught him. Meyer was as busy as ever denigrating his former pupil; his wife wrote that he ceaselessly visited people in Ansbach to persuade them that Kaspar was a lying, detestable scoundrel who had died by his own hand. In front of Dr. Heidenreich's wife, the frantic schoolmaster stabbed a large beefsteak underneath his coat to show how Kaspar had killed himself.[36] Meyer also claimed to have seen the purse, or a similar one, in Kaspar's possession prior to the stabbing. He examined the cryptic note, written in *Spiegelschrift* (mirror-image writing), which Kaspar had recently been learning, and found likenesses with Kaspar's handwriting, and a characteristic grammatical error of his. The Ansbach stationer could verify that the paper was similar to the writing paper Kaspar used and some was found in his wastepaper basket. It was folded just the way Kaspar liked to fold his letters. Unbiased witnesses later added that Kaspar was learning mirror-image writing at the time and that a similar purse had been observed in his possession.[37] Meyer had also taken down every utterance from the delirious Kaspar on his deathbed, particularly words that could be given a sinister interpretation. Kaspar had said, "Must write much with a pencil—What is written with a pencil no one can read!" and this was thought to imply the writing of the cryptic note. When asked whether he wanted to forgive some person anything, he had said, "Who am I to have a grudge against anybody, since no one has ever done me any harm!" The contradictory certificates from the medical practitioners could support any version of events and were given little attention; the court's decision was that murder was not proven. This verdict may well have been influenced by the activities of the enigmatic Lord Stanhope, who turned violently against Kaspar immediately after the boy was dead. In marked contrast to his lack of interest during Kaspar's last years alive, he now traveled ceaselessly around Germany to persuade people that Kaspar was an impostor, and published books both in English and in German proclaiming this theory.[38]


## THE LEGEND OF PRINCE KASPAR

DURING KASPAR HAUSER'S lifetime, there emerged several hypotheses about his origins, most of them assuming that he was of noble birth. As we have seen, Baron von Tucher and Lord Stanhope believed him to be a Hungarian noble. The foolish Daumer initially thought that he was the heir of a wealthy English lord. Another, no less daring contemporary hypothesis was that he was a son of Napoleon. The predominant hypothesis, first brought forth just a few weeks after Kaspar showed up in Nuremberg, was that he was the crown prince of Baden, stolen from his cot in 1812. Feuerbach was a firm supporter of this theory, and the vast majority of later writers have followed suit. The full-blown Legend of Prince Kaspar is as follows.

Old Grand Duke Karl Friedrich of Baden had three children from an earlier marriage when he morganatically married Luise Geyer von Geyersberg, who was given the title Countess Hochberg. This wicked, scheming woman was to become Kaspar Hauser's nemesis. She rapidly provided her elderly husband with three little princes and a princess, although there were rumors that their father was not the grand duke, who was in his seventies, but his son Ludwig. The countess was determined that her own children should become the rulers of Baden, to the detriment of Prince Karl, the old grand duke's only grandson from his first marriage. Karl had married Stephanie de Beauharnais, the stepdaughter of Napoleon. When, in 1812, Grand Duchess Stephanie gave birth to a little prince, the evil countess sprang into action. Impersonating a ghost, the White Lady of Baden, which was reputed to be seen just before the death of princes, she was able to enter the royal nursery, leaving a trail of frightened menials and swooning ladies, all fearful of ghosts, in her path. She stole the two-week-old prince and substituted a sickly child in his place. The changeling child soon died of natural causes, and the grand duchess was distraught. The evil countess put Prince Kaspar in the hands of two ruffians in her service, and they took him back to the family of the sickly child, substituting him for the child they had previously kidnapped. One of Countess Hochberg's court servants, Christoph Blochmann, had a son about this time, spoken of as either Johann Ernst or Kaspar Ernst in the civic records. It has been presumed that Prince Kaspar spent the first two or three years in the Blochmann family, before the evil countess executed the second part of her nefarious plot. She employed Anna Dalbonne, the swooning governess who had worked in Hungary, to take him to the castle of Beuggen, just by the Rhine. The little prince learned a few words in Hungarian from her. Further evidence for Kaspar's incarceration at Beuggen was provided by Daumer, who published a drawing of a coat of arms that Kaspar had seen in a vision. It is not unlike one that can still be seen at the Beuggen castle.

But Kaspar was not destined to remain at Beuggen for long. In 1816, a message in a bottle was fished out of the Rhine near Grand-Kemps; it contained a pathetic plea in Latin from a captive held in a subterranean prison near Lauffenburg, on the Rhine. It was signed S. Hanès Sprancio—clearly an anagram for "Sein Sohn Caspar" (His son Kaspar). The person who wrote this message must have pitied the captive little prince and hoped that this cryptic plea for his release would be deciphered by someone in Grand Duke Karl's employ. This did not happen, however, although the message was quoted in several German and French newspapers. Its meaning was not lost on the evil countess, though. Fearful of retribution, she decided to move her prisoner to another dungeon. Again, twentieth-century research has provided hints with regard to its whereabouts. When the novelist Klara Hofer bought the castle Pilsach in 1924, she discovered a secret dungeon. One of its iron bars resembled a drawing of a plant made by Kaspar in 1829. When renovations were carried out at the castle in 1982, a small wooden horse was found in an adjoining room. Thus, in the words of a recent scholar, "we now know . . . the identity of the castle in whose dungeon he lived for twelve years."[39]

While poor Kaspar was languishing in the Pilsach dungeon, the evil countess was not idle. She murdered Prince Kaspar's father, Grand Duke Karl, his uncle Friedrich, and his younger brother, Alexander, as well as numerous other people. At the time of her death, in 1820, the dynastic prospects of her own offspring seemed secure, but for one potential problem—the Pilsach prisoner. For some reason, this poor, defenseless creature was not murdered but left to grow big and strong in his tiny cell, nourished by his diet of water and bread. After the death of the countess, her accomplice Major Hennenhofer took care of the continuation of her political ambitions. This ruthless adventurer, who had risen from the ranks through his association with the countess and her evil works, again had qualms about disposing of Prince Kaspar. Instead of letting him join his poisoned relatives by slipping something into his drinking water, Hennenhofer had Kaspar released into Nuremberg in 1828. But Prince Kaspar did not become a trooper, as Hennenhofer had expected; instead he found many friends, and there was some danger that he would remember his past. As rumors were already buzzing that Kaspar was the crown prince of Baden, Hennenhofer ordered the same ruffian who had guarded Kaspar at Pilsach to murder him at Daumer's house. The brutal jailer bungled the attempt, although he was helped by the vile Lord Stanhope, the paid agent of the evil countess and her descendants, who had gone to Nuremberg on purpose to participate in the assassination. Since the two police constables were now guarding Kaspar day and night, it was not easy for Hennenhofer to make another attempt on his life. Instead, the cunning Lord Stanhope managed to outmaneuver Kaspar's friends Daumer and von Tucher and place himself in a position of authority and trust. The wild-goose chase to Hungary was just to divert suspicion and convince people that the earl was really on Kaspar's side. The spying and mistrust on the part of the earl's brutal hireling Hickel, and the lengthy incarceration with that despicable pedagogue Johann Meyer, were aimed at breaking the prince's spirit, but Kaspar stubbornly resisted the debasing influence of these loathsome guardians. It was said that Grand Duchess Stephanie wept bitterly after having read Feuerbach's book and that she expressed a desire to see Kaspar. This was not to happen. Hennenhofer and Stanhope tried the assassination game once more, this time with success. After Kaspar's death, Stanhope started his campaign of vilification, aided by the Ansbach schoolmaster. Feuerbach, who died earlier that year, was himself also murdered, by poison administered by Stanhope's own hand, and there were dark rumors that the wicked peer had disposed of others of Prince Kaspar's friends in a similar manner.

The supporters of the prince theory have claimed that some members of the house of Baden have actually accepted Kaspar Hauser as the lost prince, but the evidence is far from convincing. Prince Max of Baden is said to have promised to move Kaspar's bones to the family tomb, but this project was impeded by the Great War. A suitable last installment to this fantastic Legend of Prince Kaspar is provided by one of the seances arranged for Empress Eugénie by the celebrated medium Daniel Dunglass Home. The ghost of Kaspar Hauser appeared and introduced itself as the prince of Baden!

## HAUSERIANS AND ANTI-HAUSERIANS

MANY OF KASPAR'S friends felt outraged by the court decision hinting that Kaspar had killed himself, and particularly by Lord Stanhope's basely turning against his former foster son. Daumer, von Tucher, and others took up the cudgels in the foundling's defense, and a fierce debate was to rage for many decades to come. The Hauserians made Prince Kaspar a paragon of virtue, an almost Christlike figure untouched by his *via dolorosa* among knaves and fools; the anti-Hauserians blasted him as a brazen impostor who finally died in indignity by his own hand. He was either a prince or a vagabond—there was nothing in between. Countess von Albersdorf, a somewhat unbalanced lady of English descent who had previously denounced two innocent people as Kaspar's murderer, and who had an old grudge against Lord Stanhope, wrote a book accusing the earl of plotting his death. A certain Sebastian Sailer also had his own motives for proclaiming Kaspar the prince: he was a political radical and republican who wanted to exploit this scandal to denigrate the house of Baden for this vile dynastic crime.[40]

In 1850, the Danish physiologist Daniel Eschricht published a critical pamphlet on Kaspar Hauser.[41] His professional attendance on Danish prisoners who had been put on a water-and-bread diet left him disinclined to believe that this diet was conducive to a sturdy and

well-nourished organism. This, as well as the early observations of
Kaspar in Nuremberg, cast considerable doubt on his story of his
imprisonment. But Eschricht's knowledge of Kaspar Hauser's life was
clearly defective, since he claimed that Kaspar had been an idiot, with
the mentality of a two- or three-year-old child. There is good evidence,
however, that this is a most unfair assessment of Kaspar's intellect. He
could read and write without difficulty; several letters of his have survived and are well written and lucid. Kaspar even wrote some poetry.
Johann Meyer himself had to admit, grudgingly, that Kaspar was no
fool and that he was capable of making good progress in his studies
when he applied himself to them. Kaspar also had genuine artistic talent: several drawings and watercolor paintings of his that have survived show quite an accomplished use of color and perspective.
Furthermore, Kaspar was actually working as a clerk in the civic
administration, and even those with a low opinion of civil service
administrators would hardly consider work of this kind compatible
with the mentality of a child of two or three. Eschricht blasted
Daumer as the dupe who had willingly aided and abetted the impostor, with his ridiculous homeopathic experiments. The Nuremberg
schoolmaster, incensed by Eschricht's attack, wrote a book of his own
trying to refute the Dane's arguments, but his strange theories about
ghosts, homeopathy, and magnetism served to weaken his case.
Daumer also divulged that in 1834 Lord Stanhope had tried to turn
him against Kaspar, but when Daumer proved staunchly loyal to his
former pupil, the earl ran out of his house as if the furies were chas-
ing him. "Cannot you see he is the MURDERER!?" cried Daumer's
old mother, who was also present. Daumer was planning to write a
pamphlet against Stanhope at the time, but a mysterious villain was
pursuing him with his right hand hidden in his pocket, and the schoolmaster thought it best to preserve his life from what he presumed to
be the earl's hired assassin. When commenting on Feuerbach's trust
in Stanhope's intentions to move Kaspar to England, Daumer wrote,
in his characteristic highly charged prose, "Yes, a safe haven was given
to him, this innocent victim of the most cowardly, murderous mon-

sters: this haven was the GRAVE, and his mangled body had barely been sunk thereinto, when his 'beloved stepfather' blasted him as a worthless liar, impostor, and suicide!"[42]

The next worthwhile critical work on Kaspar Hauser came from Julius Meyer, the son of the Ansbach schoolmaster. He had inherited his father's papers, and published many observations that cast doubt on Kaspar's honesty and character, although the meanness and pedantry of his own wretched father always shines through. Meyer also trawled the archives to collect the various interrogations of witnesses in 1829 and 1834. This would have been a worthy act, had he not succumbed to the temptation to actually *improve on* these records and to falsify "proof" that Kaspar was an impostor. Young Meyer's most worthwhile contribution was that he had found a sheet among his father's papers that appeared to have traces of Kaspar's mirror-image writing.[43] Daumer again objected; in a long and rambling book of his own, the elderly schoolmaster blasted old Meyer as a torturer and his son as a lying scoundrel.[44] Shortly afterward, Daumer claimed that someone (probably an anti-Hauserian) had tried to assassinate him. In 1881, Julius Meyer published another dubious work, purporting to be a posthumous manuscript by Josef Hickel, the police lieutenant who accompanied Kaspar on his journey to Hungary. Again, this work is full of deprecatory references to Kaspar, but there is no evidence from Hickel's actions during his lifetime that he had any doubts about Kaspar's veracity.[45] When, in 1883, an impetuous German writer published a book on Prince Kaspar, containing some scurrilous observations on Johann Meyer, the son successfully took him to court for libel and had the entire edition destroyed. This series of successes for the anti-Hauserians culminated in 1887 with the publication of a long, unreliable work by Judge Antonius von der Linde, in which the entire business is reviewed through a jaundiced eye, and Kaspar blasted as a worthless scoundrel and impostor.[46]

At about this time, the interest of the British in Kaspar Hauser, dormant since the publication of the works by Feuerbach and Stanhope in the 1830s, was rekindled. Several publications reviewed the current German literature, greeting the works of the anti-Hauserians with approval.[47] Yet, in 1892, the first English-language book wholeheartedly promoting the prince theory appeared. It was written by Elizabeth E. Evans, whose ludicrous outpourings in favor of the false dauphin Eleazar Williams have already been noted. Having read the current German literature, she uncritically regurgitated many of the fantasist arguments from the Legend of Prince Kaspar.[48] Her bias against Lord Stanhope was remarkable: she called him "the most despicable actor in this fearsome tragedy." Miss Evans claimed that Stanhope had been the paid agent of a Bible society, who had neglected his family while traveling around Germany making money from religious bigotry. When contacted by the vile Major Hennenhofer, the peer had no scruples about putting his Bibles into storage and joining the conspiracy against Prince Kaspar; by the blackest treachery, he misled Grand Duchess Stephanie and spirited Kaspar away from his friends in Nuremberg. Not satisfied with blasting the earl as a murderer, scoundrel, and hypocrite, Miss Evans made the darkest interpretation of some scurrilous observations by Daumer about Stanhope's excessively affectionate behavior toward Kaspar and their frequent "kissing and embracing." She ended up by falsely claiming that on his deathbed, in 1855, the evil peer was stark raving mad and feared going to hell for his crimes. The duchess of Cleveland, Lord Stanhope's daughter, wrote a book of her own to defend her father, deploring that under English law it was not a crime to libel a dead person.[49]

In the twentieth century, Kaspar Hauser had a better press than any other pretender mentioned in this book. The bibliography of the case contains at least 400 books and 2,000 articles, the majority of them in favor of the prince theory.[50] In the 1920s, the German scholar Dr. Hermann Pies became fascinated by the mystery and decided to publish the original textual evidence. Although he was a believer in the Legend of Prince Kaspar, he did his best to stay impartial; his many books are invaluable to any serious researcher, particularly because many of the original documents were destroyed during the Second World War.[51] But Pies was also a believer in the occult and fond of drawing parallels between the life of Kaspar Hauser and that of Jesus Christ; in his view, Kaspar's via dolorosa became a symbol of human destiny. Rudolf Steiner, the founder of anthroposophy, speculated that the Jews and the Freemasons had made an alliance to construct a human being without a soul. This monstrous experiment took place in 1802, but the child (Kaspar Hauser) nevertheless acquired a soul and would have erected a new castle of the Holy Grail in Germany had the Jews and Freemasons not caught up with him. Another author speculated that God had entrusted Prince Kaspar with a mission—to unite the German states into a great kingdom that was to lead the spiritual development of humanity by setting examples of high religious and moral values. But, as we know, the forces of evil thwarted the prince; he was put in the dungeon and finally murdered. The disastrous consequences were that, instead of being ruled by the meek, gentle Prince Kaspar, Germany was united by the saber-rattling Kaiser Wilhelm. Two world wars, the Nazi atrocities, the atomic bomb, and the division of Germany into East and West could all be blamed on the failure of Prince Kaspar's great mission.[52] The historian and anthroposophist Peter Tradowsky has elaborated on this ridiculous theme: in his view, almost every major event in nineteenth- and twentieth-century history is linked to Prince Kaspar, the Christ of the modern world.[53] Tradowsky and his fellow historian Johannes Mayer later published a profusely illustrated 800-page tome that sums up the entire case from a pro-Hauser standpoint.[54] Mayer then obtained permission to study Lord Stanhope's letters and papers from the custodians of the Stanhope archives, who may have hoped that the result would be a fine biography of the earl. But in a 700-page book the bold German historian claimed that Stanhope had been a secret agent of the court of Baden on a mission to "silence" witnesses of the Kaspar Hauser affair.[55] The Kaspar Hauser revival triggered by Pies's work and fueled by the influential books of Tradowsky and Mayer has resulted in many books, films, novels, and plays about him; the large majority of them fully accept the prince theory.[56] But, as in the case of the false dauphins, this is due mainly to publication bias. People wanted to read dramatic accounts of the little prince's being kidnapped and mis-treated, and wild theories of conspiracy and murder among the aristocracy. While fantasists promoting variations on the prince theory had no difficulty getting the lucubrations of their overheated brains into print, valuable critical works were left unpublished or forever laid to rest in obscure specialist periodicals.[57]

In 1996, the American reading public was served a spicy version of Kaspar's adventures by the psychologist Jeffrey Masson, already well known as a controversial biographer of Sigmund Freud and a leading proponent of the theory of "recovered memories." Masson worked closely with the historian Johannes Mayer and had good opportunities to make a significant contribution to the study of the mystery, particularly since he had access to a recently discovered manuscript by Daumer, giving new information about Kaspar's early days in Nuremberg. Well written and controversial, his book was quite a success, probably one of the best-selling works on Kaspar Hauser of all time.[58] But Masson's uncritical acceptance of the Legend of Prince Kaspar, along with his unusual theories on child psychology, seriously flawed the book. He boldly claimed that 38 percent of all women were sexually assaulted before the age of eighteen, and that psychiatrists were overly skeptical and dismissive of their patients' reports of how they were abused as children, using the concept of the "false memory syndrome" to discredit them. Kaspar Hauser served as a metaphor for all abused, unhappy children in the world, and there was much speculation about his "recovered memories" from the twelve years in the dungeon.

## ARGUMENTS AGAINST THE PRINCE THEORY

ONE OF THE main historical arguments against the Legend of Prince Kaspar is the basic implausibility of the story. Although Countess Hochberg may have been an intriguing, unpopular lady, there is no evidence she was capable of mass murdering her own relatives in a carnage unprecedented in the annals of the German nobility. There exists no evidence they were even murdered at all; most, if not all, appear to have died natural deaths. Moreover, even if she had been capable of such bloody deeds, the kidnapping of Prince Kaspar would have been quite a futile crime, since his parents, Grand Duke Karl and Grand Duchess Stephanie, were just twenty-six and twenty-three years old, respectively, at the time; they did in fact have several more children. The little prince's uncles Ludwig and Friedrich were also still capable of siring children. And even if one accepts that the countess was poisoning her relatives wholesale, this still leaves unexplained why she did not dispose of Prince Kaspar in a similar permanent manner; after all, he posed a much greater threat to the succession of her own children. It has been suggested that she wanted to keep Kaspar alive to blackmail Grand Duke Ludwig and to prevent him from marrying, but again there is no evidence for this, or even any rational suggestion how such a blackmail could have been accomplished.

The proponents of the prince theory are right that there were rumors of foul play at the time of the death of both Grand Duchess Stephanie's sons. But medical evidence indicates that the little prince was very ill when he first saw the light of day in September 1812. Since he was a very large child, labor was difficult. He was born with congenital hydrocephalus and suffered from repeated convulsions. Grand Duchess Stephanie was herself still confined to her bed, and the little prince's grandmother Margravine Amalie looked after him. She described him thoroughly in her letters, and it is unlikely that both she and the nurse Frau Holst could be duped by an exchange of children, particularly since the little prince was an odd-looking infant with a very large head. Nor is the evidence for an exchange of children impressive; archival sources state that, far from dying as an infant, Kaspar Ernst Blochmann became a soldier and lived to be twenty-one years old.[59]

The speculative theories about Prince Kaspar's whereabouts before he entered Nuremberg do not stand up to a critical examination. There is no evidence that the message in the bottle was even remotely related to the house of Baden, and some writers have dismissed its relevance altogether, claiming that it was a prank by some students with a knowledge of Latin. The signature, Hanès Sprancio, can be interpreted as "I am a Jackass who don't know where I am!" No firm evidence links Kaspar to either Beuggen or Pilsach, and there is particular reason to doubt the evidence of Klara Hofer the novelist. She was an imaginative lady and a proponent of the Legend of Prince Kaspar; it has even been suggested that she invented the story of the wooden horse to make her family house seem more interesting. The room she proposed to have been Kaspar's prison is much larger than the measurements he himself gave in 1828. The prince theorists have blamed Kaspar's feeble mind for this inaccuracy, but it is natural for any person imprisoned in a small dungeon for many years to take particular notice of its dimensions. The Pilsach dungeon clearly never had any proper windows; again this is contrary to Kaspar's own description.[60]

Even stronger arguments come from the early observations of Kaspar Hauser entering Nuremberg, as told earlier. These accounts agree that Kaspar could walk and had enough stamina to climb a staircase of ninety-two steps and that he could speak intelligibly, though not intelligently. The prince theorists have alleged that Lord Stanhope bribed these witnesses to perjure themselves, and the admirably thorough Johannes Mayer has presented evidence that the enigmatic peer certainly bribed the shoemaker Weichmann when he traveled about to marshal the evidence against Kaspar in 1834.[61] But the affidavits presented by these same witnesses in 1829, before Stanhope could interfere with them, are damning enough. There are also numerous contradictions and inconsistencies in Kaspar's own story of his imprisonment. He said no sound ever reached him in the cell, and was greatly frightened by the first thunderstorm he heard, but the prison cannot have had soundproof walls. And can any person really learn to write in complete darkness, or learn to walk in just a few hours after spending a lifetime in a seated position? Why, if Kaspar had no concept of language, did he obey when the man told him to stop crying, and when he was ordered to go into Nuremberg? And how could he recognize the animals in the captain's stable as horses if he had never seen a real horse before? Kaspar told Hiltel that he could see a pile of wood and a tree from the window of his dungeon; he told Binder and others that the windows were always shuttered. Research from professional linguists has indicated that Kaspar spoke the quaint and characteristic Old Bavarian dialect, common in parts of Bavaria and the Tirol, but not in Nuremberg. Thus there is good evidence that, during his early days in Nuremberg, he repeatedly and intelligently used words he could not possibly have picked up in that town.[62]

There are also very strong medical arguments that Kaspar Hauser's story about his imprisonment was a complete invention. First, developmental psychologists agree that a child that has not learned to speak before the critical age of four will never learn to do so. This would, of course, tend to discredit Hauser's tale, but the more cerebral of his defenders, like Masson, have gotten around this by suggesting that Kaspar must have been brought up properly and taught to speak, and *then* shut up in the dungeon. But as the experience of similar cases of extreme deprivation shows, a child kept in total isolation for many years would become severely retarded mentally and emotionally and would certainly not be smoothly reintegrated into society.[63] All sources agree that Kaspar was friendly and outreaching when visited in the Luginsland tower, and many were impressed with his curiosity and eagerness to learn. Furthermore, at the time he entered Nuremberg, Kaspar was a stockily built, healthy-looking lad, broad shouldered and well nourished, with good teeth and a fresh complexion. This would hardly have been the case had he been fed only black bread and water for many years, since this diet is not ideal for anyone, and lethal to a growing child. Even a year or two on water and bread would have led to severe malnutrition and protein deficiency as well as rachitis because of a lack of minerals and vitamin D; a period of twelve years would surely have killed him. The earliest observations of him also agree that Kaspar walked upright and was reasonably agile. This could not have been the case had he grown up in a dungeon so low that he could not stand up, which would have led to muscular atrophy, flexion contractures of the knees, a hunchback due to kyphosis of the thoracic spine, and decubital ulcers of the behind. It was noted that he had a malformation of the kneecaps, which seemed flatter and more rectangular than usual. Doctors Preu and Osterhausen attributed this to his lengthy imprisonment, but this is in fact a recognized variant of patellar hypoplasia, a minor disturbance of the natural growth of the kneecap that has little importance for the function of the knee joint. Finally, had Kaspar been isolated from the rest of humanity for twelve years, his immune system would not have been challenged by the common infectious diseases of children, but there is no evidence he was prone to childhood infections during his stay in Daumer's house.

## THE VERDICT OF DNA TECHNOLOGY

IN EARLY 1996, it was decided to use DNA technology to put the Legend of Prince Kaspar to the test. After the inquiry into Kaspar's death had concluded, his bloodstained clothes were kept in the court archives until 1888. They were then acquired by the Historical Society of Ansbach, which stored them in a locked cupboard until 1926. The society exhibited the clothes at its own premises in early 1928, as well as at a police exhibition in Berlin. They were later transferred to the Markgrafenmuseum of Ansbach, and in 1961 a mannequin looking like Kaspar Hauser was dressed in the original clothes. It can still be seen there today. The civic authorities of Ansbach contacted forensic scientists from the University of Munich, who inspected the clothes thoroughly. The stab wound through several layers of clothing could still be clearly seen, and the entire suit of clothes seemed clean and in a good state of repair. There were bloodstains on all layers of clothing around the wound, and blood had also run down to form a substantial stain on Kaspar's underpants. This stain was cut out and subjected to blinded analysis of mitochondrial DNA in two specialist laboratories. The attempt to solve Kaspar's mystery was sponsored by the popular weekly magazine *Der Spiegel*, which obtained the rights to publish the results. The clever journalists milked the project for all the publicity and sensationalism they could get out of it. They ran regular updates on the progress of the research and reviewed Kaspar's pathetic life story, along with the evidence for his identity as the prince of Baden accumulated by various enthusiasts. The forensic scientists had secured the cooperation of two German noblewomen, both great-great-great-granddaughters of Grand Duchess Stephanie of Baden. Their mitochondrial DNA, inherited in the female line, was found to coincide. It would also coincide with that of Grand Duchess Stephanie, and any child of hers.

Throughout the summer and fall of 1996, excitement grew in Germany, particularly in the region around Ansbach and Nuremberg, where Kaspar Hauser's name was much revered. Outraged letters to the newspapers said that the cutting of Kaspar's underpants was a most wanton destruction of a historical artifact, and that a great German national myth was being dragged in the dirt by the sensationalist press. The museum curator replied that cutting off a small spot of blood from a pair of underpants was surely not such a great matter and that an expert conservator had repaired the damage.[64] He deplored the fierce letters that claimed he had murdered Kaspar Hauser a second time. There was also some newspaper debate about the originality of bloodstains on Kaspar's clothes. A joker confessed that he had himself once "improved on" the bloodstain with tomato ketchup when visiting the museum, and there was a good deal of newspaper speculation whether the project was still feasible. A newspaper cartoon depicted confounded scientists faced with the startling result that Kaspar Hauser's mother was a Dutch beef tomato. But the stern German forensic pathologists issued a statement that the substance on Kaspar's underpants was certainly blood. Then there was a second scare, after an eighty-four-year-old woman, a lifelong native of Ansbach, made a sensational confession to a local newspaper.[65] In the mid-1920s, her school had made an excursion to the Ansbach museum. She had been amazed to see that the museum janitor had brought with him some cow's blood, which he smeared on Kaspar's clothes to make the blood-

stains more impressive! Other newspapers took up this story, speculating that the reason *Der Spiegel* had not made the results public after
five months of investigation was the embarrassing finding that the
bloodstain was just cow's blood. The newspaper cartoonist published
another offering: the scientists walk into a field and approach a cow,
doffing their caps to announce that she is the mother of Kaspar Hauser.
The bull standing nearby says, "Rosa, have you cheated on me?" Una-
mused, the scientists issued another statement, to the effect that the
bloodstain they were studying was definitely human blood.

In late November 1996, *Der Spiegel* was finally ready to publish the
results. The magazine cover had a large reproduction of the original
drawing of Kaspar Hauser, as he looked when entering Nuremberg in
1828, but it had been cleverly retouched so that he was holding not his
letter to the captain but a computer floppy disc. The caption was "The
Bewitched Prince KASPAR HAUSER. Geneticists solve the Riddle of
Centuries!" Many people probably bought the magazine believing the
Legend of Prince Kaspar had finally been vindicated, but the results,
also announced on live TV and in a press conference in the Ansbach
Orangerie on November 23, was that Kaspar could not have been a son
of Grand Duchess Stephanie.[66] There was general surprise and dismay
among the adherents of the Legend of Prince Kaspar. Some of them
admitted that they had been wrong and that Kaspar was no prince of
Baden.[67] Others blasted *Der Spiegel* for its distasteful exploitation
of what they called the DNA farce. Further criticism was directed at
the museum curator; thanks to his irresponsible actions, Ansbach had
lost its foremost tourist attraction. Kaspar Hauser's life story had an
almost religious symbolism for some people; they furiously wrote to the
newspapers that although Kaspar's life had been taken in 1832, these
modern vandals and technocrats had murdered his soul by wantonly
disproving the legend of this suffering, blameless youth.[68]

Some of the diehard supporters of the prince theory mounted a
counterattack, claiming that the bloodstain was not from Kaspar's
blood. These arguments would have carried more weight if they had
been presented prior to the DNA analysis, but they nevertheless

deserve consideration. One author rightly pointed out that what was proven by the DNA analysis was just that the individual whose blood was on the underpants was not related to Grand Duchess Stephanie in the female line. Surely, these underpants had traveled much during their career as a museum exhibit; someone might have switched them for his own as a practical joke and added a suitable bloodstain.[69] Another author noted that when the antiquary Adolf Bartling examined the clothes in 1927, Kaspar's socks and flannel undercoat were missing. Both these garments are present today, and this, of course, raises the question about the authenticity of the other pieces of clothing.[70] Other historians have retorted that the underpants are marked C.H. and certainly appear to be authentic early nineteenth-century examples. They were photographed in the late 1920s and looked very much as they did in 1996, except that the bloodstain had faded somewhat; this adds evidence to the view that no substitution had been made during this period of time. It was discussed in the media, but apparently never seriously considered by the scientists, that comparison of the mitochondrial DNA from the bloodstain on the underpants with that from Kaspar's skeletal remains might be a valuable undertaking, since it would remove these lingering doubts.[71] But some of the most diehard Hauserians, people whose trust in the Legend of Prince Kaspar had an almost religious aura, would still take some convincing. In a speech made in 2000, the Ansbach scholar Rudolf Biedermann claimed that the house of Baden had stolen Kaspar's body from the grave many years ago and also substituted a replacement pair of underpants to confound the forensic scientists. A powerful conspiracy of noblemen, editors, politicians, businessmen, Freemasons, and Rotarians was keeping the truth about Prince Kaspar from coming to light.[72]

## RIVAL THEORIES

SO IF HE was not a prince of Baden, who was Kaspar Hauser? As we know, the anti-Hauserians held that he was an impostor who faked the attempts on his life, but who overdid it when stabbing himself in the chest, with the result that he actually killed himself. But if Kaspar was a deliberate impostor, he was surely one of the least opportunistic ones ever. He spurned repeated opportunities to steal from his benefactors and never showed any signs of dishonesty apart from telling the occasional harmless lie. It is not the least remarkable fact about this boy of mystery that, throughout his fifty-three-day incarceration in the Luginsland tower, Kaspar ate only black bread and drank only water. If he was an impostor, as Lord Stanhope and the anti-Hauserians maintained, he was certainly a determined one. And if it was Kaspar's intention to improve his lot in life through this deception, he failed miserably, since his existence as a lodger in Meyer's joyless house must have been dismal indeed. A German psychiatrist has instead suggested that Kaspar suffered from pseudologia fantastica, a syndrome characterized by an unconscious desire to deceive other people, that is not connected with external reasons such as malingering or financial gain.[73] This hypothesis has more to recommend it, but again there are serious counterarguments. We know that some of the people involved in the case, like Daumer and Preu, were foolish enthusiasts, but would men like the skeptical Hiltel, the stern von Tucher, and the brilliant Judge von Feuerbach really be taken in by such an impostor, for a period of more than five years? Most people with pseudologia fantastica are extrovert con artists, causing all kinds of misery to those who are deceived by them; contemporary accounts agree that Kaspar was meek, humble, and obedient.[74] And as for Kaspar's purported suicide, the historical and medical evidence concerning his death indicates that he was actually murdered. In 1838, a formidable-looking dagger was found in the park not far from the Uz memorial, along the possible escape route of the assassin. This "French bandit's dagger" has been presumed to have been the murder weapon, although firm evidence is lacking; given to the Ansbach museum in the 1920s, it was stolen by rioters in 1945 and has not been seen since.[75]

So, if Kaspar was not a prince and not an impostor, who was he?

Independent thinkers have supplied a few suggestions. In 1834, a certain Ritter von Lang suggested that Kaspar had belonged to a traveling troupe of Gypsies and vagabonds.[76] He knew that there were numerous bands of vagabonds near Nuremberg, and he had probably seen some youngster put on a display as a piteous cripple or helpless simpleton to gain compassion and money. This would explain much of Kaspar's extraordinary behavior when he came to Nuremberg, and his success in duping Hiltel and Daumer. Kaspar might also have done equestrian tricks with the Gypsies, and this would explain his familiarity with horses and talent for riding. The archivist Ivo Striedinger, one of the more astute twentieth-century Kaspar Hauser scholars, brought forth a similar theory: Kaspar had belonged to the so-called *Kärrnersleute*, a band of German Gypsies who put up permanent winter quarters during the cold season.[77] These theories also provide an explanation for the two attempts on Kaspar's life: it was, of course, one of the wicked Gypsies who came back to take revenge on this deserter from their ranks. But the theories of Ritter von Lang and Striedinger also have their shortcomings, some of them serious. First, all accounts agree that Kaspar was a meek, innocent, timorous youth when he came to Nuremberg; this is unlikely to have been the case if he was brought up by a band of vagabonds. Nor did Kaspar ever commit any dishonest act apart from lying. The arguments about his motives, as presented above, again stand fast: after a week with the martinet schoolmaster Meyer, any Gypsy lad would have taken the opportunity to return to his carefree life as a clown or an equestrian performer. The strongest argument against Lang's hypothesis is that twice, when Kaspar was found and after his death, large rewards were offered to anyone who might know where he was from or who murdered him. This information was disseminated throughout Germany by means of handbills and cheap newspapers. Gypsies and vagabonds are not noted for their affluence or loyalty; had Kaspar been one of them, they would certainly have given information about his origins. And if he had in fact been acting the clown or performing on horseback, what about all the people who had seen his performances?

In 1966, another constructive hypothesis concerning Kaspar Hauser's origins was presented by Dr. Gunther Hesse, a neurologist and psychiatrist active in Karlsruhe.[78] Dr. Hesse's medical knowledge made him disbelieve Kaspar's story of his imprisonment, and he reinterpreted the available data concerning his medical history. Records agree that when Kaspar came to Nuremberg, his hands and feet were extraordinarily soft, and at this time walking for half an hour produced severe blistering. Occasionally, he also suffered from a skin disease causing facial rash and hair loss. Dr. Hesse diagnosed him with epilepsy as well: twitching in the left side of the face, absence attacks, and also attacks of "convulsions" that resembled Jackson epilepsy. Dr. Hesse claimed that Kaspar's intelligence was that of an eleven- or twelve-year-old child and that he suffered from hallucinations and a tendency to confabulation. On autopsy, one doctor suggested that he had microcephaly. In Dr. Hesse's opinion, all these observations fitted with a hereditary disease called epidermolysis bullosa. Kaspar's epilepsy also neatly explained the presence of the key, the gold dust, the devotional tracts, and the rosary in his pockets: in nineteenth-century German folk medicine, all these objects were used as prophylactics against the falling sickness. Kaspar's thick country dialect implied that he had been a native of the Tirol district, and some words in the letter he had brought with him to Nuremberg were also in this dialect. Dr. Hesse knew that a form of epidermolysis bullosa was endemic in this district. He believed that Kaspar was just a poor boy from one of the villages in the Tirol. His name could have been taken from that of a local freedom fighter against the Bavarians; the monument honoring this Kaspar Hauser can still be seen in Kitzbühel. Kaspar had been vaccinated against smallpox, as was obligatory in the Tirol at the time. When looking through the old vaccination ledgers, Dr. Hesse found the name Kaspar Hechenberger, the fatherless son of the maid Maria Hechenberger in the village of Rattenberg. He was the right age, and a portrait of his uncle bore some likeness to Kaspar Hauser.

The descriptions of the blistering on Kaspar's hands and feet certainly resemble the modern concept of epidermolysis bullosa.[79] It would appear that the tendency to blistering actually decreased with age, as has been described in the medical literature; an alternative explanation may be that after Kaspar left Daumer's house, there was less fussing about his health. Unlike most patients with the more severe forms of epidermolysis bullosa, Kaspar could walk considerable distances without difficulty. Moreover, there is no evidence he had any of the other common stigmata of epidermolysis, namely nail dystrophy, atrophic scars over bony prominences, dental changes, and hyperkeratosis. The available portraits of him do not suggest that he had any marked degree of hair loss. Dr. Hesse is right that there is a subtype of epidermolysis bullosa with microcephaly, but this is extremely uncommon; nor is it proven that Kaspar really had microcephaly, since the most competent doctor at his autopsy thought his brain was perfectly normal. It may well be that Kaspar had an epileptic seizure after the 1829 attack, but this was probably post-traumatic. Modern medical knowledge does not support a link between epidermolysis bullosa and epilepsy; in fact, Kaspar's facial spasms are more likely to have been nervous tics. Thus, although it is possible (but by no means proven) that Kaspar had a benign version of epidermolysis bullosa, this does not give any particular lead with regard to his origins, and the remainder of Dr. Hesse's theory is mere speculation.

## A NEW THEORY

LET US FIRST summarize the small amount of hard knowledge pertaining to Kaspar Hauser. We know that his story about his imprisonment was untrue, but it is likely that he had little contact with other people throughout his youth. His soft hands indicate that he had done no manual labor for quite some time before entering Nuremberg. His dialect indicated that he came from a small, isolated village in the Tirol countryside, near the Bavarian frontier. As for the 1829 attack, there is no conclusive evidence that it was faked. The intention of the attacker, apparently, was not to kill Kaspar, since this could easily have been achieved when he lay helpless, but to frighten or intimidate him. As for the 1833 stabbing, forensic evidence indicates murder, and the witness testimonies agree that Kaspar met someone in the Hofgarten that day, probably a person he knew already. But then Kaspar's own story of what happened that day was clearly untrue, and there is evidence that he actually wrote the cryptic message himself and put it in a purse belonging to him.

The furor caused by Kaspar's arrival in Nuremberg was so great that it is reasonable to assume that his description would have been known by some person, had he not been brought up in near-complete isolation. The cause for this is easy to guess: he was the illegitimate child of a respectable woman. She had been seduced by one of the soldiers of the Schmolischer regiment, who were serving in the Tirol in 1812, but this soldier had deserted her. Kaspar's mother lived with her own parents at an isolated farm, and they decided to make Kaspar's existence a secret. He spent nearly all his time indoors, playing with his wooden horses and his wooden dog; sometimes, he was taken out to his grandfather's stables to admire the five farm horses. He was a sad, neglected, clumsy child, afflicted with nervous facial jerks, which his grandparents tried to cure with folk medicine prophylactics. The family was poor, and Kaspar rarely ate salt or meat. Perhaps it is true, as Kaspar himself said in Nuremberg, that for a time he attended a school across the Bavarian frontier, where he learned to read and write. Perhaps, when Kaspar was sixteen years old, his mother gained another suitor, who promised to make her an honest woman. Kaspar's grandfather decided that this awkward "Hauser" must be gotten rid of, since there was no longer any chance of hiding him away. His helper in this scheme was an individual we may call the Evil Vagabond, a criminal known to Kaspar's family. The Vagabond suggested that Kaspar follow the same career as his father and become a trooper. He wrote a letter containing the true facts that the boy's name was Kaspar, that he was the son of a trooper in the same regiment, and that his mother was a poor unmarried woman. Kaspar's mother could not write, so the Vagabond wrote another letter for her, at her dictation.

The Vagabond offered to accompany Kaspar to Nuremberg, and to make sure the slow-witted lad was delivered to the regimental depot. This was not due to altruism on his part, however. Kaspar was a ludicrous-looking figure in his odd clothes, and the Vagabond realized his potential as a professional beggar: surely, this pathetic boy would fill his purse, particularly if he was taught some heart-wrenching stories about how he had been abandoned and mistreated. But Kaspar's dormant mind and lack of money-getting talent doomed this scheme to failure, and during the weeks they spent trudging toward Nuremberg, the Vagabond got tired of his slow-witted companion and sometimes treated him cruelly. Kaspar had a bruise from a blow on his arm when he came into Nuremberg. Reverting to the original plan, the Vagabond deserted Kaspar inside the town walls of Nuremberg, himself making a hasty exit. Poor Kaspar was more confused than ever, since he had never seen such a large town before; the buildings, the throngs of people, and the bullying policemen frightened him out of his senses. He did his best to play the idiot, pretending that he was unable to walk or speak, and later told his story of being kept imprisoned on water and bread, just as the Vagabond had taught him. He flinched at the unaccustomed meat and beer, and then noticed that this gained him attention. After a lifetime of neglect and deprivation, he was almost childlike in his receptiveness of human kindness, as noted by Feuerbach and others. In the hands of Daumer, the credulous, fanatical enthusiast, Kaspar played his role better and better. The homeopathic experiments taught him to lie and deceive to gain the reward that was forthcoming when the quacks thought their experiment a success. The reason he made such giant strides in learning to read and write was, of course, that he was recapturing skills he had been taught already.

The only person capable of responding to Mayor Binder's proclamation was the Evil Vagabond, but he did not do so. Amazed that his stolid, uncomplaining charge was becoming a local celebrity, he instead made plans to exploit Kaspar's success in Nuremberg. The Vagabond crept into Daumer's backyard and surprised Kaspar sitting in the outhouse. Bursting the door open, he gave his former partner in crime the shock of his life. Grinning at the terrified boy, the Vagabond suggested that he open a door that night to enable burglars to enter Daumer's house. But the naïve Kaspar had learned much about humanity in the few months he had stayed in Nuremberg, and this included a healthy mistrust of the violent, unpredictable Vagabond. When he threatened to cry out for help, the Vagabond struck at him with a sharp knife, before quickly running off, being spotted only when he exited the house and when he later washed the blood off his gloves. We then know what happened: after being deserted by Daumer, who doubted the results of his experiments, Kaspar was turned over to von Tucher and then to the exuberant Lord Stanhope, who filled his mind with vanity and conceit. In the Hungarian-language investigation, Kaspar did just what Daumer had taught him in the homeopathic experiments; he played along with the earl and pretended to recognize some phrases, but Stanhope saw through him and began to doubt his sincerity.

In late 1833, when Kaspar was living in Meyer's house in Ansbach, the Evil Vagabond again showed his face. Having suffered poverty and hardship in the intervening years, he was filled with anger toward Kaspar for being well fed, well dressed, and secure. Amazed by the rumors that Kaspar was a prince or a nobleman, he realized that there might be some profit in this for himself, by means of threatening blackmail. After all, he was the only person who knew the truth, apart from Kaspar's family back in their isolated village. One morning, he stalked Kaspar on his walk to the chancery. Jumping out from an alleyway and grabbing the unsuspecting boy, he swore that unless Kaspar delivered a large sum of money to him, he would tell Meyer and Stanhope that the Child of Europe was just a common country yokel. Kaspar was in a desperate quandary. He still trusted Stanhope and believed that the earl would one day take him to England. He could not tell any person for fear of betraying his past in the Tirol, and it was equally impossible for him to accede to the blackmail, since Meyer had taken care of the money left to him by Stanhope. This earlier threat from the Vagabond may also explain one or two minor mysteries. First, Kaspar said that the workman had actually come to the chancery to invite him to see the clay specimens on one previous occasion; this might refer to the Vagabond's visit. Second, Meyer thought Kaspar had been very worried and dejected about two weeks before the stabbing; was this because he had received a threat?

For some days, there was no further sighting of the Vagabond, and Meyer noted that Kaspar was gradually growing more cheerful. But when Kaspar had left Pastor Fuhrmann and was walking toward the Stichaner residence, the Vagabond came up and ordered him to keep quiet and walk to the Hofgarten. Petrified, Kaspar did as he was told, being observed by several people on the way. The Vagabond crept after him, taking care not to be seen; it is curious that one witness, the forester Friedrich Rauch, saw him hide his face in his cloak. Only the workman Leich actually observed the two together. The Vagabond demanded money and became angry when Kaspar said he had not been able to get hold of any. Kaspar then produced the purse with the cryptic message from his pocket; he had written it in advance (in *Spiegelschrift* so that Meyer would not be able to read it) and carried it with him to thwart his old opponent, should he reappear. Kaspar threatened that unless the Vagabond made himself scarce, he would tell Meyer that his jailer had returned, and deliver the note to him. He could easily fill in the name of the village, the river, and the Vagabond's full name. . . . But this allusion was lost on the brutal Vagabond, who had no understanding of mirror-image writing: believing he was being made a fool of, he furiously stabbed Kaspar in the chest and then sped off through the park, throwing the dagger away as he ran. He was last seen by two witnesses walking quickly out of the Hofgarten into the Eyber Strasse and then toward the post station Windmühle.

In the meantime, the persistent rumor that Kaspar was the lost prince had reached the court of Baden. Although unfounded, this rumor was an embarrassment that needed to be dealt with. The obvious answer was to approach the capricious Lord Stanhope. He had become tired of Kaspar, whom he had not seen for almost two years, and when the court officials offered to reward him well if he could prove Kaspar was an impostor, the peer readily agreed to help them out. As we know, he had doubted Kaspar's story ever since the failure of the Hungarian experiments and employed his creature Meyer to spy on him. This also explains the earl's energy in denigrating Kaspar as an impostor after the boy's death.

## THE IMMORTAL KASPAR HAUSER

EVEN WHEN THE Legend of Prince Kaspar is viewed merely as a historical mystery, as we have done here, it is still apparent that the various writers on the Kaspar Hauser enigma have used it as a wider-ranging metaphor. To Daumer, he was a wonder child, a noble savage with remarkable powers; to Feuerbach, he represented a great and heinous crime that had to be solved. To the nineteenth-century German radicals, Kaspar served as a timely reminder of the perfidy of the ruling house of Baden. To other commentators, he was a "wild boy," comparable to children nurtured by wolves or other animals. These enthusiasts have wondered why, in contrast to all other genuine examples of this phenomenon, he acquired a language, was quite intelligent, and reintegrated into society without difficulty.[80] The obvious explanation, that his story was a complete fabrication, eluded them. To Herman Pies and other pious Hauserians, he was an almost Christlike figure; Peter Tradowsky and other anthroposophists made him a mythical hero along the lines of Wagner's Parsifal. To Jeffrey Masson and other psychologists, Kaspar Hauser was a symbol of child abuse. There is even a "Kaspar Hauser syndrome" of extreme deprivation in childhood, a very dubious addition to the medical nomenclature.[81]

The story of Kaspar Hauser shares several themes with the traditional fairy tale: the imprisoned prince, the simpleton with extraordinary powers, and the orphan in search of his real origins. That the fairy tale has no happy ending seems to have fascinated rather than repelled. In literature and the arts, Kaspar Hauser has taken on a life of his own.[82] Shortly after Kaspar's death, the first representations of him in fiction appeared in a German gothic novel entitled *Kaspar Hauser, or The Walled-in Nun*. By the 1840s, several novels had appeared, both in German and in French. There were none in English, but at the Theatre Royal in Edinburgh, Moncrieff's play *Caspar Hauser, or The Wild Boy of Bavaria* was quite a success at the time. Kaspar's fame even crossed the Atlantic: billed alongside the Feejee Mermaid at P. T. Barnum's Boston Museum was "Kaspar Hauser, the Wild Boy of the Woods, Half Man Half Monkey"; inside was a gibbering, retarded child dressed in a fur costume.[83]

Many novelists have since readapted the sentimental, highly charged story of Prince Kaspar, realizing that even the most stony-hearted misanthrope, who could smile at the sufferings of Little Nell and laugh heartily at the misadventures of the pathetic Smike, would get the handkerchief ready when reading about Kaspar's via dolorosa. It is in fact curious why Charles Dickens did not use the story either in his fictional works or in his journalism, but perhaps he was influenced by Stanhope's skepticism, like most people in England at the time. The great Kaspar Hauser novel was instead written by the Austrian Jakob Wassermann, who had been fascinated by the Hauser figure for many years.[84] His main theme was that of the pure-hearted innocent ruined by the selfishness and egocentricity of all the people he encounters; the novel's subtitle is *Inertia of the Heart*. The novel is well written and the narrative fast moving. Wassermann milked the Legend of Prince Kaspar for every drop of sentimentality and even added some "improvements" of his own to spice it up. Throughout the novel, wild threats are uttered, cryptic messages delivered, and mysterious clues found. The real Kaspar Hauser enjoyed a platonic friendship with Karoline von Kannawurf, a lady from Feuerbach's circle; in the novel, they fall madly in love, and Kaspar is filled with despair when she defers to social conventions and ends their relationship. The cruel Ansbach schoolmaster is presented as a cross between Fagin and Wackford Squeers; to evade the litigious Meyer family, Wassermann changed his name to Quandt in the book. Another Dickensian creation is the villainous Lord Stanhope—a debauched pederast, who is finally overcome by Kaspar's innocent candor and commits suicide. In his memoirs, Wassermann related how he narrowly escaped a lawsuit from the earl's grandson. Translated into many languages, Wassermann's novel has remained a classic particularly in the German-speaking countries; it has become the prism through which the majority of later interpreters of the story have seen Kaspar and his misadventures.

The best-known representation of Kaspar Hauser in poetry is Paul Verlaine's *Gaspard Hauser chante*, ending with these words:

> Suis-je né trop tôt ou trop tard?
> Qu'est-ce que je fais en ce monde?
> O vous tous, ma peine est profonde:
> Priez pour le pauvre Gaspard!

Translated as

> Am I born too soon or too late?
> What am I doing in this world?
> All of you, my sorrow is profound:
> Pray for the poor Gaspard!

Verlaine's theme is one of alienation. He wrote the poem while in prison for a drunken assault on his friend and fellow poet Rimbaud, and probably saw himself as Kaspar in his dungeon, shut away from the rest of the world. A similar motive emerges in the German poet Georg Trakl's *Kaspar Hauser Lied*: Kaspar is an outsider, excluded from conformist society. The Kaspar Hauser revival triggered by the works of Hermann Pies served as a catalyst for a vast production of novels, plays, and poems. Just as many of the historical writers used Kaspar as a metaphor for their own pet interests, the writers and artists have done the same. Kaspar has served as a Christlike redeemer, a wild child, an innocent learning to communicate, or an outcast eager to rejoin society. There have been Kaspar Hauser films, musicals, and plays, including a postmodern revamping of the story, where a defiant

Kaspar fires a pistol at his tormentors. By far the most famous fictional adaptation of the Kaspar Hauser legend since Wassermann's novel is Werner Herzog's prizewinning film *The Enigma of Kaspar Hauser*. The title role is played by the eccentric street performer Bruno S., who was at least thirty years old at the time; still, this awkward-looking individual is brilliantly cast and turns in a memorable performance. Herzog's main inspiration is probably Wassermann's novel, but he wisely turned his back on the romantic overtones of the prince legend: the film's interest is in Kaspar himself rather than in the speculation about his origins. The characters are more true to the originals than Wassermann's: the kindly prison guard Hiltel, the pedantic enthusiast Daumer, and the vainglorious Lord Stanhope. They all contribute to the natural man Kaspar's being thrust into a both repressed and repressive society. Like Wassermann, Herzog emphasizes how the insight and visions of the noble savage Kaspar threaten the establishment. The story progresses toward the logical conclusion, and Kaspar is killed by the unknown assailant. His many appearances in European twentieth-century culture indicate that in spite of the prince legend's being crushed by science, Kaspar Hauser will live on as a metaphor for many years to come.

# 3

---

## *The Emperor and the Hermit*

REMEMBERED AS THE tsar of Tolstoy's *War and Peace*, Alexander I is one of the most appealing figures in Russian history. His persistent struggle against the French invaders in 1812 and 1813 saved Russia.[1] But there was a darker side to Alexander I. As a youth, he had taken part in the conspiracy to dethrone his unbalanced father, Paul I, and for the rest of his life he would be tormented with guilt for having acceded to the murder of his own father. Toward the end of his long and successful reign, he became something of a religious mystic and told some of his friends that his real desire was to abdicate to lead a life of prayer and austerity. Since the 1860s, there has been a persistent legend that Alexander I did just that—that after faking his own death, in 1825, he lived on for thirty-nine more years in the guise of the pious Siberian hermit Feodor Kuzmich. The mystery of the Emperor and the Hermit soon became Russia's national enigma; despite the work of many scholars, it remains unsolved.[2]

## THE LIFE OF ALEXANDER I

ALEXANDER WAS BORN in 1777, the son of Tsarevitch Paul and the grandson of Catherine the Great. His powerful grandmother Catherine hated her own son, the ugly and paranoid Paul, but she doted on the good-looking, precocious Alexander and carefully groomed him for his future role as ruler of Russia. He was provided with a French teacher who introduced him not only to fluency in the French language but also to liberal and democratic political thought. Catherine may well have planned to skip her own son in the succession, but her untimely death in 1796 made Paul the new tsar. In a five-year reign of terror, this unenlightened despot introduced censorship of all letters leaving Russia, prohibited foreign travel and the importation of foreign books, and put in place the most intricate and ridiculous laws controlling daily life. People who invited too many guests to a dinner party, who did not curtsy deep enough to their superiors, or who kept dogs that did not wear regulation dog collars were harshly punished. Paul also changed Russia's foreign policy completely: he hated revolutionary France, but also made plans for war with Britain and an invasion of India. He summarily dismissed his mother's favorites and had her lover Potemkin's body dug up and flung into the Neva. In 1801, there was a conspiracy of nobles to dethrone the tsar. It is certain that Alexander, who was well aware of his father's disastrous foreign policy and petty tyranny, was sworn into this conspiracy and that he agreed to take over the throne. It is unlikely, however, that the young tsarevitch was aware of the murderous plans of the more ruthless conspirators. They burst into Paul's bedroom and spied the detested tsar skulking behind his bed; it was impossible for him to escape into his wife's rooms, since he had ordered the door nailed shut out of fear she would poison him. Paul tried to break free, but was promptly knocked down and strangled. Some of the conspirators came rushing into Alexander's rooms shouting "Hooray! Hooray!" They then informed him that his father was dead and that he was the new tsar of Russia. Poor Alexander,

An equestrian portrait of Alexander I in his prime.

distraught at the notion that he had taken part in the murder of his father, pleaded with them that he wanted to abdicate, but they gruffly told him to do his duty and reign.

Outwardly, at least, Alexander's reign started under the brightest of auspices. People were dancing in the streets to celebrate the death of the tyrant Paul, and the simple expedient of revoking all his father's

unpopular laws greatly endeared the handsome young tsar to his subjects. The conspirators of 1801 had, of course, hoped to remain in
posts of influence, but Alexander had more willpower than they had
thought, and he excluded them from power. Although Alexander had
hoped gradually to introduce liberal reforms into the Russian constitution, both the Orthodox Church and the aristocracy opposed him,
and he eventually realized that Russia was not ready for anything
resembling democracy. For many years, Alexander I was absorbed by
the war against Napoleon. After the defeats at Austerlitz and Fried-
land, the Russians made peace at Tilsit in 1807. The tsar and the
French emperor met face to face and got on quite well. It appears that
Alexander admired Napoleon's plans for a united Europe, although he
was naturally wary that the huge French empire would expand farther
eastward. He pretended to agree with Napoleon's plans for reshaping
the map of Europe and closed all Russian ports to British ships. But
when, in early 1812, Napoleon finally invaded Russia, Alexander's
armies were ready for him. The French advanced far enough to burn
and plunder Moscow, but the tsar's resolution never failed. By this
time, he saw Napoleon as an Antichrist who had to be defeated. After
some bloody battles, this was achieved with help from the bitter Russian winter. In 1814, Alexander I entered Paris in triumph, the most
powerful man in Europe. He hoped to establish a "Holy Alliance" of
European states, but the cunning Austrian statesman Prince Metternich opposed him. In the end, the tsar's utopian concept became
much diluted by the reality of European politics.

As the years went on, Alexander became increasingly bitter and disappointed. He took little pleasure in the great successes of his life, but
ruminated on the things that had gone wrong. He lamented that his
plan for a united Europe had failed and that Russia's dominant position in European politics was gone. Moreover, revolutionary elements
in Russia forced him to adopt a quite repressive, reactionary policy
after the wars, and this also saddened the lonely tsar. He became
more religious and introverted. In 1824, a series of disastrous events
lowered his spirits further. Early that year, he developed erysipelas, a

cutaneous infection in his left leg, which had been injured some time previously by a kick from a horse. After several weeks of convalescence, he gradually recovered. It then became apparent that Empress Elizabeth was also severely ill, with a heavy cough and difficulties in breathing. Some months later, Alexander's illegitimate daughter, to whom he was very devoted, died of tuberculosis. Then there were rumors of civil unrest, and Alexander's spies warned that a conspiracy of military officers were plotting an uprising. In November of that fateful year, the Neva flooded large parts of St. Petersburg, and the Imperial Palace appeared almost like an island in the middle of an ocean. Many lives were lost, and the damage to property was immense. As the tsar inspected the disaster site, an old man called out, "God is punishing us for our sins!" "No, not for your sins, but for mine!" replied the gloomy emperor.

## TSAR ALEXANDER GOES TO TAGANROG

IN EARLY 1825, Alexander's primary concern was the failing health of the empress. As a young man, he had treated her badly and entertained numerous mistresses, but in middle age he became devoted to his long-suffering wife. The tsar's personal physician, the Scotsman Sir James Wylie, advised that Elizabeth spend the summer months in a warmer climate.[3] Alexander decided that they should go to Taganrog in the Crimea. This small town near the Sea of Azov would hardly strike anyone as particularly suitable for an invalid, however. Its wet and windy climate was considered particularly unhealthy. Large swamps were nearby, and violent fevers raged among the local inhabitants. Other members of the imperial family tried to make Alexander change his mind, but he was obdurate. It may well be that the tsar, who liked visiting the outposts of his great empire, wanted to see Taganrog and its surroundings, and that this desire guided his choice. Before leaving the capital, he attended mass at the Alexander Nevsky monastery, as was his habit before beginning any long journey. After the service, the metropolitan took him to see a starets (Russian holy man): a monk who spent all day praying in solitude. A wild-looking character, the monk commanded Alexander to pray and admonished him for the lax state of public morals in Russia. When asked where he slept, the monk pointed to an open black coffin and shouted, "Look! That is my bed, and not mine only! In it we shall all be lying some day, and we shall sleep deeply!" Alexander was profoundly moved by the exhortations of this gloomy monk. As the tsar's carriage left St. Petersburg, the coachman was puzzled that Alexander ordered him to stop at the outskirts of the city. The tsar stood up and silently surveyed his capital, as if he were saying farewell.

After Alexander finished the 1,400-mile journey from St. Petersburg to Taganrog, his mood changed. The weather was fine and the scenery beautiful, and he made long trips to see the local sights. The empress, who did not share her husband's predilection for traveling at breakneck speed, joined him ten days later. Many in the imperial entourage noticed that Alexander, having neglected his wife for many years, had become much closer to the empress after she had fallen ill. The tsar himself appeared as vigorous as ever. On November 4, he rode twenty-five miles to visit a Tatar village. The head of the local Tatars had suffered from an intermittent fever for some time, but the local governor, Count Vorontsov, had dispatched his personal physician, the Englishman Robert Lee, to treat him with quinine, a novel medication at the time.[4] The tsar spent the night in this village, sleeping in a common little Tatar cottage. The next day, Alexander rode along the coast with his entourage. He was so impressed with the magnificent scenery that he arranged to buy a country estate where he could spend winter with the ailing empress. That evening, a strange incident occurred. When Alexander was opening an oyster, he was dismayed to observe some species of marine worm in its shell. Dr. Wylie was consulted, and he pronounced the worm "quite common and harmless." Although few people today would pronounce such a diseased crustacean a dish fit for an emperor, Alexander took the advice of his physician and ate it. During the following days, he seemed fit and well. He kept traveling at high speed, riding on horse-back thirty miles a day, and inspecting various military and religious establishments.

While riding in his carriage on November 16, Alexander was seized with a fit of violent shivering, and his teeth began to chatter.[5] After his return to Taganrog, Wylie noted that the tsar's complexion was quite yellow. He had an insatiable thirst and was drowsy because he was running a high temperature. Alexander's friend Prince Volkonsky bluntly told him that his violent exertions on horseback had caused his illness, particularly as the weather had become rather cool in the evenings and the tsar was without cloak or overcoat. At first, neither physicians nor laypeople seem to have been particularly alarmed by the tsar's illness. He was in good cheer, the bouts of fever were only intermittent, and the empress thought he was recovering. But Wylie had misgivings about the outcome. His diagnosis was "bilious remit-tent fever" of a variety endemic in the Crimea. His friend Robert Lee had recently treated two hundred cases of this "Crimean fever," includ-ing two members of Count Vorontsov's entourage. "Bilious remittent fever" is an archaic term for various infectious diseases causing relaps-ing fever and jaundice. Some cases were due to malignant malaria, some to typhus, typhoid, yellow fever, or other infectious agents. A notable specialist in the field declared himself convinced that the Crimean variety of bilious remitting fever was due to malaria, and this agrees well with Lee's observation that patients with a disease like the emperor's responded well to quinine.[6] Another possibility is that the diseased oyster the emperor ate might have carried typhoid. But what-ever was wrong with Alexander, he was not a good patient. Although he had the greatest respect for Sir James Wylie, he refused to take any medicine. It must be admitted that the therapy proposed—bloodlet-ting and purgatives—was likely to have done him more harm than good. It is not known with certainty whether Wylie had access to quinine or any other antimalarial concoction at the time.

## THE DEATH OF ALEXANDER I

IT WAS NOT until November 22 that Empress Elizabeth became alarmed about her husband's health. He was growing very weak and at times was delirious with fever. Alexander's chief of staff, Baron Diebitsch, sent couriers to St. Petersburg to inform the imperial family that the tsar was gravely ill.[7] Wylie consulted his colleagues Drs. Tarasov and Stoffregen, but the tsar refused to take any medication, apart from drinking cordials. The empress and Prince Volkonsky begged him to accept medical treatment, but the tsar could not be persuaded. On November 25, the emperor seemed much stronger, and he worked at his desk all morning. The next day, he suddenly collapsed just after ordering hot water for his morning shave. Coming to,

The tsar receives Communion a few hours before his death.
A print from the *Album Cosmopolite*.

The tsar's deathbed. An engraving by T. Kulakov in 1827,
from A. S. Rappoport, *The Curse of the Romanovs* (London, 1907).
It should be noted that there is also a curious drawing of the dead tsar
with his jaws bound up, in Grand Duke Nicholas Mikhailovitch's
*L'empereur Alexandre 1er*. Prince Alexis Troubetzkoy further informs me
that he has seen what was purported to be the tsar's death mask.

he was as irate as ever with the doctors, cursing them bitterly as they
tried to persuade him to accept leeches and medication. When Wylie
offered him muriatic acid in some water, the tsar shouted, "Get out!"
Wylie was so upset that he burst into tears. Alexander then said, "Forgive me, my dear friend. I hope you are not angry with me. I have my
reasons." Prince Volkonsky had an idea how to get the stubborn tsar
to accept medication, however. The empress prevailed upon him to
take Holy Communion the next day, and the priest argued that by not
accepting treatment, he was in essence committing suicide. Alexander immediately turned to Tarasov and accepted whatever therapy the
doctors saw fit to recommend. He was put to bed, and thirty leeches
applied to his neck and behind his ears. The following day, mustard

plasters were applied to his legs in a futile attempt to reduce the fever. But on November 30 Wylie saw that all hope was lost. The tsar grew steadily weaker and was unconscious most of the time. The next morning Wylie recorded that at ten minutes to eleven "the great Monarch stepped into eternity."

On December 2, the assembled doctors performed a careful autopsy.[8] It was noted that the liver was enlarged and dark in color and that the gall bladder was distended by a great quantity of "deteriorated bile." The official autopsy protocol records that the spleen was normal, but Wylie told his colleague Robert Lee that the spleen was enlarged and softened in texture.[9] According to the protocol, the brain was congested with blood, and there was an increased amount of serous fluid in the ventricles of the brain. In some areas, the dura mater (the covering of the brain) adhered solidly to the skull. The autopsy completed, the tsar's body was to be embalmed. Neither Wylie nor Tarasov, both of whom had known Alexander well, wanted to take charge, so the task was left to a team of four local doctors and an apothecary, with their helpers. A military man who attended the procedure gave a vivid description of their activities. Four surgeons were cutting away at the body, and two of the physicians were busy boiling grass and herbs in spirits, with which to stuff the body cavities. The doctors were puffing at strong cigars in a vain attempt to escape the pungent odors of putrefaction. At first, the four doctors were pleased with their handiwork, but they soon noted that the body was decomposing quickly. They blamed this on the lack of clean sheets and sufficient quantities of alcohol, but their own competence in embalming would appear to have been very questionable. The tsar's face became very black and almost unrecognizable. Wylie was called in, and he saw that the state of the putrefying body was such that cooling seemed to be the only way of preserving it. Accordingly, all windows were opened, and a container of ice put under the bed. On December 11, Alexander's body was moved to a local monastery, where a ceremony was held. Robert Lee, who was present, specifically noted that the coffin was exposed at the head.

While the doctors at Taganrog were busy trying to keep the tsar's corpse looking presentable, pandemonium reigned in Moscow. Alexander had secretly arranged that his brother Constantine would renounce the throne in favor of their younger brother Nicholas, but the people did not know this, and it was widely anticipated that Constantine would become tsar. A secret society tried to use this interregnum to stage a full-scale rebellion, but Nicholas called in the military, which scattered the rebel forces by artillery fire. Not until December 29 did Nicholas order the transferral of his brother's body to the capital. Tarasov was put in charge of monitoring the state of the body during the lengthy journey to St. Petersburg. The body was regularly inspected through a hatch in the coffin, and boxes of ice were placed under the casket when the temperature rose above freezing. In every town or village, masses of mourners turned out to pay their last respects to the popular tsar. Curiously, near the town of Tula, there were rumors that factory workers were planning to stop the procession and force open the coffin, because stories had been circulating that the body in the casket was not that of the tsar. When the workers appeared, however, they were full of reverence for the dead tsar; after unharnessing the horses, they pulled the heavy carriage more than three miles into the city cathedral.

On February 3 the procession finally reached Moscow, where the coffin was put on a catafalque in the Kremlin and seen by many thousands of people. After three days, the metropolitan Philaret led a service, and the procession set out for St. Petersburg. On March 1, once the procession had reached Tsarskoye Selo, Tarasov was asked whether the coffin might be opened so that the imperial family could pay their last respects. The dowager empress was very moved by the appearance of the corpse and exclaimed, "Yes, this is my dear son, my dear Alexander. But how thin he has become!" She was not the only member of the imperial family to be deeply shaken by the appearance of the corpse. The body was then placed in an ornate bronze casket that was taken into St. Petersburg and placed in the Kazan cathedral. Tsar Nicholas was appealed to for permission to open the casket, but he refused, according to Tarasov because the face was so discolored. On March 13, the casket was interred in the fortress of St. Peter and St. Paul, the final resting place of the tsars.

## THE LEGEND OF FEODOR KUZMICH

AS WE HAVE SEEN, there were fleeting rumors in early 1826 that Alexander was not dead and that the coffin that traveled across Russia contained the body of an unknown man. Some authors have alleged that the British newspapers reported these rumors, but this appears to be untrue. In fact, the *Times* and other papers were more concerned with the rumors that Alexander had been poisoned. A curious manuscript in the Bodleian Library argues against the hypothesis of poisoning, but again mentions nothing about a substitution of bodies.[10] Nor does any other source from 1825 until 1850 seriously discuss the possibility of Alexander's surviving his deathbed in Taganrog. But all this changed after the appearance of the Siberian hermit Feodor Kuzmich.

In September 1836, eleven years after the tsar was supposed to have died, a mysterious stranger rode into the village of Krasnoufimsk.[11] This village was situated on the main road through the Perm district, used by the parties of convicts and exiles who were herded to Siberia. An elderly man with a military bearing, the stranger looked about sixty years old. He was dressed in simple peasant clothes, but his face was austere and rather handsome and his bushy gray beard well trimmed. He made his way to the local blacksmith's shop and asked to have his horse reshod. Soon, some rowdy peasants came into the shop and tried to question the stranger about his travel plans. The old man gave nothing away, and the inquisitive countrymen thought he might be a fugitive from justice. It aroused further suspicion that the stranger's manner of speech was that of an educated gentleman and that his horse was a fine animal. The peasants grabbed him and marched him to the police station for additional questioning. The secretive stranger replied that his name was Feodor Kuzmich—

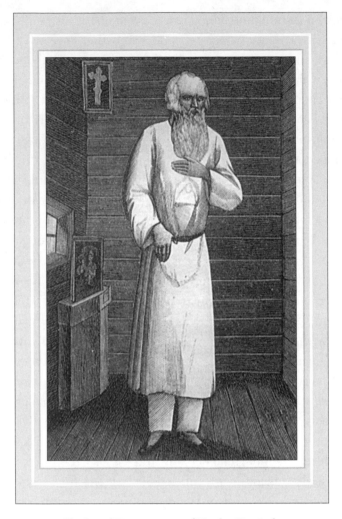

The best-known portrait of Feodor Kuzmich.
From the collection of Prince Alexis Troubetzkoy,
reproduced with permission.

that is, Feodor son of Kuzma—according to the Russian system of nomenclature; he did not give his family name. The horse belonged to him, he said, and he was on his way to Siberia. When cross-examined, he said he had no fixed address, supported himself with casual labor, and could not read. He was a member of the Russian Orthodox Church. Kuzmich, who had no identification documents whatsoever, maintained a stubborn silence when asked about his family and his past activities. The exasperated policemen then arrested him as a vagabond, and he was sentenced to twenty blows with the whip, followed by exile to Siberia; this was the usual punishment for any tramp unlucky enough to fall into the hands of the Russian authorities.[12] In October, Feodor Kuzmich, also known as convict no. 117, accompanied a transport of prisoners bound for Bogoyavlensk. For five months, he trudged through snow and mud, surrounded by thieves and vagabonds; yet he seemed oblivious to the squalor and hardships of his enforced journey. On arrival, he was set to work in a vodka distillery. It did not take long, however, for Kuzmich to become quite a local celebrity. People were impressed with his courteous manner, his religious piety, and his great ability as a storyteller. Rumors began to circulate that he was some important person who had been exiled, perhaps even a member of the imperial family.

Feodor Kuzmich lived in a little log cabin, and was revered as a starets by the local people, who brought him food and supplies. In return, he taught the children history and geography and advised their parents on agricultural questions. His cabin, or rather hermitage, was furnished with a wooden bed without any mattress, a small table and three stools, a small stove, and a few icons in one corner. Despite his statement to the contrary when questioned in Krasnoufimsk, he could definitely read, although he had only three books: the Bible, a book of prayers, and a religious work entitled *Seven Words from the Savior*. He wrote many letters, most of them in Russian, some in foreign languages, but always hid his chest of writing material when any stranger called. His letters were entrusted to the wandering pilgrims who often visited him; this was not the quickest of mailing systems, but the starets was above such matters. His habits of life were very simple: he spent his days working in his garden and tending his bees, and devoted long hours to prayer in front of his icons and crucifix. He ate mostly bread and vegetables, but accepted meat and fish when he was asked to dinner. Once, the bishop of Irkutsk tried to persuade him to divulge his true identity, but Kuzmich refused, saying that his penance had been approved and blessed by the metropolitan Philaret of Moscow. Many of his visitors relished Kuzmich's endless stories; he had an intimate knowledge of the court of Catherine the Great and often spoke of the grand parties arranged in St. Petersburg on the Alexander Nevsky holiday, with parades, gun salutes, and illuminations. He sometimes also talked of the battles in the great war against Napoleon, praising General Kutozov but rarely mentioning Alexander I. Once, an old soldier knelt before Feodor Kuzmich, claiming to have recognized him as Alexander I, but the starets gruffly told him off.

In 1858, a gold prospector named Khromov persuaded the elderly Feodor Kuzmich to move to Tomsk, where a new hermitage was built for him. Khromov's daughter Anna became fond of the old starets and left some remarkable stories about him. Once, she and her father saw a handsome young officer and a lady leaving his cabin. Feodor Kuzmich accompanied them to their carriage, and they could be overheard conversing in a foreign language. The starets did not divulge the identity of his visitors, but said, "A long time ago I was known by my grandparents, and now it is the turn of my grandchildren." The Khromovs later surmised that this officer might have been Tsarevitch Alexander, visiting his uncle the hermit. Another time, Anna Khromov's younger sister was reading aloud from a historical work. When she read a statement Alexander I was supposed to have made to Napoleon, an angry voice shouted, "I never said that!" This cry had come from the room where the starets was staying, but when the Khromovs opened the door, they found him in fervent prayer. Another of Feodor Kuzmich's friends was a young orphan girl named Alexandra Nikiforovna, whom he taught history, religion, and geography. When she was twenty years old, she wanted to make a pilgrimage to various holy places. While visiting a monastery in Kiev, she carried a letter of introduction from Feodor Kuzmich to Countess Osten-Sacken. Here she met Tsar Nicholas I, who was making a tour of inspection; he spoke kindly to her and said that Feodor Kuzmich was indeed a holy man. When returning to Siberia, she once remarked how much Feodor Kuzmich resembled a portrait of Alexander I that she had seen in Count Osten-Sacken's study. Again the starets appeared embarrassed and angry at being challenged.

In 1864, the old starets fell ill and seemed to be close to death. Khromov tried to persuade him to tell his name and those of his parents, but Kuzmich refused. He indicated a small bag hanging on the wall and said, "In there is my secret." After the death of the starets, this bag was opened and found to contain six small pieces of paper with enigmatic text. The only sentence that could be clearly read recorded Kuzmich's arrival in Siberia in 1837. Just as the German scholars tried to decipher the obscure message in the pouch given to Kaspar Hauser, Russian historians have spent years poring over these slips of paper. Some have suspected them to be written in a code used by Freemasons, giving Alexander, alias Feodor Kuzmich, the secret name of Strufian as a Freemason pseudonym. Others have created sentences saying, "When Alexander is silent, he has no qualms of conscience about Paul" or "Nicholas I has treacherously sent his brother away." Another hypothesis is that one slip of paper is a message from Paul to his mistress that Alexander and Count Pahlen were conspiring against them, and that they must hide. The most plausible suggestion is that the slips of paper are actually the code to a cipher used by Feodor Kuzmich in his secret correspondence. Much effort has also gone into comparing the handwriting on the notes with that of Alexander I; some "experts" have found resemblances, but others have not. Some Russian letters changed their appearance in the early 1800s; Tsar Alexander used the new typography, but Feodor Kuzmich did not.[13]

After the death of the old starets, Khromov spent much time spreading the word about him, emphasizing his great piety and the wonders he had worked. Archbishop Benjamin of Siberia noted that Khromov was obsessed with the idea that the hermit who had lived and died on his estate was none other than Alexander I. Throughout the 1860s, Khromov worked to spread the fame of the starets. He had a small chapel built on the hermit's grave, and pamphlets describing his holy life soon became widespread in the neighborhood of Tomsk.

It is recorded that in the late 1860s Khromov applied for an audience before Tsar Alexander II. He was received by a courtier, who was impressed by his obvious sincerity. Khromov did not ask for money or favors; he just wanted to tell the tsar about his conviction that Alexander I had survived as Feodor Kuzmich, and to hand over some relics of the starets. Accounts differ on whether Khromov ever met the tsar, but it is certain that Feodor Kuzmich's skullcap, Bible, and chaplet were given to a courtier, along with some handwritten notes of his.[14] In the meantime, Khromov's pamphlets had become popular enough to be known in Moscow and St. Petersburg, with the result that rumors started to spread and that the police began to investigate what they called the untrue stories about a so-called Siberian holy man. In particular, they were outraged that religious services had been held in the Tomsk chapel, in front of a cross with the inscription "Alexander the Blessed." The state procurator had the pamphlets suppressed, and admonished the local clergy for their ignorance and idolatry. This had the desired effect, particularly since Khromov died not long afterward, but the rumors about the Emperor and the Hermit were never completely silenced.

Toward the end of the nineteenth century, Russian society became somewhat less repressed, thanks to liberal reforms. The passage of several decades since Kuzmich's death led to his being seen more as a historical curiosity than as a present threat, and the debate about the death of Alexander I was rekindled. It was rumored that the body of a courier named Maskov, who had died in an accident at Taganrog, had been put in the coffin after the tsar had faked his own death. Another story had it that a soldier on guard at Taganrog had seen a tall man walk out; he had recognized the tsar and saluted him. The other soldiers ridiculed him, since it was known that the tsar was too ill to leave his bed, but the soldier persisted in his belief. The two great nineteenth-century biographers of Alexander I, General N. K. Schilder and Grand Duke Nicholas Mikhailovitch, both refuted the legend in their published writings, but privately hinted that they were far from convinced. A very typical installment of the Feodor Kuzmich saga held that

Schilder was working late one evening on his great biography. He fell asleep, and in his dream a tall specter rose before him, demanding, "Well, don't you recognize me?" It was the ghost of Feodor Kuzmich, and the shaken general changed his mind on the spot and admitted there might be something in the old legend after all. The grand duke noted that Nicholas I had seen to the destruction of many letters and documents regarding Alexander I's last days. Several members of the imperial family, particularly Tsar Alexander III, had an active interest in the legend. One account stated that he had a small portrait of Feodor Kuzmich on the wall of his study, next to a portrait of Alexander I. In 1925, Prince Vladimir Bariatinsky published the first full-length book directly claiming that the Emperor and the Hermit were one and the same person. In later years, it is notable, the majority of academic historians, including Alan Palmer and Henri Troyat, the two leading biographers of Alexander I, have been wholly unconvinced of the legend's veracity. On the other hand, a Soviet academician and a Russian prince have argued that Alexander I survived as Feodor Kuzmich. The latter, Prince Alexis Troubetzkoy, once heard from Grand Duchess Olga, the sister of Tsar Nicholas II, that she and her family had no doubt that Alexander I had survived as Feodor Kuzmich.[15]

## HISTORICAL ARGUMENTS

TO ACCEPT THE legend of the Emperor and the Hermit, one needs a valid motive for Alexander's wanting to disappear into obscurity. Historians are divided over whether this was the case. Those in favor cite his religious and mystical musings, and his sense of guilt from his father's murder. There is no doubt that he felt depressed in 1824 and 1825, as various calamities struck him and his family. Alexander often spoke of abdicating when he felt depressed, but he vacillated, depending on his mood, and there is no evidence he was ever sincere and determined enough to approach his younger brothers on this vital matter. At Taganrog, before he fell ill, Alexander said to Prince Volkonsky that when he abdicated, he would purchase an estate in the Crimea and employ the prince as his librarian. But the wretched hermit had only three books in his possession. Could Alexander, with his voracious appetite for news and literature, have changed so completely? Moreover, as an experienced statesman, would he really have faked his own death? This would have made every law and edict from his successors null and void, had any person discovered he was still alive, with disastrous consequences for Russia. It is also highly questionable whether a sincerely religious man like Alexander could have gone through with a mockery like burying a dead soldier in his place; this would have been the utmost sacrilege in his eyes. It would also have been out of character if the pampered tsar, surrounded by every luxury since an early age, willingly submitted to a brutal flogging, followed by harsh treatment as a convict. And would he willingly have deserted his ailing wife, whom he rightly presumed to be seriously ill?

If the question about a possible motive for Alexander to disappear remains unresolved, we are on safer ground with regard to the question of his death in Taganrog. There are five well-known firsthand accounts of the last days of Tsar Alexander: the letters of the empress, the personal memoranda of Prince Volkonsky, the diary of Sir James Wylie, the memoirs of the physician Tarasov, and an unsigned manuscript called "Official History of the Illness and Death of Tsar Alexander I."[16] I have discovered Wylie's original description of Alexander's last illness and death in the archives of the Wellcome Library in London.[17] This important original document was written in German by Dr. Stoffregen at Wylie's dictation. Its section on the autopsy is virtually identical to the official autopsy report, but its account of the disease adds that Wylie believed the tsar to have been the victim of typhus or a similar acute febrile illness. A seventh important source is the diaries of the physician Robert Lee. Where these are today is uncertain, but in the 1960s they were owned by the medical historian Dr. Norah H. Schuster. They tell that Lee was summoned to Taganrog by Wylie, but he was in Odessa at the time and arrived too late. Wylie dictated to him the full report he intended to send to St. Petersburg, and Lee took it down in shorthand. He confided enough details to his diaries for Schuster to conclude that there was no doubt Alexander I died at Taganrog in 1825, and of natural causes.[18] When it is considered that Tarasov wrote his account of Alexander's illness many years after the event, relying on his memory rather than on notes made at the time, the other descriptions of his illness tally relatively well. There are several sources of contributory evidence: letters from a colonel in the imperial entourage and from an English Quaker who visited Taganrog, and memoirs from various people involved in the autopsy and embalming.[19]

The discovery of Wylie's original postmortem account and Lee's diaries add much evidence that Alexander really died in Taganrog, and that the cause of death was the "Crimean fever," a malignant form of malaria. It can be speculated that the malarial parasite involved may well have been sensitive to quinine; the tsar's obstinacy in refusing any medication until he was in extremis may well have carried a high price. If there had really been a conspiracy to fake Alexander's death, it would have had to involve quite a few people. Wylie, Lee, Tarasov, and Stoffregen would have had to be sworn into the plot, as would Prince Volkonsky. The account of the embalming shows that it was done not by Wylie or Tarasov but by three local doctors and their helpers; these men would also have been in on the secret. Empress Elizabeth would have had to be a key member of the conspiracy, and her role in the cover-up would have demanded feats of cunning and duplicity wholly inconsistent with her character. A letter of hers, written not long after Alexander's death and discovered in a Finnish archive, says that she did not expect to survive long after the loss of her irreplaceable husband.[20] As for the theory that the corpse of an officer named Maskov was put into Alexander's coffin, it is recorded that this individual died in an accident not less than fifteen days before the tsar; it would hardly have been possible to keep the body fresh for such a period of time.

Staunch believers in the legend of Feodor Kuzmich also need to explain how the tsar left Taganrog. Early rumors had it that an English nobleman had taken Alexander on board a ship in the harbor. There are several theories regarding the name of this elusive peer. A certain General Balinsky claimed to have made inquiries at Lloyd's in the 1890s and found that only one foreign ship, the yacht of the diplomat Lord Cathcart, was in Taganrog at the relevant time. The yacht's log did not contain either the date of her departure from Taganrog or her destination. But when the historian Prince Troubetzkoy contacted the Cathcart family, he learned that the first earl was seventy years old at the time and not a yachting man, and that there was no evidence that he traveled abroad in 1825.[21] Another suspect, supported by more than one Russian historian, is the diplomat Lord Augustus Loftus, but this turns out to be another red herring. Loftus was just eight years old in 1825, and thus a very unlikely candidate. Yet another candidate for the mystery peer is the diplomat Sir Stratford Canning, who was in Russia in 1824–25. He was received in audience by Alexander on April 4, 1825, and could thus have been sworn into the conspiracy. But it is known that Canning left London in late October 1825, traveling to Constantinople via Italy. He got the news of the death of Alexander when receiving a Greek delegation on board a British man-of-war. Finally, the third marquess of Lansdowne has been tentatively suggested as the mystery peer, but he was in session with the House of Lords at the time, and there is no evidence he was a yachting man.[22]

After seeing the yachts of the four British noblemen sinking into the Black Sea before their eyes, the adherents of the legend of Feodor Kuzmich are in even more trouble when asked to explain where Tsar Alexander spent the eleven years between his presumed death in 1825 and his appearance as Kuzmich in 1836. There are suggestions that the mystery peer took him to Palestine, or that he lived as a hermit in a small Finnish village; a more sinister variation is that he was imprisoned in the dungeons of the fortress of Sveaborg, like some Russian Man in the Iron Mask.[23] There is no evidence to support any of these fantasies. On the other hand, that Feodor Kuzmich knew various priests and religious establishments in southern Russia suggests that he spent much time in these parts, possibly as a pilgrim relying on the hospitality of the church. Had the tsar tried anything of the kind in the years following 1825, he would immediately have been recognized.

Much of the evidence that Feodor Kuzmich was Alexander comes from his adherents in Siberia. There is no doubt the old starets was an educated man who spoke at least one foreign language; he had probably spent time at the court of Catherine the Great and had knowledge indicating that he had taken part in the war against Napoleon. Profoundly religious, he knew much about the Russian Orthodox Church and corresponded with bishops and noblemen. A number of tales of dubious veracity claim that a soldier recognized him as Alexander, that he was visited in Siberia by his brother Tsar Nicholas I and by Tsarevitch Alexander, and that Alexander I's marriage certificate was observed among his private papers. Not enough is recorded about Kuzmich's stories to allow for a serious comparison of his knowledge and opinions with the Tsar's, but Alexander I's biographer Alan Palmer has pointed out that Kuzmich often praised the actions of General Kutozov, a great popular hero of the war against Napoleon, of whose merits Alexander had always been unconvinced.[24] There is also a strange statement of Kuzmich's that Alexander I had ridden into Paris in triumph in 1814, with Count Metternich at his side. It is true that Alexander entered Paris on March 31, 1814, riding on his charger surrounded by his personal guard. But Metternich, who had actually been made a prince by this time, was nowhere to be seen, and the tsar would certainly have objected to sharing his great moment of triumph with a man he was already beginning to distrust.

The adherents of Feodor Kuzmich have had nothing but praise for his first apostle, the prospector Khromov, but some historians have looked into his activities with a critical eye. Khromov worked ceaselessly to spread the word about the holy man, but his stories about Kuzmich's miraculous prophecies, the sweet smell emanating from his beard, and the brilliant light seen surrounding his body are very similar to the tales about other Russian holy men. Khromov praises Kuzmich's great cleanliness, but the bishop of Tomsk noted that the starets never bathed or washed himself, except his feet once a year.

The German historian Martin Winkler has suspected that Khromov invented the various stories about Feodor Kuzmich to make the chapel and other relics of the famous starets a popular site for monks and pilgrims, thus enriching the Khromov family, which had a lodging house nearby.[25] But although some of Khromov's stories seem exaggerated, the available evidence for him as a rogue does not stand up to scrutiny. All who came into contact with him were impressed by his sincerity and his almost monomaniacal belief in the legend of Feodor Kuzmich, and there is no evidence that he ever derived any monetary benefit from his activities.

## MEDICAL ARGUMENTS

PRIOR TO THE age of fingerprinting, blood group analysis, and molecular biology, the forensic principles of identification were based mainly on anthropometry and applied pathology, comparing variables like height, cranial shape, dental health, and surgical scars. We know a good deal about what Alexander I looked like: he was more than six feet tall and had handsome features, including a straight nose and blue eyes. His fair hair had started to gray at the time of his supposed death in 1825, and portraits also show that he was balding. Alexander was slightly deaf as a youth, and this deafness worsened with age. Some accounts claim that his eyesight was poor, but there is no evidence that he used eyeglasses. His health was always excellent, and he was never touched by the surgeon's knife. The only physical mark on his body was an indentation on the left thigh that was the result of a kick from a horse that was complicated by attacks of erysipelas, and led to a permanent limp.

There is a deplorable lack of medical and anthropological information about the old starets, however. The most solid data is from his police examination as a vagabond in 1836, as discovered by the Russian historian E. Hessen. Feodor Kuzmich's features were unremarkable, and his age less than sixty-five years. It is curious that he is described as being just five feet nine inches tall; more so that his back bore the marks of wounds that could have been the result of an earlier flogging. Many later observers described the starets as being more than six feet tall, however. This renders it questionable whether the Feodor Kuzmich who was arrested in 1836 was the same one who was active in Siberia in the 1840s and 1850s.[26] There is no mention that Feodor Kuzmich suffered from a limp or had any injury to his thigh. It has been suggested that Kuzmich had a full head of hair in 1836, in contrast to the balding tsar, but the police examination mentions only that his hair was fair but graying; later accounts hint that Kuzmich, too, had a receding hairline. The only other remarkable thing in Kuzmich's medical history is that he gradually became very stooped. The romantics attributed this to the old man's brooding about his past imperial glory; a pathologist would instead suspect osteoporosis secondary to a deficient diet, lacking in minerals and vitamin D.

Some historians have made much of the fact that both Alexander and Kuzmich had calluses on their knees (from diligent praying), but such calluses are found in many people, housemaids as well as monks and nuns. The portrait of Feodor Kuzmich reproduced in this book certainly depicts a tall, thin individual, and many historians have marveled at how much he resembles an elderly Alexander I. But the truth appears to be that the stubborn old Feodor Kuzmich did not care much for having his portrait painted; he refused every offer of having his likeness kept for posterity, and this portrait was actually done after his death by a local artist, using a picture of Alexander I as guidance. A Russian historian claims to have seen a second portrait done by the same artist, showing a coarser-featured Feodor Kuzmich lying in his coffin. Those who knew Kuzmich thought this portrait, which bore no direct resemblance to Alexander I, much more accurate.[27]

## CAN DNA ANALYSIS SOLVE THE RIDDLE?

THE READER WHO has been impressed with the way modern DNA technology has shed light on the mystery of the Lost Dauphin and the riddle of Kaspar Hauser would, of course, recommend that the same techniques be applied to the remains of Alexander I and Feodor Kuzmich. It is a matter of some complexity, however, whether material for such an investigation will be available. We know that Feodor Kuzmich was buried in the Bogoroditsko-Alexeyevsk monastery in Tomsk. Khromov erected a chapel over the grave that was either rebuilt or added to in 1902.[28] The year thereafter, repairs to the grave showed that Kuzmich's remains were in situ.[29] It would appear that the monks took good care of the final resting place of the old starets, but the Soviet administrators had much less reverence for religious monuments. In the 1930s, the chapel was torn down to provide bricks for a local school; it is not known with certainty what happened to the grave. In the 1990s, the chapel was rebuilt in its original form. A

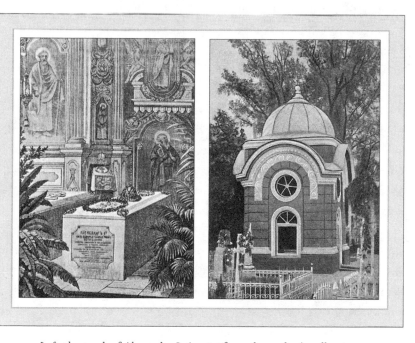

*Left,* the tomb of Alexander I. A print from the author's collection.
*Right,* the chapel over the grave of Feodor Kuzmich.
From the collection of Prince Alexis Troubetzkoy,
reproduced with permission.
Do they hold the solution of the mystery?

recent historian adds the important information that the remaining monks disinterred Feodor Kuzmich's remains and transferred them into the monastery church. They found that more than one-third of the skeleton was missing, including the skull.[30] Provided that they dug up the right skeleton, this would indicate that Kuzmich's grave had been disturbed on at least one previous occasion, possibly by the Bolshevik vandals in the 1930s. There is also a story that at some time before 1914, when repairs were made to the tomb, it was found to contain no coffin; the workmen surmised that it had been taken to St. Petersburg to be reinterred in the imperial tomb.[31]

There are reports that on several occasions the tomb of Alexander I in the fortress of St. Peter and St. Paul in St. Petersburg was opened and found to contain no human remains. A noblewoman told the Russian historian Lev Ljubimov that her father and Tsar Alexander III had inspected the tomb sometime in the 1880s. The lid was lifted by four soldiers, and the tomb turned out to be empty.[32] It is very questionable, however, whether only four people, even strong Russian guardsmen, could shift the lid of this massive tomb, and this story must be suspected to be a mere invention. The statement is often repeated that in 1921 the Bolsheviks plundered the imperial tombs looking for valuables. The short accounts in the contemporary Russian newspapers did not indicate that anything extraordinary was observed.[33] But some years later articles in many European newspapers held that Alexander I's coffin had been opened in 1921 and found empty; not a few of the journalists took this as evidence that the old story of Feodor Kuzmich was now proven to be true. The story spread abroad and was widely quoted as fact. The German historian Martin Winkler doubted its veracity, however. He strongly suspected the whole thing was a hoax, since the story emanated not from Russian sources but from unreliable German newspapers.[34] He knew that sensational stories about Russian affairs were often invented by unscrupulous German journalists, and that there was considerable interest in historical mysteries, like that of the Emperor and the Hermit. The historian J. G. Lockhart read a similar story in several British newspapers in 1929: all the imperial sarcophagi had been opened in 1927, in front of many witnesses, including foreign newspaper correspondents. That of Alexander I was the only one to be found empty. Lockhart wrote to the Soviet authorities, who replied that the story was a complete invention.[35] In 1965, the historian Ljubimov discounted the stories that the tomb of Alexander I had been opened in the 1920s. Instead, he demanded that the Soviet government exhume the body in the tomb to find out whether it appeared to be that of a forty-eight-year-old man (Alexander) or that of an octogenarian (Feodor Kuzmich). This advice does not appear to have been acted upon.[36]

The adherents of the legend have accepted the story of the missing body as reality and have, of course, presumed that the body of the soldier given out as Alexander's was found unworthy of this exalted resting place and buried in obscurity elsewhere. There is another account, however, stating that Alexander I's tomb was opened as early as 1866. Somewhat dishearteningly, this story comes from the aforementioned General Balinsky, whose other researches into the mystery, including his story of Lord Cathcart's yacht, appear somewhat fanciful.[37] Balinsky never published his results; his archive was destroyed by fire, and he was himself murdered by the Bolsheviks in 1920. Balinsky claimed that his father, the famous psychiatrist Ivan Balinsky, had employed a soldier as a janitor in his clinics. On his deathbed, this soldier confessed to the elder Balinsky that he had been among a troop of soldiers employed to open Alexander I's tomb in 1866. Closely supervised by Tsar Alexander II and a group of generals, they had lifted the lid of the tomb. Balinsky told various people different versions of what happened next: one said that the tomb was empty; another that a coffin was removed and a different one substituted in its place.[38] Most later writers have preferred to rely on a third version, that the coffin was taken out and buried in the cemetery of the Alexander Nevsky monastery, leaving the imperial tomb empty. The adherents of the legend have taken this story as evidence that Alexander II had decided to get rid of the soldier's body, but have given no explanation why he should have chosen to do so. The historian Alan Palmer, who rather surprisingly also gave Balinsky's whimsical account the benefit of the doubt, instead supposed that Alexander disliked the traditional burial place of the tsars and that he wrote a secret will indicating that he wanted to be buried in the Alexander Nevsky monastery, where he had so often prayed.[39] An expert on the imperial tombs and their construction has expressed strong doubts whether any nineteenth-century expedition could have opened these immense tombs. This would have been a tough undertaking even with modern lifting technology, and well-nigh impossible with nineteenth-century methods.[40]

Although I do not share the belief in the legend expressed by the historian Prince Troubetzkoy, whose excellent book on the subject has recently been published, I fully agree that a forensic analysis of the remains of the Emperor and the Hermit would be a worthwhile undertaking. Unlike the learned prince, I do not consider any of the stories of Tsar Alexander's tomb being opened worthy of much credit; in fact, the question of the authenticity of the bones of the old starets is more of a concern. Still, the interpretation of the results would be somewhat difficult. If the tomb of Alexander I is found to contain human remains, it should be verified that these remains appear to be around 180 years old and that they come from a middle-aged person. If they are instead the remains of an octogenarian, one would suspect that a swap of coffins was performed and that the remains of Feodor Kuzmich were placed in the imperial tomb at some stage. If the remains in Alexander's tomb are those of a forty-eight-year-old Romanov, as verified by DNA testing against other members of the imperial family, it would prove that Alexander I really died in 1825. If these remains are not those of a Romanov, and those of Feodor Kuzmich are, there is a high likelihood that Alexander lived on as Kuzmich after his supposed death in 1825. Skeptics may invoke Balinsky's story, suggesting that the tsar was buried somewhere else, but they would have difficulties explaining why a non-Romanov was put in the tomb in his place. Those of a skeptical turn of mind could also object that Kuzmich could have been an illegitimate son of Paul I, as some historians have suggested. The situation would be much the same if Alexander's tomb is empty and Kuzmich's remains are those of a Romanov: this would suggest that Balinsky's story was true and that the body of the soldier was removed from the tomb. The final alternative, that the tomb is empty but that Kuzmich's remains are not those of a Romanov, would give much needed support to Palmer's hypothesis that Alexander's corpse was removed from the tomb and buried somewhere else.

## WHO WAS FEODOR KUZMICH?

IT SHOULD BE made clear that, unlike the false dauphins, Feodor Kuzmich was no pretender: he himself never claimed to be the tsar and reacted gruffly when others did so. All accounts agree that he was a remarkable personality who for some reason had chosen to accept a great penance. One can only speculate about what had driven this intelligent, educated man to live as a hermit among common people in a desolate area. In 1986, the synod of the Russian Orthodox Church made Kuzmich a saint, and he is revered particularly in the area around Tomsk.[41]

My interpretation of the historical and medical evidence does not support the notion that Alexander I and Feodor Kuzmich were the same person. But who, then, was Feodor Kuzmich? One would have thought it a worthwhile enterprise for the late nineteenth-century doubters of the Kuzmich legend to search for other individuals who matched the characteristics of this mysterious hermit. But just like the German historians obsessed with the idea of Kaspar Hauser as the lost prince of Baden, their Russian colleagues seemed to reason that if Feodor Kuzmich was not the tsar, they did not care who he was. Some writers, impressed by the (unverified) stories that Kuzmich corresponded with the imperial family, and was visited by them, have found it likely that he was an illegitimate son of some royal personage. Another line of inquiry was to look for a possible link with the family of Count Osten-Sacken, with whom Kuzmich corresponded. It was found that the count had been married to the daughter of a certain General Usjakov.

Her sister was the mistress of Alexander's father, Paul—the royal connection!—and they had a son called Simeon Veliki, probably born in the early 1770s. This young man attended the St. Petersburg naval academy and then went to Britain, where he joined the Royal Navy. One account has it that he died of a tropical disease in the Caribbean; another, that he drowned in the Baltic during a visit to Kronstadt; historians have found no clue to verify either version, and he is not mentioned in the relevant naval records. Another interesting circumstance was that the names Feodor and Kuzma were common among members of the Usjakov family; one was even named Feodor Kuzmich. But Simeon Veliki would have been too old to fit in with the relatively vigorous-looking Feodor Kuzmich who surfaced in 1836, and he would have died at the age of well over ninety.[42]

Another approach has been to take Kuzmich's knowledge of the battles in the war against Napoleon to indicate that he was an officer during that war; this method of deduction has led to another suspect. The nobleman Feodor Uvarov, born around 1790, became a cavalry officer and served with great distinction throughout the wars against France. He was wounded several times and gained a number of Russian and foreign decorations. In 1816, he was wounded in a duel and later invalided out of the army, because he could no longer ride. Although made a chamberlain at the imperial court, he lived mostly at his large country estate, where he was known for his cruelty to his serfs. Uvarov was an active Freemason, and some observers have found hints in Kuzmich's arcane writings that he had knowledge of Masonic rituals. Uvarov disappeared from his house in St. Petersburg in 1827. No trace of his whereabouts was ever found. His wife claimed that he had drowned in the Neva, but the police suspected she knew more about his departure than she was willing to tell. She sometimes described herself as a widow, sometimes as a married woman, although she apparently never remarried. It was notable that all portraits of Feodor Uvarov had also disappeared, along with all his letters and his entire private archive. This would indicate that he was not murdered and did not commit suicide, but deliberately sought to disappear, either taking his personal effects with him or destroying them to keep clues to his whereabouts from being found. With his knowledge of foreign languages, his firsthand memories of St. Petersburg and the imperial court, his extensive military experiences, and his agricultural expertise as a country squire, he matches many of the known facts about Feodor Kuzmich. A historian found a cryptic note in the diary of a certain Bishop Foti, who apparently knew Uvarov, stating that he had blessed the penitent Feodor, to make him ready for an important undertaking.[43]

Although the case for Feodor Uvarov seems rather stronger than that for Veliki and other candidates, there is not one shred of strong evidence linking him with Feodor Kuzmich. As befits a holy Russian starets, Saint Feodor Kuzmich will remain a man of mystery in a house of sanctity. As he himself stipulated as part of his great penance, his true identity is unlikely ever to be known.

# 4

—

## Princess Olive, Hannah Lightfoot, and George Rex

And finally, to crown the whole,
The Princess Olive, Royal soul,
Shall from her bower in Banco Regis,
Descend, to bless her faithful lieges.
And, mid our Union's loyal chorus,
Reign jollily forever o'er us.

—THOMAS MOORE,
*"Proposals for a Gynæcocracy"*

IN THE YEAR 2002, Queen Elizabeth II of Great Britain celebrated her diamond jubilee. Although her fifty-year reign has sometimes been a rocky ride, with the divorce of the Prince of Wales and Princess Diana as a low water mark for the royalists, the queen herself has remained popular. In a time of great political and social change, she has represented a sense of tradition appreciated by many of her subjects. The Labour Party is governing the country, the House of Lords has been reformed, and the pound is threatened by the euro, but the British monarchy is still going strong.

Or is it? For more than two hundred years, a legend has been told and retold that, as a teenager in the early 1750s, King George III married Hannah Lightfoot, a young Quaker girl. Queen Hannah, as some have called her, was definitely a historical person, and some evidence suggests that she was the mistress or wife of a person of high rank.

George III as king. An engraving
from the portrait by A. Ramsay.

What is purported to be their marriage certificate is still kept at the
Public Record Office in Kew. If this document is genuine, the king's
later marriage to Princess Charlotte of Mecklenburg-Strelitz was bigamous, and all other sovereigns after George III nothing but usurpers.
Instead, the children of George III and Queen Hannah would be the
true heirs of the throne. The best-known of their putative descendants
is George Rex, who moved to South Africa and subsequently became
very rich. He had many children with two native women, and their
descendants are still living. In theory, Britain might thus gain a black

royal family instead of the present one, a change unlikely to be appreciated by the traditionalists. The claim of the Rex descendants is weakened, however, by the fact that George Rex never actually married either of his "wives." But even if the South African Rexes are disqualified, numerous other families claim descent from George III and Queen Hannah. Some of them sincerely believe that they are Britain's true royal family.

## GEORGE III AND QUEEN VICTORIA'S WICKED UNCLES

THE POPULAR IMAGE of King George III of Great Britain has been very much tainted by the well-known film *The Madness of King George*, which depicts a raving lunatic wildly rushing about in the corridors of his palace, with the queen, the Prince of Wales, and numerous attendants carrying straitjackets in hot pursuit.[1] In the United States, he is known as the "bad guy" of the War of Independence. In fact, though, George III was for many years a reasonably competent monarch, an affectionate husband and father, and a man of high moral values, opposed to the vicious social customs of the time. His predecessors, the Hanoverian kings George I and George II, had both been unpopular rulers, neither of whom had been able to speak English; his father, the buffoon Frederick, Prince of Wales, had been widely detested. When George III ascended the throne in 1760 at the age of just twenty-two, he was the first Hanoverian monarch to become even moderately popular with the middle and working classes.[2] In the ensuing years, it was in fact King George who was a sane and steadying influence within a royal family renowned for its immoral tendencies. The antics of Queen Victoria's wicked uncles and granduncles, the brothers and sons of George III, were notorious in their day.

Edward Augustus, duke of York, George III's younger brother, was a dissipated, profligate young man, plunging into every kind of excess, before suddenly dropping dead in 1767 after having danced all day and night in the palace of the prince of Monaco. His brother William Henry, the duke of Gloucester, was known as Silly Billy for his feeble intellect. He married the widow of the earl of Waldegrave, and was promptly cut off by George III for this misalliance. The duke was never forgiven, and had to wander the Continent for many years, in a state of semipoverty. The youngest brother, Henry Frederick, duke of Cumberland, was the worst of the lot. A foolish, strutting little man, he was known as the Royal Idiot. He had many mistresses, all of whom he treated badly. One of them, Polly Jones, took him to court for selling furniture he had given her. The duke then turned his attentions to Lady Grosvenor, and this affair soon became talked about in London. The actor Samuel Foote wittily said that while King George had created Sir Richard Grosvenor a lord, his brother had created him a cuckold. Either to maintain secrecy or to add to the titillation of his latest adventure, the duke often met his paramour at various country inns and taverns; he was disguised as a squire, a farmer, or a village idiot. But Lord Grosvenor still managed to track him down and had his brother and a body of servants follow the duke to his love nest, where they caught him in the act with Lady Grosvenor. Frightened that he would be beaten up, the duke fled in terror, screaming that he had done nothing wrong. Lord Grosvenor successfully took the duke to court for seducing his wife, and the jury gave him £10,000 damages; poor George III had to pay the bill.[3] Cumberland next got involved with the Irish beauty Anne Horton.[4] Her brother Colonel Luttrell was a rough character who objected to his sister's becoming a kept woman. It was rumored that he compelled the duke to marry her at the point of a pistol. The craven duke then knelt before George III, weeping and begging his brother's forgiveness, but the king gruffly ordered him to make himself scarce. Banished from George III's court, the disgraced duke went to France with his duchess. Later, they set up house in London, where the duchess for several years kept a fashionable gambling den; the young Prince of Wales lost much money there.[5] Disgusted by the actions of his irresponsible, pleasure-loving brothers, George III introduced the Royal Marriage Act in 1772 to keep any member of the royal family from marrying without his consent. This meant in practice that none of George III's sons would be able to marry according to their own inclinations, but that a suitable German princess would be selected for them.

George III was himself a model husband and father. In 1761, he married Princess Charlotte of Mecklenburg-Strelitz, and they had fifteen children, all but two surviving to maturity.[6] He became known as Farmer George, for his simple habits and interest in agricultural pursuits. George III's eldest son, George, Prince of Wales, was handsome, dashing, and clever, but he quarreled bitterly with his father and did everything he could to annoy him. Extravagant and vicious, the prince wined and dined, gambled to excess, and kept a string of mistresses. In open violation of the Royal Marriage Act, he married the actress Maria Fitzherbert in 1785. By the early 1790s, the prince had accumulated debts of £400,000. George III offered to pay his debts, but only if he married a princess of the king's choice; his previous marriage was to be regarded as unlawful. The prince grudgingly complied and married Caroline of Brunswick in 1795. As could be expected given its unpromising beginning, this marriage was not a happy one, and the queen soon moved abroad, leaving the prince to continue his wicked ways. George III's favorite son was Frederick, duke of York, who is today best known for his disastrous career as a military tactician in the war against revolutionary France. After retiring from active duty in the field, he became commander in chief of the army. But the duke allowed his mistress, the courtesan Mary Anne Clarke, to sell military promotions, which he himself signed according to her request. In 1809, this scheme was exposed, and the duke had to resign from his military appointment in disgrace. Several of George III's other sons refused to marry according to their father's wishes. In 1817, Princess Charlotte, the only child of the Prince of Wales, suddenly died. This meant that at the age of seventy-nine George III did not have a single legitimate grandchild alive, and there was a real risk of the dynasty's becoming extinct. The elderly royal dukes had to be provided with suitable wives to prevent this from happening. The duke of Clarence already had ten children with the actress Mrs. Jordan; when he eventually married Princess Adelaide of Saxe-Coburg-Meiningen in 1818, he brought his illegitimate children along to live in the same house. The duke of Kent, who had lived with his French mistress for twenty-seven years and had several children with her, also had to marry for the sake of the succession; his eldest daughter was to become Queen Victoria.

It was at about this time that the royal family appeared to gain a new recruit: Princess Olive, duchess of Lancaster. She claimed to be the daughter of George III's scapegrace brother, the aforementioned duke of Cumberland, in a secret marriage. Both George III and the duke had promised to support her, but neither had made good his promise, and the princess was now near-destitute. She claimed to have evidence of her royal descent and to own various other documents concerning skeletons in the royal cupboard of the most sensational nature.[7]

## PRINCESS OLIVE

NOMINALLY, AT LEAST, Princess Olive was the daughter of Robert Wilmot, who she claimed was an artist but whom others described as a simple house painter. A native of Warwick, he had originally succeeded his father as county treasurer, but had fallen into disgrace for embezzling funds. He decided to try his luck as a painter and decorator in London, and sent his ten-year-old daughter, Olive, to board with his brother James, who had become rector of Barton-on-the-Heath in Warwickshire. Olive was to reside at the rectory for quite a few years. According to some accounts, her uncle taught her privately, and she became quite a scholar. A more hostile source claims that James Wilmot was a dotard and that the frivolous Olive had the run of the rectory, where she bullied the servants and henpecked her ailing uncle. She spent much time in the library, reading "works which paternal duty should have kept from her hands, and female modesty

Olive Serres. From M. L. Pendered, *The Fair Quaker* (London, 1910).

have closed up with disgust."[8] In 1789, Olive rejoined her father in London. As a young woman, she was quite good-looking and vivacious, with luxuriant brown curls and expressive dark eyes, although her figure was somewhat inclined to embonpoint. She showed an early talent for painting and became a student of the celebrated artist John Thomas Serres. In 1791, Serres married her. James Wilmot, who conducted the ceremony, is said to have called out, "Serres, she is now your wife, but keep her employed, or she will be plotting mischief!" In spite of this gloomy prophecy, all seemed well during the early years of their marriage. Serres loved his wife dearly, and they had two children to whom he was devoted. Olive several times exhibited paintings at the Royal Academy of Arts and the British Institution, and was praised by none less than the Prince of Wales. But her extravagant habits were not suited to life as the wife of an impoverished artist. All accounts agree that she had ideas far above her station in life and was financially reckless in the extreme. Olive bought things on credit from tradesmen without her husband's knowledge and even forged his name on bills and bonds when he was away. It was told that once, when a creditor came to demand money, she pulled down the fine curtains in her front room, telling him to take them to the pawnshop. Things went so far that both the Serreses were imprisoned for debt.

According to the anonymous biographer of John Thomas Serres, Olive was a termagant who bullied and henpecked her weak-minded husband mercilessly. When Serres found out that she had conducted several affairs when he was away on painting expeditions, he had had enough. Their divorce in 1804 was an acrimonious one; disgusted when she was given just £200 a year by her husband, Olive seized several of his paintings that were for sale at various galleries, and took her two daughters away. Because of penury, the artist George Fields, a friend of Serres, had lived with the family for some time just before their divorce. When Serres learned that Olive had given birth to an illegitimate child a few months after their separation, he realized that Fields had shared more than his house.[9]

On her own in London, Olive managed to keep poverty from the door by selling her paintings and by writing several books of plays, poems, and essays.[10] In a book published in 1813, she made the audacious claim that her uncle, the Reverend Dr. James Wilmot, had written the *Letters of Junius*, a famous political commentary from the 1760s and 1770s, noted for its hostility to the sitting government.[11] Four years later, she wrote a letter to the Prince of Wales claiming that she was a natural daughter of the duke of Cumberland by Dr. Wilmot's sister Mrs. Olive Payne, and asking the prince for financial support. In 1820, after the death of both James and Robert Wilmot,

Olive expanded on her heritage, claiming that she was actually the duke's legitimate daughter. Far from being a lifelong bachelor, her clergyman uncle James Wilmot had secretly married the Princess Poniatowski, the sister of King Stanislas of Poland, whom he had met during his Oxford studies. The only daughter of this marriage had married the duke of Cumberland, and given birth to Princess Olive in April 1772, before dying from a broken heart as a result of the duke's

Prince George as a youth. From M. L. Pendered,
*The Fair Quaker* (London, 1910).

second bigamous marriage, to Anne Horton. James Wilmot had sworn his brother Robert to secrecy and consigned the infant Olive to him, to be brought up as his own child. But in spite of all this secrecy, George III knew of his immoral brother's activities, Olive claimed. He gave Princess Olive £5,000 in cash and a yearly pension of £500 for life; he provided a further £15,000 for her in his will. Olive's kinsman the king of Poland gave her another £5,000. Princess Olive claimed to have solid documentary evidence for all these financial claims. Another of her documents, signed by George III in May 1773, created Princess Olive duchess of Lancaster. The duchy of Lancaster, an appendage to the crown and a source of income for royalty, should thus become her dominion.

Princess Olive's first official act was to have herself rebaptized in 1821 as the daughter of the duke of Cumberland at Islington Church. She wrote several letters to the newspapers announcing her parentage, as well as a short pamphlet.[12] The duke of Kent had been one of her supporters, she claimed, and even made her the guardian of his daughter Victoria. Princess Olive seems to have been quite a well-known London character in the early 1820s. A corpulent, middle-aged lady, well dressed and with a haughty, dignified manner, she was often accompanied by a much younger gentleman. At the Lord Mayor's banquet in 1820, she insisted on sitting at the right hand of the Lord Mayor, as befit a princess of the blood, and the procession into the dining hall was halted for ten minutes while her claim was debated. After much altercation, she was compelled to sit at a different table. Another time, she wanted to travel through Constitution Gate, a way normally reserved for royalty, on her way home from a party. Amazingly, the royal servants gave way, and Princess Olive majestically went past them in her carriage, which had the Royal arms emblazoned on the door panels, her servants wearing elegant green-and-gold liveries. Another amusing story has it that Olive became the mistress of the earl of Warwick.[13] He once introduced her to the duke of Sussex, another of the sons of George III, and Olive called him "cousin" and treated him with much familiarity. She wanted to impress the duke with her remarkable likeness to the royal family, but he was not impressed. Olive, who might have been the worse for liquor, then pulled off her large wig and said, "Why, did you ever in your life see such a likeness to yourself?"

But Princess Olive lacked the financial means to keep up her royal pretentions. In 1821, she was arrested for debt, but with characteristic spirit claimed that, as a member of the royal family, she could not be put into prison. Nevertheless, she had to languish in the King's Bench prison for quite some time, neither the first nor the last of her incarcerations in this debtor's prison. She managed to raise some money by having a poster entitled "The Princess of Cumberland in Captivity!" put up all over London. It claimed that the late king had bequeathed her £15,000 in his will but that the government had kept the money for itself. The princess was thus left to rely on the generosity of the great British public. In 1822, Olive published a pamphlet describing her claim in detail.[14] She was ignorant of her royal descent until 1815, when the earl of Warwick and the duke of Kent visited her to tell her the truth. According to her pamphlet, all three were weeping profusely, and when Olive exclaimed, "Would I was more worthy of the high rank it has pleased Divine Providence to call me to!," the Duke replied, "I will protect you, Olive, with my heart's best blood, and see you yet restored to your royal rights!" In spite of its dramatic touches and highly charged language, the pamphlet failed to impress the reading public. Olive had an affair with Sheriff J. W. Parkins, a well-known London eccentric, and hoped to involve him in her claim. But they quarreled after she failed to return some money she owed him, and he turned against her with a vengeance. It particularly annoyed the sheriff that his successor in Olive's affections was a dashing young man who called himself William Henry FitzClarence, supposedly an illegitimate son of the duke of Clarence. The jilted sheriff contacted John Thomas Serres and learned the sordid story of his marriage to Olive. In a letter, the sheriff deplored "the machinations of your wicked & worthless wife," and Serres agreed that "it is high time such fraudulent humbug should be completely put a stop to."[15]

Olive next managed to persuade Sir Gerard Noel, an elderly parliamentarian, to demand an inquiry into her claim. Olive's various documents were examined by Parliament, and Sir Gerard delivered an impressive speech in her favor. But documents in the Public Record Office make it clear that by this time the royal family was fighting back. The duke of York was employing Sheriff Parkins and the clergyman Joseph Brett as agents to disprove Olive's royal pretentions.[16] They found her birth certificate and a document signed by Robert Wilmot saying that he was her natural and lawful father. Parkins was clever enough to write to Princess Poniatowski, who assured him that neither of King Stanislas's sisters had ever been to England. A man named John Deuley, whom Olive had cheated out of £19 for some books she had bought on credit, testified that he had provided her with autographs of Lord Chatham and the duke of Cumberland—for use in forging documents? It is very likely that the findings of Parkins and Brett were presented to the prime minister, Sir Robert Peel. In a powerful speech in response to Sir Gerard Noel, Peel blasted her documents as forgeries and her story as full of fabrications. To add insult to injury, he quoted a document stating, "The Princess Olive, only child of Henry Frederick Duke of Cumberland, and bred up by my brother Robert, may be known by a large brown spot"; there was ribald laughter and cries of "Where? Where?" It was concluded that Mrs. Serres was either a most impudent imposture or the innocent dupe of others. Parkins and Brett hoped that she would be prosecuted for forgery, but their royal master was content to let the matter rest.[17]

Poor Princess Olive sank low during her later years, and more than once had to write begging leaflets to get out of the debtor's prisons where she languished. Her daughters had to fend for themselves, and her illegitimate son became a tramp.[18] In 1830, she published her last pamphlet on her claim to royalty.[19] It appears she was by this time relying on tips from wealthy people who came to see her as a curiosity. After the death of Princess Olive, in 1834, her eldest daughter inherited her titles. This lady had previously been leading a quiet middle-class existence, but after becoming Princess Lavinia, she divorced her husband and devoted the remainder of her life to pursuing her claim.[20] In 1844, she tried to take the duke of Wellington to court for having ignored the prior will granting Olive £15,000 when he acted as executor of George III, but without success. In 1850, she published a pamphlet directed to Queen Victoria.[21] Unless the queen gave proper attention to her claim, she threatened, she would divulge the great state secret she and her mother had previously guarded so scrupulously. Since she had been cruelly persecuted for thirty-eight years, and lived in poverty and distress, she also asked for financial help from the royal purse. She had six children dependent on her, and one son was "almost reduced to a skeleton." But in spite of this pathetic touch, the queen's secretary curtly denied her any pecuniary assistance. It was not until 1866, when she was sixty-nine years old, that Princess Lavinia finally managed to take her opponents to court: she asked the Court of Probate and Divorce to pronounce her the legitimate granddaughter of the duke of Cumberland, and to award her the £15,000 left to her in George III's will. Her barrister was Dr. Walter Smith, who was opposed by Attorney General Roundell Palmer; the hearing was conducted by the lord chief justice, Sir Alexander Cockburn.[22]

The mainstay of Dr. Smith's argument was a bundle of 108 documents, left by Princess Olive to her daughter and containing remarkable information. Here, signed by George III, the earl of Chatham, and the earl of Warwick, were the certificates of Olive's royal birth and the various pecuniary donations to her. Amazingly, a handwriting expert testified that both King George's signature and that of James Wilmot were genuine. Although he declared himself uncertain about the others, this was an important victory for the princess. It also turned out that Olive's story that the duke of Kent had supported her was nothing but the truth. One of the duke's porters testified that he had often seen her visit the duke, and had delivered letters and presents from the duke to her house. Most memorably, he had brought her a piece of Princess Victoria's christening cake and a vial of wine in 1819. The duke used to speak of Olive as "my cousin Serres" and gave every indication of believing her story. Dr. Smith ended his presentation of the case with a flourish. Boldly, he claimed that, before his marriage to Princess Charlotte, George III had been privately married to the Quaker Hannah Lightfoot. The startled lord chief justice queried what this daring pronouncement had to do with his case. When Dr. Smith began to explain that neither George IV nor her present majesty Queen Victoria would have any right to the throne, he was rudely interrupted. These things must not be gone into, the judges warned him, and it was a great indecency to make such uncouth and unverified statements about the royal family.

After his successful start, Dr. Smith soon got into difficulties when he was trying to explain why George III had signed one certificate as George Guelph, a most unconventional signature. Nor could he explain why William Pitt had signed several certificates as Chatham and Lord Brooke several others as Warwick before they had succeeded to their respective earldoms. In spite of the handwriting expert's testimony, the attorney general roundly proclaimed the bundle of documents a pack of forgeries, done by Olive herself or by some artist friend of hers. He also pointed out that nobody had ever seen Dr. Wilmot's Polish princess, nor was there any evidence she had ever existed. The same was true of her daughter who had purportedly married the duke of Cumberland. These many difficulties notwithstanding, Princess Lavinia conducted herself well in the witness-box. An unremarkable-looking lady of seventy, tidily dressed in black, she seemed the very antithesis of her flamboyant mother. Interrogated at length, she avoided contradictions with considerable skill and adroitness; the impression was certainly that she believed every word she was saying. After a grueling cross-examination about Olive's certificates, which she survived very well, the attorney-general gruffly said, "I have done with these documents, madam, but not with you!" "I am very glad to hear it!" replied the princess calmly. When asked about the activities of a genealogist employed by Princess Olive to draw up her pedigree, her similarly tranquil response was "that Mr. Bell was an Irishman, and Irish people are very apt to invent things." The attorney general questioned her at length about the Reverend Dr. Wilmot and his curious partiality for secret marriages, but again with little effect on the elderly plaintiff's remarkable sangfroid. He then brought up the letter written by Princess Olive to the Prince of Wales in 1817, where she begged him "to consider the situation of your late uncle's natural daughter in London, who in every trial has maintained her sexual dignity." Princess Lavinia replied that, under the Royal Marriage Act, her mother thought she might be considered illegitimate although she was born in wedlock. To the gruff query "And do you imagine the jury will believe this?" she defiantly replied, "Yes, I do!"

The outcome of the case could only be one, however. Although the court found Lavinia the legitimate daughter of John and Olive Serres, it could not consider her the granddaughter of the duke of Cumberland. The court had no power to prosecute her, since she protested that she had believed implicitly in the genuineness of her mother's documents and had intended no deception. Princess Lavinia never gave up her claim. She wrote another pamphlet to lambast the judges who had cheated her out of her birthright, and before her death, in 1871, she even tried to get her case reheard by the House of Lords.[23] The antiquary W. T. Thoms pointed out the many inconsistencies of her story.[24] In particular, her story of the Polish princess is almost certainly a falsehood, there being no evidence that any such exalted personage ever visited Oxford, or any other part of the British Isles, at the time Dr. Wilmot was supposed to have married her. It is true that Stanislas Poniatowski, elected king of Poland in 1764, had visited England in 1754, but he spent just one day in Oxford. He did have two sisters, but they were both married in the 1740s and never came to England. I have examined Princess Olive's bundle of documents at the Public Record Office in Kew, and they certainly appear to be forgeries.[25] The vast majority resemble scrap paper, and they look very unlike the important documents of state they purport to be. Documents said to be of very different age, like Hannah Lightfoot's marriage certificate and the affidavits from the duke of Kent, consist of suspiciously similar paper. Indeed, a recent expert has found that the style of paper indicates it was manufactured in the period from 1795 to 1810; this agrees very well with the notion that Olive forged the documents or had them forged.[26] The analysis of handwriting evidence is an inexact science, but it has been pointed out that the signatures of George III and the earl of Chatham on Olive's documents look very unlike their authentic signatures.[27] There was a rumor at the time that Princess Olive had teamed up with a disreputable solicitor named Knight to blackmail the royal family and that Olive's young boyfriend Mr. FitzClarence, who was quite a calligrapher, had forged the letters involved.[28]

Thus there is no reliable evidence whatsoever that Princess Olive was the legitimate daughter of the duke of Cumberland. Her biographers gave her the benefit of the doubt, however, and found it not unlikely she was the duke's illegitimate daughter, as she herself claimed back in 1817.[29] The duke's flighty character was well known, and Olive would not have been his only bastard child. Olive's undoubted support from the duke of Kent also indicates that her claim to royalty may well have had some foundation. Yet it should be remarked that the duke was a silly, well-meaning character, easy to fool by a scheming adventuress. Olive's story that the duke provided her with pecuniary support must also be looked upon with great skepticism, given his own financial embarrassment at the time. Another drawback for her claim is the date of her birth—1772, the year after Cumberland had (bigamously?) married Anne Horton. Records agree that the duke was very much in love with his wife, at least for a few years after they married, and that he gave up his philandering ways. In fact, their marriage lasted until his death, in 1790; in his real and undoubted will, he left his entire estate to her.

The strongest objection to Princess Olive's claim is her own character. She delighted in inventing romantic stories about herself.[30] One of her favorites had to do with burglars who broke into her uncle James's house while she was staying there. In one version, the robbers were so impressed by her beauty and courage that they spared her jewelry. In another version, told at length in her biography of James

Wilmot, the entire gang of burglars broke into the house, intent on murder and mayhem. Armed with "various instruments of destruction," they surrounded Olive's bed, but she stoutheartedly refused to tell where the doctor kept his gold. The servants were nailed up in their rooms, and the burglars were ransacking the place, when Olive saved the day by leaping through a window dressed only in her petticoats, and running barefoot through the snow to gather assistance from the villagers. The robbers were caught, and the neighboring gentry all came to congratulate the heroine of the day; they even printed a handbill to celebrate her courage. From an early age, she was obsessed with the royal family. She wrote letters to the Prince of Wales and the duke of Kent, asking them for money and giving them unwanted advice. Once, she offered to lend the prince £20,000, much more money than she herself or anyone in her family had ever possessed, but fortunately he did not take up her offer. Another time, she told her husband she was having an affair with the duke of Cambridge, but according to the long-suffering Serres, this was as untrue as her other royal fantasies. Olive's sense of pathetic drama is also vividly illustrated by the ludicrous scene when the duke of Kent and the earl of Warwick told Olive about her royal past. She later improved even on this masterpiece by stating that it was actually Lord Warwick's ghost that had told her the story first, adding that this was not the only time this noble specter had come to visit her. Sheriff Parkins knew more about Olive's sinister side, and her predilection for untrue and malicious gossip about royalty. George IV, she had told him, had killed a groom by stabbing him with a pitchfork, the duke of Kent had committed adultery with his own sister, the duke of Clarence had murdered two men, and the dukes of Cumberland and Sussex were both homosexuals. As for the paterfamilias himself, George III had stolen a necklace from the queen to give to the Princess of Wales, and he was in the habit of having "criminal connection with his niece and his sister-in-law on a couch."[31]

## HANNAH LIGHTFOOT

THE MOST REMARKABLE feature of the 1866 trial was the obscure
and enigmatic mention of King George III's previous marriage to Hannah Lightfoot, which caused so much stir among the legal luminaries
involved. This was a story known to the London gossips since the late
eighteenth century.[32] One day when Prince George, later George III,
was traveling through London in his sedan chair, on his way to the
opera, he saw a young woman sitting in the window of a linendrapers
shop at the corner of St. James's Market. She was very beautiful and,
unlike most people at the time, had a face unblemished by smallpox.
Prince George fell in love with her at first sight. He found out that her
name was Hannah Lightfoot and that she came from a poor but
respectable Quaker family. Although just thirteen years old at the time,
George immediately set about making plans to seduce Hannah, plans
worthy of an experienced Casanova. He arranged for Elizabeth
Chudleigh, one of his mother's ladies-in-waiting, to arrange a meeting. She did so with the help of a certain Jack Emm, who appears to
have been some kind of high-class pimp in charge of a house of ill
repute in Pall Mall. After meeting the lovesick young prince, Hannah
agreed to become his mistress. But later in 1751 Prince George's father
died, and he became heir to the throne. Fearful of scandal, he wanted
Hannah to be married, and so did his mother, who had found out about
the affair and wanted it to end. On December 11, 1753, Hannah Lightfoot married a young grocer named Isaac Axford, who had been lured
by the promise of a generous dowry. But legend has it that Prince
George changed his mind: he swooped past the doors of the chapel in
his coach and abducted Hannah in front of the startled wedding procession. Axford jumped onto a horse and desperately pursued the royal
coach, but in vain. There were numerous toll stations along the road,
and while the prince shouted "Royal Family!" and was let through without stopping, Axford had to stop and pay at every one of them. Later,
Axford waited for the prince to come by in Kew Gardens; the wretched
grocer knelt in silent supplication, but the haughty prince just rode

Sir Joshua Reynolds's portrait of "Miss Axford,
the Fair Quaker," alleged to be of Hannah Lightfoot.
From M. L. Pendered, *The Fair Quaker* (London, 1910).

past him. The prince installed Hannah as his mistress in a house in
the outskirts of London. One version says Kew, another Hackney, a
third Tottenham; the latter adds that Dr. John Fothergill, a Quaker doctor who was a skilled accoucheur, was once taken there blindfolded
to deliver a child. Hannah and the prince were very much in love, and
according to one of Princess Olive's certificates, he married her on May
27, 1759. They were joined in holy matrimony by that specialist in
secret weddings—Olive's alleged grandfather the Reverend James

Wilmot—and the witnesses were Prime Minister William Pitt and Anne Taylor the bell ringer at St. James's Palace. In another of Princess Olive's documents, James Wilmot and Lord Chatham solemnly certified that George and Hannah had two sons and a daughter. Legend has several different versions of Hannah Lightfoot's final fate. Princess Olive's collection contains another scrap paper document, namely the will of Queen Hannah, written in 1762 after George had become king. One version tells that she herself died soon after making this will, another that she was sent abroad to facilitate George's second marriage, to Queen Charlotte. There is complete disagreement where she went; some say to Germany and others to America or South Africa. A particularly romantic ending has her installed in a large dome-surmounted house in France, near a lake with many swans; the brokenhearted queen could be seen walking there as the day's shadows grew longer. According to a more prosaic version, she went back to England and lived to be a hundred years old.

After Princess Lavinia's 1866 trial, the librarian to the House of Lords, W. T. Thoms, published a pamphlet about the case. He pointed out that the entire story was a fable and that no such person as Hannah Lightfoot had ever existed. But another antiquary, J. Heneage Jesse, managed to prove that she had definitely existed, and today we know a fair amount about her.[33] Hannah Lightfoot was born in 1730 in the East End of London. Her father was the shoemaker Matthew Lightfoot, who had married Mary Wheeler in 1728; his shop was in Execution Dock, Wapping. After Matthew's death, in 1733, Hannah's uncle Henry Wheeler took care of his sister and niece: they were allowed to live with his large family and help with the daily chores in his successful linendrapers business in St. James's Market. Both the Lightfoots and the Wheelers were respectable members of the Society of Friends, also known as the Quakers. During her residence with the Wheelers, Hannah signed the birth certificate of one of her cousins as a witness. The next known date in her life is her marriage to Isaac Axford in 1753. The parents of Hannah's husband were both Baptists, but other family members were Quakers. There is evidence that he worked as a "shop-man" assisting in the grocery business of a certain John Barton. But something was not right with this marriage.[34] We know from the minute-book of the Westminster Quakers that Hannah was actually expelled from the Society of Friends in 1756. The reason was that she "did Enter into a State of Marriage by a Priest with one not of our Society" and had since gone away and could not be spoken with. Her mother testified that she was not fully satisfied that Hannah was separated from her husband. The name of this husband is not stated.[35] It may have been a reference to Isaac Axford, since there is no evidence he was a Quaker. It is a fact that Hannah and Axford married in Dr. Keith's marriage chapel in Mayfair, and not in any chapel of the Society of Friends. Thus there is good evidence that Hannah left her family and the Quaker congregation; she may have left her husband and could have been living with someone else. The next corroborated fact is that in 1757 a certain Robert Pearne gave "Mrs. Hannah Axford, formerly Miss Hannah Lightfoot," an annuity of £40 a year in his will. The will was carefully drawn up so that Isaac Axford would not be able to access the money, which was obviously meant for Hannah alone—another indication that all was not well between Hannah and her husband. It does not mention any children of Hannah Lightfoot. Not much is known about this Robert Pearne, except that he was a wealthy, unmarried gentleman owning estates in both England and Antigua.[36] He is unlikely to have been a relation to the Lightfoot family or a family friend, and it is natural to speculate whether Hannah might have been his mistress. One of Hannah Lightfoot's biographers claimed to have seen some of her letters. In these undated letters, Hannah assures her mother that all is well and that her protector, whom she refers to only as "the Person," will soon help the Lightfoots with their financial trouble.[37] There is also the question of a portrait of "Miss Axford, the Fair Quaker," painted by Sir Joshua Reynolds in 1758. It depicts a beautiful, wistful-looking woman aged around thirty. She is not dressed in the simple Quaker attire, but is wearing an elegant dress in satin and lace. The origins of this portrait can be traced back to the 1790s, and many writers have presumed it to be a portrait of Hannah Lightfoot; this is possible but by no means certain.[38] Isaac Axford remarried in December 1759. He referred to himself as a widower, indicating that Hannah was dead by this time. The last certain thing we know about her is that her mother, Mary, herself died in May 1760 and that she left her property to Hannah in her will. She stated in this will, made in January 1760, that she did not know whether her daughter was alive or dead, since she had not heard from Hannah for about two years.[39]

The known facts about Hannah Lightfoot thus show surprising agreement with some of the legendary stories about her, with one exception: she could hardly have given birth to three legitimate children if she died in 1759, the same year she married, according to Princess Olive's certificate. Furthermore, there is no contemporary evidence that Hannah Lightfoot ever met Prince George. Far from being a precocious youngster, capable of seducing a twenty-one-year-old mistress at the age of just thirteen, the young prince, sources agree, was a shy, awkward lad, hardworking rather than intellectual, but nevertheless immersed in his studies. George was also sincerely religious already in his teens. His correspondence with his personal tutor, the earl of Bute, gives ample evidence of his immaturity, his preachy and verbose religious outpourings, and his narrow sense of morality. In another letter, the prince confessed to Bute that the first time a woman touched his heart was in late 1759, when Lady Sarah Lennox came to court.[40] One would also have thought that contemporary society gossip and court diaries would have delighted in speculating about Prince George's illicit affair, but, with one exception, they are silent on this topic. This exception is a letter from Lady Sophia Egerton to her uncle, mentioning that the prince "kept a beautiful young Quaker for some years, that she is Dead, and that One Child was the produce of that intrigue."[41] This letter was written in December 1759 and thus agrees well with the known facts about Hannah Lightfoot. In 1770, the *Public Advertiser* newspaper published an article about the duke of Cumberland's seduction of Lady Grosvenor; it contained a reference to a spurious "new publication entitled *The Letters of an Elder*

*Brother to a Fair Quaker.*" The first mention of Hannah's name in connection with that of royalty occurred six years later, in a similarly enigmatic note in the *Citizen* newspaper about a forthcoming publication
entitled "The History and advances to Miss L . . . thf . . . t (The Fair
Quakeress), Wherein will be faithfully portrayed some striking pictures
of female constancy and princely gratitude which terminated in the
untimely death of a young lady. . . ." In 1779, yet another publication
alluded to George's Quaker mistress.[42] Interestingly, the affair is said
to have been divulged in the Quaker proceedings—again something
that fits in well with what we know about Hannah Lightfoot.

From 1779 until 1820, there was complete silence about Queen
Hannah. In a time not noted for reticence with regard to royal failings
and blessed with a vigorous newspaper press and plenty of scurrilous
pamphleteers, a scandal of this magnitude should have attracted more
notice. Not until the early 1820s, however, was there much correspondence about Hannah Lightfoot in the *Monthly Magazine* and
other London periodicals.[43] Some of it may have emanated from the
busy pen of Princess Olive, but by no means all, since some people
wrote in their personal reminiscences of the Lightfoot and Axford
families. It was at this time that the legend of Hannah Lightfoot gradually took form: the dashing teenage prince, the demure but lovely
Quaker girl, the abduction from her husband, and, not least, the several young royal children. There exist several variations on the main
theme: one writer said Hannah was still alive, but the majority agreed
she was dead, and the number of children varied from one to five. No
one was audacious enough to claim that George had actually married
Hannah, however. This final touch to the legend was added in a vulgar publication entitled *Authentic Records of the Court of England*,
which was quickly withdrawn because of a libel on the duke of Cumberland, who was wrongly accused of murdering his own valet. This
squib has been attributed to Lady Anne Hamilton, an audacious lady
pamphleteer with a grudge against the royal family, but there is evidence Princess Olive had a hand in it as well.[44] Its preface declares
that the history of England does not present two reigns equal in enor-

mity to those of Queen Charlotte and her infamous son George IV:
"*Baseness* of every kind was practiced, and *murder became an every-day
occurrence. Deception* and *villainy* were esteemed *virtues,* while *incest*
and *adultery* proved passports to *Court favour* and *promotion.*" The
section about Queen Hannah is equally dramatic and highly charged.
It is first claimed that Prince George and Hannah were legally married in 1759, at the Curzon Street Chapel, Mayfair. This disregards
the fact that this chapel had been closed in 1754. But the government
learned of the prince's secret marriage, and the weak-willed George
was beguiled by the cunning politicians, who assured him that his
marriage to Hannah could be secretly nullified. He promptly married
the wicked Princess Charlotte, the basest and most abandoned of
women, and "thus was this ill-fated prince doomed to imbecility, des-
peration, and madness!" The queen heard about George III's secret
marriage and demanded that Hannah be disposed of. The evil politicians accomplished this by offering the young gentleman Axford a
large sum of money, payable upon the consummation of his marriage
with Hannah. The poor king, very much put out by Hannah's disappearance, dispatched Lord Chatham to prowl about in disguise to
discover where she had been taken, but the distinguished prime minister failed to accomplish this secret mission. In 1765, the queen
insisted that her marriage to George III again be solemnized (after
Hannah's death?); this was done in secret by the ubiquitous James
Wilmot.

Many historians have pondered the legend of Queen Hannah. The
twentieth-century biographers of George III, and indeed the vast
majority of professional historians, have tended to disregard it as a
fable.[45] The amateur historians have shown much more credulity.
Many of them have been disposed to believe that there was something
in the legend after all; some have accepted the notion that Hannah
was Prince George's mistress.[46] A few have swallowed the story whole,
including the marriage and the claim to the throne by Hannah's
alleged descendants.[47] But we have seen that the story of the marriage
was added to the legend in the 1820s by Princess Olive, and it can be

wholly discredited by the same arguments we used above to demolish Olive's own claim. The only palpable evidence, the couple's alleged marriage certificate at the Public Record Office, is certainly a forgery. But there are also strong arguments against the claims of some historians that Olive invented the whole story of Hannah Lightfoot. We know that Hannah was a historical person, that the known facts about her life show a remarkable resemblance to some features of the legend, and that there was something mysterious about her marriage to Axford and her exclusion from the Society of Friends. Moreover, we have evidence that, already in the 1760s and 1770s, there was some talk about the king's mistress, who was named as Miss Lightfoot in 1776. The articles from the *Monthly Magazine* of 1821 show the existence of a remarkably strong oral tradition in London that Prince George had kept a Quaker mistress named Hannah Lightfoot. Princess Olive thus used a preexisting tradition about the king and the fair Quaker, and there is no question of her having invented it. To these arguments, a skeptic might retort that there is no clear evidence from contemporary sources that Prince George and Hannah Lightfoot ever met. The rumor going around may have been a mere short-lived fabrication by some individual who wanted to make fun of the prudish prince by alleging that he was having an affair with an equally ostentatiously virtuous Quaker. The contemporary writers of court gossip and memoirs, like Horace Walpole and Fanny Burney, never mentioned the prince's affair. Most important, what is known about the young prince's character speaks strongly against his having conducted any affair as a young teenager.

To finally lay the ghost of this phantom queen to rest, it would be important to find out what finally happened to her and, if possible, to trace her grave. An early tradition has it that Hannah Lightfoot was buried in Islington Churchyard in 1759, in a tomb with the name Rebecca Powell. But in 1949 a genealogist found that there really was a Rebecca Powell, daughter of the Reverend Zachary Powell, born twenty-three years earlier, just as the tombstone indicated.[48] Despite numerous other hypotheses about what finally happened to her, the ultimate fate of Hannah Lightfoot remains a mystery.[49]

## GEORGE REX AND QUEEN HANNAH'S
## OTHER CHILDREN

IF WE ACCEPT as a faint possibility that Prince George and Hannah Lightfoot were lovers, then what about their putative children? The contemporary sources have little to add, except that the 1759 letter of Lady Sophia Egerton says, "One Child was the produce of that intrigue." By the 1820s, the number of children had risen. The correspondents of the *Monthly Magazine* in 1821 agree that George and Hannah had a son; one writer adds another son and claims that Hannah moved to Germany with her children; another claims they had several children; one or two of whom became generals in the army. A third writer knew of a gentleman named Dalton, who had married a daughter of Hannah Lightfoot, by the king. By the mid-nineteenth century, there was some agreement that George and Hannah had had three or four children: the eldest son, George Rex; the daughter, Catherine Augusta, who married Dr. James Dalton; a son named Sir Samuel Parks; and possibly a younger son who became a general in the army.

By far the best known of Queen Hannah's alleged children is George Rex, first alleged to have been her son in 1861. He went to South Africa, where he became marshal of the Vice Admiralty Court at the Cape of Good Hope in 1797. All sources agree that George Rex was a clever, farsighted man. He bought property cheaply and set up a vast country estate in Knysna, where he farmed successfully for many years. The profits from this farm and various other successful business ventures made him very rich; he lived in splendor and entertained magnificently. No portrait of George Rex survives, but he was said to resemble George III very closely. George Rex's family life was somewhat peculiar. From 1800 onward, he cohabited with a black slave woman named Johanna Rosina and had four children with her. In 1808, George Rex separated from Johanna Rosina and instead invited her fifteen-year-old daughter, Carolina Margaretha, his own stepdaughter, to share his bed and palace at Knysna. Although they, too, never married, records agree that they lived happily for thirty-one years and had nine children, the youngest of whom George sired when he was sixty-nine. After Rex's death, in 1839, his will specified that all his children were illegitimate, but he nevertheless provided well both for them and for his wife. The reason for this, it was rumored, was of course that his father, George III, had forbidden him to marry; any legitimate son of George Rex would become the true heir of the British throne. Some South African historians have accepted the entire story of Hannah Lightfoot and George Rex, backed by the descendants of George Rex still inhabiting these parts.[50] But in 1975 Professor Ian R. Christie, of University College London, established that, far from being in any way related to George III or Hannah Lightfoot, George Rex was the son of the London distiller John Rex.[51] Born in 1765, George Rex had a sister named Sarah, with whom he corresponded for many years, and a brother named John Rex. His name was thus not a Latin pun but a proper family name, inherited for several generations. The documentation brought forward by Professor Christie and others thus proves with certainty that George Rex of Knysna was no son of George III. His amazing success in South Africa, suspected to be due to financial support from the king, was entirely owing to Rex's own cleverness and business acumen. From humble beginnings, he made his fortune in South Africa at a time when rich pickings were to be had as the British administration sold land cheaply to investors.

It is curious that there was another George Rex, whose descendants also claim George III and Hannah Lightfoot as their progenitors.[52] The second George Rex was born in 1750, but it is not known where he came from. He emigrated to America in 1771, settled in Bucks County north of Philadelphia, farmed successfully for many years, and had twelve children. A quiet, religious man, he was known for his pro-British views, which made him somewhat unpopular with his neighbors. George Rex left quite a fortune when he expired in 1821. At the end of the nineteenth century, one of his descendants, the American writer Aline Shane-Devin, claimed to be the granddaughter of Rex's daughter Hannah Lightfoot Rex, the granddaughter of George III. This view is still widely held by Rex's descendants, whose numbers have grown at an amazing rate.[53] In 1933, Leda Farrell Rex published a 250-page book listing them and restating the claim of royal descent, discreetly disregarding that this would have made Prince George a very virile young man indeed, capable of siring a child at the age of just twelve. Furthermore, local archives indicate that George Rex had in fact been a private soldier fighting on the American side in the War of Independence. He had previously been working on his father's farm, and his grandfather George Rex had a farm in Bucks County as early as 1742.[54]

Another alleged child of Prince George and Hannah Lightfoot was Catherine Augusta Ritso, who married Dr. James Dalton in 1801 and who died in Madras in 1813.[55] Curiously, Burke's *General Armoury* makes this same lady a daughter of Henry Frederick, duke of Cumberland, and thus a sister of Princess Olive! In the year 2000, archaeologists working in the parish church of St. Peter in Camarthen, Wales, found the vaulted tomb of Charlotte Dalton, the daughter of James Dalton and his wife, Catherine Augusta.[56] It was promptly announced that the tomb of George III's secret granddaughter had been discovered. Much was made of the fact that the church's fine eighteenth-century organ had originally been intended for the Chapel Royal at Windsor. The Welsh enthusiasts speculated that George III had in some strange way foreseen that his granddaughter's remains would rest in this obscure country church, and decided that it should at least have a proper organ. They disregarded, however, the reality that Catherine Augusta Ritso was actually born in 1781; this would have made Hannah Lightfoot a mother at fifty-one, a most uncommon occurrence at the time. There is also good evidence that Catherine Augusta Ritso was actually the daughter of George Frederick and Sophia Ritzau, who were private German secretaries to Frederick, Prince of Wales, the father of George III. Her brother became a captain in the Royal Engineers, and a fair amount is known about him. There is no evidence at all to support the hypothesis of her royal birth, except for an old and unverifiable oral tradition.

As we have seen, an early feature of the legend is that one of Queen

Hannah's sons became a well-known general. This individual was later identified as General John Mackelcan, who made a quick career in the army although he never took part in any military action.[57] He was born in 1759, and so would at least fit in with the known facts about Hannah Lightfoot's short life. It was claimed that the name Mackelcan was unknown prior to this time, but a genealogist has since discovered earlier naturalization papers for a Harman Mackelcan. Furthermore, when he wanted to insure his life in 1817, the general himself stated that his father lived to the age of nearly eighty, that his mother lived to be about sixty, and that his grandmother reached the venerable age of ninety-two. He also had a fifty-six-year-old sister, married to a fellow officer. These facts make the family tradition about his royal descent less likely. Another of Hannah's alleged sons was Samuel Lightfoot, born in 1760, who became a London merchant.[58] His descendants have added that he changed his name to Samuel Parks, although they themselves were still called Lightfoot. A more fanciful addition is that Samuel was knighted Sir Samuel Parks, and that both he and his family received large sums of money from the king to give up certain documents they held. An American lady added a further ludicrous touch. Hannah's firstborn was christened Parks, after the beautiful parks nearby. His family went to America and multiplied there. Genealogists have found, however, that although Samuel Lightfoot was a historical person, he was in fact the grandson of Hannah's uncle. There is no record that any Samuel Parks (or Lightfoot) was knighted.[59]

The legend of Hannah Lightfoot and her children with George III has traveled well: wherever emigrants from Britain came, it was sure to follow. There are auxiliary royal families in Tasmania, Australia, South Africa, and the United States. In the twentieth century, the number of alleged children grew exponentially, and today there are more than fifty known "children" of Prince George and Hannah Lightfoot. The claims of many of these families are even weaker than those related above, resting on recent family traditions only. Some of better-known claimants were put to the test in 2002, when a TV documentary tested DNA from fourteen people belonging to the South African and Australian Rexes, and the U.S. Mackelcans, against DNA from the earl of Munster. The first earl of Munster had been an illegitimate son of William IV, a son of George III, and the pattern of the Y chromosome would thus have been inherited in the male line. The results indicated that neither the Rexes nor the Mackelcans could have been descendants of George III.[60] But the story of the prince and the fair Quaker will live on. After all, kings and queens are mere mortals, but it is difficult to kill off a good story.

# 5

—

## The Tichborne Claimant

Sir Roger was a youthful knight,
A youthful knight with a gallant air,
Who left his stately ancestral halls,
And all for love of a lady fair.
He sailed away o'er the ocean wide,
He sailed away from his native land,
Until in three weeks he stepped ashore,
And in the port of Rio did stand.

—"Sir Roger: A Tichborne Ballad"[1]

THE TICHBORNES WERE one of the oldest and most respectable Anglo-Catholic families.[2] Their pedigree, with many intermarriages with other wealthy Catholic families, extends back to before the Norman Conquest. At her deathbed, the thirteenth-century Lady Mabella Tichborne asked her husband to help the deserving poor. Her hard-hearted spouse replied that he would give as much land as she could crawl around while a torch burned. To everyone's astonishment, she roused herself and crawled around twenty-three acres of land, the yield from which was afterward given to the poor. Lady Mabella threatened that if these alms were not distributed according to her wishes, evil times would come to the house of Tichborne: seven sons would be succeeded by seven daughters, and the family would become extinct. In the 1790s, the Tichbornes nevertheless ordered this ancient custom to cease, since it attracted vagabonds and undesirables from all over the country. But by 1829 Sir Henry Tichborne's six sons had no male heir, and the oldest had seven daughters; the Tichbornes then found it wise to resume this ancient custom, to avoid Lady Mabella's curse.

At this time, the family's only hope of dynastic survival was James Tichborne, Sir Henry's fourth son. He had married, at the mature age of forty-three, a lady named Henriette Felicité Seymour. The illegitimate daughter of a wealthy magnate, she had spent her entire life in France and had a low opinion of English customs.[3] Soon she also developed a poor opinion of her stolid, portly husband, and she henpecked and bullied him cruelly. After many angry scenes between this mismatched couple, she settled in Paris with her young sons, Roger and Alfred; her husband was left to sit brooding at Tichborne Park, lamenting his wife's fierce and unreasonable disposition. Henriette Felicité Tichborne's eccentric notions extended to dress and upbringing, and she kept her son Roger in frocks, like a little girl, until he was twelve years old, and generally spoiled and mollycoddled him. By 1845, when Roger Tichborne was sixteen, he had seldom left the family house, rarely been out of Paris, and never ventured outside France. His mother believed him to be weak and sickly and frequently dosed him with various homeopathic remedies; she also believed that his mind should not be overtaxed by too much study, and, as a result, Roger's general knowledge was very poor. His native language was French, which he could not yet write properly.

By the mid-1840s, it was clear that James Tichborne would soon inherit the family title and wealth and that the lack of male heirs would mean that the entire fortune would one day pass on to Roger. But reports of Roger's progress were not laudatory. His father feared that his prolonged residence in Paris had made him into a spineless milksop, who preferred sitting in the boudoir drinking café au lait and eating fricassée to enjoying a hearty meal of roast beef and brown ale, and who eschewed foxhunting, fly-fishing, and the other hearty outdoor pursuits of the English country squire. His fears were by no means allayed when he saw that Roger was a short, thin, unmanly-looking youth, who could barely express himself fluently in English. James Tichborne saw no other means to regain the control over his

Sir Roger Tichborne in 1854.
From E. V. Kenealy, *Introduction to the Tichborne Trial* (London, 1875).

son than to actually abduct him during Roger's visit to England for the funeral of his uncle Henry. He sent young Roger to Stonyhurst, a respectable Catholic public school. Furious, Henriette dispatched a French servant to bring Roger back to Paris, but when confronted, he declared that he wanted to stay at Stonyhurst. The Jesuits at this venerable school were unable to install much academic ambition into Roger's dormant mind, but at least he gradually became fluent in the English language, although with a strong French accent.

After three years at Stonyhurst, Roger Tichborne narrowly passed the examination to become an army officer, and joined the Sixth Dragoon Guards (the Carabineers), based in Ireland. He was an odd-looking cavalry officer, thin and knock-kneed; his hips were so narrow that he had to fasten his sword belt to his suspenders with hooks so that it would not fall down. When first presented to the colonel with his cornet's commission, he was mistaken for the cook's assistant and sent on his way to the kitchen. Roger was ragged a good deal by his fellow officers, who ridiculed his French accent and lack of athletic ability. But Roger gradually toughened up, becoming a good shot, a competent horseman, and a tolerably efficient officer, although some of his colleagues maintained that his feeble mind was never able to grasp the intricacies of cavalry drill. To emulate his peers in the regiment, Roger began smoking and drinking excessively. He would have liked to serve abroad, but a planned sojourn in India came to nothing, and he resigned his commission in 1852.

After leaving the army, Roger planned finally to realize his dreams of traveling widely to see the world. There was another reason for this decision, namely that his advances to his first cousin Katherine Doughty had been rebuffed by her parents. Lady Doughty thought Roger a feckless, immature young man, who drank heavily and lacked the steadying influence of a sincere Catholic faith. Although Katherine Doughty admitted that she was fond of her cousin, and although Roger was, after all, heir to a title and a great fortune, her mother forbade them to marry. The snobbish lady did not completely reject Roger's suit, however, shrewdly keeping this wealthy candidate standing by in case her daughter did not receive any better offers of marriage. Disgusted by her actions, Roger went to South America in March 1853, sailing from Le Havre to Valparaiso. He brought with him one of the Tichborne servants, John Moore, to serve as his valet. From this time onward, not much is known about his activities. He wrote occasional letters home, mostly complaining about his mother's nagging and Lady Doughty's prejudice against his drinking habits. In one letter, he made plans to stay permanently at Tichborne Park after his father's death and to pay his mother an annuity if she stayed away. A more palpable reminder of Roger was a collection of tropical birds he had shot, which was shipped back to Tichborne Park along with some old paintings he had purchased from a monastery. In Santiago, he bought two daguerreotypes of himself and sent them to his parents and aunt, bragging of his healthy, tanned appearance. Some evidence suggests, however, that his habits were as dissipated as ever and that his servant Moore deserted him as a result. Roger spent his travel funds quickly, and when he wanted to journey from Rio to Kingston, Jamaica, on the ship *Bella*, he had to borrow money to pay for his passage. The *Bella* sailed on April 20, 1854, and was never seen again. Some weeks later, the ship's longboat was spotted off the coast of Brazil, along with some wreckage. No survivors were ever found at the time.

## SIR ROGER RESURRECTED

Then to Wagga Wagga Sir Roger went,
On his way to Woolomoloo
For he had set out with a trusty friend,
To hunt the Kangaroo.

At the Bush Hotel one night they stopped
Some Kangaroo Steak to fry
And on the Buxom Cook-maid there,
Sir Roger cast his eye.

—"Courtship and Marriage of Sir Roger"

WHEN NEWS OF Roger's being lost at sea reached Tichborne Park, where the ailing Sir James Tichborne had been reunited with his quarrelsome wife, they were both devastated. Although Sir James seemed to recover from the tragedy, and to center his dynastic hopes on the younger son, Alfred, Henriette Felicité became obsessed with the thought that Roger was still alive. Vincent Gosford, the agent at Tichborne Park, wrote that Sir James's declining years were embittered by his wife's obstinate refusal to accept that Roger was dead. Moreover, the actions of young Alfred Tichborne did nothing to raise the old baronet's spirits; there were worrying signs that this foolish, reckless youth was no better than Roger. After old Sir James's death, in 1862, Sir Alfred wasted thousands of pounds on various harebrained schemes, before drinking himself to death at the age of twenty-six. The family would have become extinct had not Alfred's widow been pregnant; to everyone's delight, she gave birth to a son, and the succession was saved. After Alfred's death, Lady Tichborne redoubled her efforts to find her dear Roger. She thought that lifeboats from the stricken *Bella* might have reached Australia, and imagined Roger living there. In spite of all her inquiries, however, made through various Australian agents, no trace of Roger had been found by late 1865, more than eleven years after the shipwreck of the *Bella*.

But in the small township of Wagga Wagga, situated in a remote part of New South Wales, things were beginning to happen. A local attorney named William Gibbes had seen the advertisements for Roger Tichborne in the Australian newspapers, and he and his wife began to suspect a local butcher who called himself Thomas Castro. A strong burly fellow, Castro had spent many years in Australia, going walkabout in the bush and working as a hired hand when he felt like it, before settling down in his Wagga Wagga butcher's shop. He married a sluttish, illiterate woman who had already borne an illegitimate child to another man; the pair also had a young daughter together. Castro's business was not particularly successful, and Gibbes helped him in filing for bankruptcy because of considerable debt. One day, Castro asked him whether certain property in England, to which he was entitled, should be included in his list of assets. He also mentioned that he had once survived a shipwreck after spending days in an open boat. His pipe was carved with the initials R.C.T!

When Gibbes challenged Castro with being Roger Tichborne, the butcher reluctantly admitted that he was indeed the missing baronet,

The Claimant's hut in Wagga Wagga.
From a contemporary stereoscopic photograph.

although he implored Gibbes to keep his discovery quiet, because he
did not want to make himself known after all his years in Australia.
Gibbes and Lady Tichborne's agent managed to change his mind, however, and these two wrote to her ladyship announcing the joyful news
that Roger had been discovered in darkest Australia. Lady Tichborne
was delighted, particularly since this happened not long after the death
of her younger son, Alfred; the recovery of Roger after an absence of
almost twelve years seemed like divine intervention. The family solicitor Mr. Bowker was much harder to convince. He immediately suspected an imposture and impeded Lady Tichborne's attempts to send
money to Australia for the Castros' travel expenses. Although Castro
(hereafter called the Claimant) wrote her a heartfelt, but quite illiterate, begging letter, no money was forthcoming until well into 1866. By
that time, the Claimant had gone to Sydney to try to raise travel money
from other sources. There he met an old Tichborne servant, the West
Indian Andrew Bogle, who had been pensioned off by the family with

a small annuity. Bogle willingly recognized the Claimant as Roger Tichborne, and the two became firm friends, spending much time together discussing the old days at Tichborne Park. Two other people in Sydney who had previously met Roger Tichborne also recognized the Claimant as the lost baronet. These successes made it possible for the Claimant to borrow money in Sydney for his travel expenses to London, and he arrived late in 1866, together with his wife and child and the servant Bogle. He promptly secured the services of the young London solicitor John Holmes and set out to recover his lost fortune.

The solicitor Bowker had already begun to orchestrate the opposition from the Tichborne family, and even before the Claimant's arrival in London, there had been hostile articles in the newspapers. Holmes realized that it was imperative that the Claimant see his mother as soon as possible, and they quickly traveled to Paris. On the day he was to see Lady Tichborne, the Claimant felt ill. He received his alleged mother lying fully dressed on a bed, with a white handkerchief over his head. When Lady Tichborne saw the big hulking fellow in this position, she lifted the handkerchief and exclaimed, "Oh, my dear Roger, is it you?" The Claimant wept with relief, and they embraced fondly. The solicitor Holmes promptly had affidavits made up that Lady Tichborne had recognized the Claimant as her son. This was a heavy blow for the rest of the Tichborne family. Except for the solicitor Bowker, who made a last-minute dash to Paris to try to bring the eccentric lady to reason but arrived too late, they had not expected things to come to this. The family fortune was held in trust for Sir Alfred's posthumous son, and they sensed that there was a very real risk that the claim would actually go to court and the infant baronet be expelled from Tichborne Park. The Tichborne family's fears were not allayed by a steady stream of sinister news from Hampshire, where the Claimant was now staying. In a triumphal tour through the old Tichborne strongholds, he had been recognized by Colonel Lushington, the tenant of Tichborne Park, by the antiquary Francis Baigent, an old family friend, by J. P. Lipscomb, the Tichborne family doctor, and by Edward Hopkins, the old family solicitor. Country gentlemen, old Tichborne tenants, and

officers and soldiers from the Carabineers followed in droves. They
were all impressed with his detailed recollection of Tichborne Park,
its gardens and grounds, and episodes from Roger Tichborne's boyhood and military life. Guildford Onslow, a local member of Parliament, was astonished by the Claimant's knowledge of local lore and
old hunting incidents and became an instant convert as well as a longtime friend. The Claimant was an expert fly-fisherman, and the local
fishing tackle salesman was amazed that he ordered exactly the same

A contemporary stereoscopic
photograph of the Claimant.

dry flies that Roger Tichborne had wanted fifteen years earlier. One of the few dissenting voices came from a blacksmith named Etheridge. The Claimant had approached and bought him a pint of beer, later asking him whether he thought he was Roger Tichborne. "No, I'll be damned if you are. If you are, you've turned from a race-horse into a cart-horse!" was the forthright reply.

Awaiting the legal action that was to follow, the Claimant settled down in a house in Croydon. Henry Seymour, Roger Tichborne's uncle, who had very little confidence in his sister's identification of the Claimant as her son, went to see him there. The Claimant cut a sorry figure during this interview, for he failed to recognize an old Tichborne butler whom Seymour had brought with him, did not know Sir James Tichborne's handwriting, and said he could not understand French at all. After Roger Tichborne's disappearance, his old sweet-heart Katherine Doughty had married Sir Percival Radcliffe and had several children. She and her mother, Lady Doughty, were both allied with the Tichborne family interest. Her husband decided to try to fool the Claimant by proposing that he meet his aunt Lady Doughty and his cousin Katherine, to see whether he could recognize the love of his youth. But at the meeting the Claimant was confronted by another aunt, Mrs. Nangle, and by one of Katherine's cousins. The confused and angry Claimant said that he knew neither of these ladies, his face contorting spastically as he realized that he had been tricked; Radcliffe hastily withdrew when his burly opponent advanced toward him with clenched fists. Katherine Radcliffe herself also had a look at the Claimant during this confrontation; at first, she thought he resembled Roger, but later turned against him, in view of his gross ignorance of his own family and relations. Disaster struck for the Claimant in March 1868, when Lady Tichborne suddenly died. Not only did he lose his most impressive supporter, and the pension of £1,000 a year she had settled on him, but all her papers were impounded, including all the letters he had written to her, letters that would do him considerable harm at a later stage.

## EVIDENCE FROM AUSTRALIA AND FROM CHILE

The snob that measured Orton, he was a knowing card,

He knew him by his wopping feet, that measured just a yard,

His head was like a pumpkin, for pretty girls to ponder,

And his mouth it was a beauty, and reached from here to yonder.

One witness swore young Orton, he well remembered him,

And naked in the water they together used to swim,

He said that he would know by, and was just a-going to shout,

When the Judge he was disgusted, and turned the blackguard out.

—From the handbill "Have you seen the Claimant? The Big Fat Man!"

WHEN ASKED WHAT he did after the wreck of the *Bella*, the Claimant said that he was in one of the lifeboats that had not been overturned, along with several other sailors. After some days in the open boat, they were rescued by a ship named the *Osprey*. When landed at Melbourne, none of the shipwrecked sailors made themselves known, but preferred to join the Australian gold rush and quickly dispersed into the interior of the country. The Claimant also decided to try out the Australian way of life for a while. He changed his name to Thomas Castro and was employed as a cowboy for several years, before drifting to the Wagga Wagga butcher's shop.

After it had become apparent that the Claimant meant business, the Tichborne family dispatched a solicitor named John Mackenzie to Australia, charged with finding out the truth, or lack of it, in the Claimant's story.[4] He immediately struck lucky at the Melbourne stockyard where the Claimant said he had been employed: the owner had been careful in keeping his books, and they contained no record of any cowboy named Castro or Tichborne. Instead, the man recognized a photograph of the Claimant as that of a cowboy named Arthur Orton, who had worked at the stockyard for some time. Mackenzie then went on to Wagga Wagga, where several witnesses testified that Orton and Castro were one and the same person. One of them had praised Castro's skill in butchery, and Castro had replied that he had learned his trade at Newgate Market in London. It turned out that Orton's family came from Wapping in the East End of London; Arthur was the youngest of twelve children and had come to Hobart Town, Tasmania, in 1852 before drifting to the Australian mainland. In early 1868, Mackenzie alerted the clever private detective John Whicher, who was charged with tracking down the London Ortons. This he did without any difficulty, and soon he could report some news that must have cheered the beleaguered Tichborne family. Not long before, on Christmas night, a heavily built stranger had arrived at the Globe public house in Wapping High Street, near the Orton home. He showed much knowledge of the Orton family, and the landlady remarked that he looked very much like old George Orton, and presumed he must be the Arthur Orton who went to sea many years earlier. The stranger evasively explained that he was a great friend of the Orton family and eager for information about what had happened to it in recent years. He gave her several letters directed to the Orton sisters. The Claimant (for it was really he) then showed her photographs of his own wife and child, saying they were the wife and child of Arthur Orton. Whicher also found a letter sent by Thomas Castro asking for information about the Orton family. He went around to the Orton sisters, but they were adamant that the Claimant was not their brother; the detective, of course, suspected that they had been sworn into the plot. Orton's former sweetheart Mary Ann Loder readily identified the Claimant as Arthur, however.

The suggestion that Castro and Orton were one and the same person made many of the Claimant's friends deeply uneasy. They lacked the money to send detectives to Australia to make similar inquiries, and it was not until 1869, when a commission was formally sent to look into the Australian evidence, that the matter of Castro's identity was again looked into. This commission began in Tasmania, where several witnesses spoke of Arthur Orton's arrival and subsequent work as a butcher. The Claimant was adamant that he had never set foot in Tasmania, but the witnesses gave a description of Orton that tallied well with his own appearance, and they recognized photographs of him. In Sydney, the testimony was divided, and the Claimant's side believed that one of the key witnesses had been bribed by Mackenzie to change his evidence. In Wagga Wagga, several witnesses had known Arthur Orton under the name of Thomas Castro. He was always bragging about his noble descent and his being the heir to large estates. Some other witnesses swore that Orton and Castro were two different people. In the Australian bush, there was much lawlessness at this time; in this free-and-easy society, men changed their names as they liked and drifted in and out of occupation. It was hinted that there were many reasons for Arthur Orton to change his name, one of them being to escape prosecution for horse stealing. At other times, Orton called himself Smith, and there was another shady character named William Cresswell, who on occasion went under the name of Orton. There was also some extraordinary evidence about a man called "the Foreigner," thin and gentlemanly in bearing, who had been seen with Orton in the gold diggings.

When asked why he had called himself Thomas Castro, the Claimant replied that during his South American tour he had met a man called Tomas Castro in Melipilla, Chile, and later decided to use his name. The solicitor Holmes suggested that he write to Castro with a view to providing evidence that Roger Tichborne had been in Melipilla, and to any other witnesses who could identify the Claimant as Tichborne. The Claimant willingly did so, producing a list of fourteen people he could recall, but the response was not what he had wanted. It turned out that no one in Melipilla could remember any person called Tichborne staying there. Instead, they recalled a sailor boy named Arturo, who had run away from a ship where the captain had ill-treated him. Some time before 1851, Arturo had arrived in the village and stayed for well over a year. He became quite popular, since many of the Chileans pitied his youth and forlorn appearance. Arturo said that his father was a butcher in London and that he had several sisters. When another commission was sent to Chile, the Tichborne family's solicitors again held the upper hand.[5] Tomas Castro and four other witnesses made depositions that they had known Arturo well but never met Roger Tichborne. It was presumed that Arthur Orton had tried to fit his previous stay in Melipilla in with his imposture as Roger Tichborne, but that the Chileans had not understood the meaning of his letter and instead confessed the truth. The Claimant's friends proposed that the family's solicitors had spent thousands of pounds bribing the Chilean witnesses to perjure themselves.

## THE FIRST TRIAL

**C** stands for Claimant, he knows what he's about
And in spite of judge and jury, he'll see the trial out.

**H** stands for Hampshire, and the Tichborne tenants there
The fat man is Sir Roger, the people they can swear.

**R** stands for Radcliffe, his cousin says she never will
Confess she danced the can-can with Roger in the mill.

**S** stands for Secret packet, they made such a fuss about
Roger's cousin she disowned him so he let the secret out.

—Extracts from "A New Alphabet on the Tichborne Trial"

TO PAY FOR the coming trial, the Claimant's friends had hatched a scheme at once novel and brilliant. The Claimant had himself been declared bankrupt in 1869, and none of his backers were ready to sponsor his adventure in court out of their own pockets. The solution was to print Tichborne bonds, on which the Claimant promised to pay the holder £100 within a month of obtaining possession of the Tichborne estates. The bonds sold for around £20 and greatly appealed to the British public's sporting instincts and fondness for gambling; in all, not less than £40,000 was obtained from this scheme. The government and the upper classes stood aghast at this novel system of raising funds. Could any penniless adventurer challenge the landed aristocracy with impunity, and was every skeleton in the family cupboard to become a potential commercial enterprise?

With their newfound wealth, the Claimant and the solicitor Holmes

lost no time in securing a first-rate legal team, headed by the experienced William Ballantine.[6] As the trial began in May 1870, Ballantine
called eighty-five witnesses in favor of his client. He had not been
greatly impressed with the Claimant's intelligence and demeanor, and
hoped to impress the jury with this vast amount of evidence before he
surrendered his client for cross-examination. First, several of Roger
Tichborne's fellow officers recognized the Claimant as their lost
brother in arms. One of them, Major Heywood, said he had remembered a not very subtle practical joke played on poor Roger: all his pos-
sessions had been thrown out through the window. The major had
asked whether anything had been left inside the room; the Claimant
had immediately answered that there was one thing—the chamber-
pot! This had convinced Heywood that in spite of more than doubling
his body weight since they had last met, the Claimant was the right
man. Roger Tichborne's old servant John Moore told a similar story
about the Claimant's detailed recollections of some incidents during
their journey to South America. Anthony Biddulph, the only member
of the Tichborne family who was supporting the Claimant, had been
very much impressed with his detailed knowledge of the topography
around Tichborne Park and of Biddulph's past contacts with Roger
Tichborne. Other witnesses also testified that the Claimant had
recalled various odd little incidents from Roger's past life, details that
would have been very difficult for an impostor to learn.

When the Claimant finally took the stand for the cross-examination,
on June 5, things still looked relatively bright from his point of view;
none of his witnesses had been seriously shaken, and Ballantine
appeared to have things under control. The family's legal team, Sir
John Coleridge and Henry Hawkins, had had ample time to prepare
their onslaught, however. There was immediate drama when
Coleridge raised the subject of Roger Tichborne's departure for
South America. Vincent Gosford, the Tichborne agent, had sworn
that Roger had given him a sealed packet just before leaving; its con-
tents were said to relate to Katherine Doughty. The Claimant mum-
bled something about an event he hoped had not happened, and

then was goaded into admitting that this event was "the confinement of my cousin"!

"Do you mean to swear, before the judge and jury, that you seduced this lady?"

"I most solemnly to my God swear that I did."

There was immense tension in the air when Coleridge pointed to Mrs. Radcliffe, who was actually sitting in court at the time, asking, "This lady?" "Yes, that lady," replied the Claimant, and then volunteered that the intercourse had taken place near a local mill. He caddishly continued that she had pressed him very hard to marry her, but that he had resisted, since he suspected that she was lying about the pregnancy. The cross-examination moved on to Roger Tichborne's early life in Paris. Here the Claimant was in great difficulties, and tried to excuse himself with talk of illness and loss of memory. Encouraged by this show of ignorance, Coleridge decided to spend two days examining the Claimant about his time at Stonyhurst. Now the trial entered the realm of high buffoonery, as the gloating Coleridge tormented the Claimant at length. The burly, awkward-looking fellow could not recollect a single word of Hebrew or Greek, thought Caesar was a Greek writer, and denied that Euclid had anything to do with mathematics. He had never heard of the Asses Bridge or ever tried to cross it; there was much laughter in court when Coleridge went on to ask, "Do you know where it is? How far from Stonyhurst?" The Claimant knew nothing of the plays in which Roger Tichborne had acted at Stonyhurst, and his ignorance of the simplest Catholic customs astounded those present. When faced with questions about his movements in Australia and Chile, the Claimant fared better. As Ballantine had probably instructed him, he admitted that he had known Arthur Orton in Australia, and that they had both been accused of horse stealing. Orton had also been in trouble for bushranging, and the Claimant had written to the Orton family because he wanted to inform them that Arthur was still alive and well. When faced with difficult questions, the Claimant either pleaded loss of memory or alleged that the incriminating affidavits and documents put forth had been forged. After a lengthy recess, court action was resumed on November 7, with Ballantine calling another hundred or so witnesses. As stalwart as ever, Bogle performed well in the witness-box. But the second key witness, the antiquary Francis Baigent, was severely shaken by Coleridge's cross-examination and came across as a silly, bewildered busybody.

In his opening address, Coleridge appeared quite confident; he crowed over the Claimant's ignorance and blasted him as a brazen impostor, helped by rogues like Bogle and fools like Baigent. He depicted the real Roger Tichborne as a cultured and virtuous young man—shy, gentle, and literate. Could this educated aristrocrat have degenerated into a human hippopotamus, coarse-featured and illiterate, and cunning and blackguardly in manner? And even if it was accepted that Roger Tichborne could triple his body weight and lose his memory, could he also forget being a gentleman? Coleridge found it an absurd impossibility that a baronet would seek work as a butcher, that typical lower-class trade, and that he would marry a sluttish woman like the Claimant's wife. But as he confessed in his private diary, Coleridge was actually quite uncertain about the outcome of the case. By no means convinced that the Claimant was Arthur Orton, he speculated that he might be an illegitimate member of the Tichborne family.[7] Most of the evidence against the Claimant was evidence that he was Orton, however, and it was vital for the case to use the material linking the two, from Australia, Chile, and Wapping. As a surprise witness, Coleridge introduced Lord Bellew, a contemporary of Roger Tichborne's at Stonyhurst, who testified that Roger had been tattooed on his left arm. The Claimant had no such tattoo, and other family witnesses went on to swear that they had seen this tattoo on Roger's arm on several occasions. Coleridge had promised to call more than two hundred witnesses, which would mean that the case would go on for almost a year. Everyone from the judge down was heartily tired of the lengthy and repetitious proceedings. This included the Claimant's own legal team, since in spite of the huge sum gained from the Tichborne bonds, he had run out of money and none of them were receiving their fees. On March 4, the jury indicated that it had heard enough evidence to give a verdict. This was bad news for the Claimant's side, and Ballantine elected to be nonsuited, namely that his client abandoned his case. This resulted in an automatic decision for the defendant, but avoided any formal verdict. But Judge Bovill told the jury that he entirely agreed with its view and ordered the arrest of the Claimant for willful and corrupt perjury. This was not at all the outcome Ballantine had hoped for, but it was now too late for him to do anything to save his client.

The Claimant was released on bail, but his prospects looked dim. Far from being in a position to demand a retrial, he was now himself facing criminal proceedings that could lead to a long prison term. The London newspapers crowed with delight, ridiculing the Claimant and his friends. Baigent was a fool, Bogle was a liar, and Onslow and Biddulph were scoundrels hoping to make money from the case. Poor old Lady Tichborne's maternal instinct was likened to that of a hen that had been tricked to sit upon a duck's egg. Most of the opprobrium was reserved for the Claimant himself, the dirty, vulgar butcher from the convict colonies. His poor performance in the witness-box was much ridiculed, particularly his ignorance of the classics.

But among the working classes there was a different reaction. Here, even before his arrest, sympathy for the Claimant had been growing. His huge bulk made him an easily recognizable figure on the London streets, and his jovial manner and sporting tastes won him many friends. Was he not a rebel against wealth and authority, and did he not challenge the social order? And had he not been crushed by the aristocracy and established society, and had the Catholic Church not had a sinister influence? The establishment newspapers gloating over his ill-bred manner and lack of education annoyed many people; they thought Sir Roger was persecuted because he was like themselves. As the Claimant toured the country and received a rapturous welcome by the people, establishment politicians and judges became uneasily aware that he was turning into a rallying point for political radicalism.

## THE SECOND TRIAL

Of virtue, science, letters, truth
They talked till all was blue,
Of Paul de Kock, the bane of youth,
Of Bamfylde Moore Carew.

If fools are oftner fat than thin,
Which first forgot their tongue,
Why all tobacco, mixed with gin,
Is poison to the young.

—Lord Bowen, a poem on the Tichborne Case

AFTER THE FIRST trial, it was not easy for the Tichborne Claimant and his friends to find another legal team to argue their cause. The notoriety of the Claimant and the scandalous libel of Lady Radcliffe counted against him, and the fact that neither Holmes nor Ballantine had received the fees due to them was unlikely to influence any member of the legal profession in the Claimant's favor. But in March 1873 Lord Rivers, one of the Claimant's respectable supporters, managed to secure the services of Dr. Edward Vaughan Kenealy to act as defending counsel in the forthcoming criminal trial. Kenealy, a fifty-three-year-old native of Ireland, was a gifted and eccentric individual.[8] Throughout his life, he had dabbled in politics, religion, law, and literature, but without much success. In 1850, his life had been permanently soured when a court of London magistrates sentenced him to a month's imprisonment for severely beating his illegitimate son. Even before this dismal experience, Kenealy had been an obstinate, rebellious character; after leaving prison, he developed into a full-blown paranoiac, with grudges against the Catholic Church, the legal establishment, and many politicians in both England and Ireland. He also had manic-depressive tendencies. At his highs, he nurtured expansive political ambitions, and wrote Bible-length tomes depicting himself as a messiah sent to cleanse the British Isles from

Dr. Kenealy.
From E. V. Kenealy, *Introduction to the Tichborne Trial* (London, 1875).

immorality, corruption, idolatry, and tyranny. At his lows, he wrote poison-pen letters to reviewers of his books and imagined vast conspiracies against himself. Kenealy's legal career was something of a sideline among his manifold activities; in spite of his learning and eloquence, he was mostly a supporter of lost causes and desperate actions in the law courts, often with little success. He claimed to be a doctor of law from Trinity College in Dublin, but this distinction could not be verified by his biographer from the records of this venerable university.[9]

With its political and religious overtones, the Tichborne case was just what Dr. Kenealy had wished for. Eager to free the poor Claimant from the hypocritical tyrants who opposed him, the doctor accepted his brief with alacrity. A vanload of legal documents was delivered to his door, and he began to digest them with his usual monomaniacal energy. Unlike Ballantine, Kenealy had an unshakable belief in the veracity of the claim, and he devoted all his time to mastering every detail of the great case. He was not particularly impressed with the Claimant's silly, overenthusiastic friends, several of whom acted as amateur detectives to find witnesses and often did more harm than good. And in spite of his reverence for the great man himself, Kenealy could not help reflecting that the Claimant was behaving quite oddly. Although he faced a stiff prison sentence if found guilty, the Claimant appeared quite unconcerned about his fate and gave obtuse and unhelpful answers when Kenealy asked him about his eventful life. The great hulking fellow had become a familiar man about town, and the people cheered and shouted "Wagga-Wagga!" when they saw him coming in his elegant brougham, puffing at his huge cigar as he went. He was a crack shot and won several pigeon-shooting matches to great public acclaim. The Claimant was wining and dining to excess and steadily putting on more weight. In spite of his bulk, he also vigorously sought female company in the low music halls he frequented, and some donors of money to the Tichborne cause would have been aghast to find out how the Claimant had spent it.

As the second trial opened in Westminster Hall on April 23, 1873, in front of the lord chief justice, Sir Alexander Cockburn, Kenealy had high hopes of success. Determined to prove that the Claimant was really Sir Roger Tichborne, he eschewed the suggestion that it would be sufficient to prove that his client was not Arthur Orton for him to be acquitted. Kenealy's tactics were bizarre, to say the least. In a monthlong, rambling peroration, he attempted to rewrite the modern history of the Tichborne family. Roger's father had been a brutal, drunken wife beater, he asserted; his wife, a saintly woman who doted on her eldest son. Young Roger Tichborne had been little

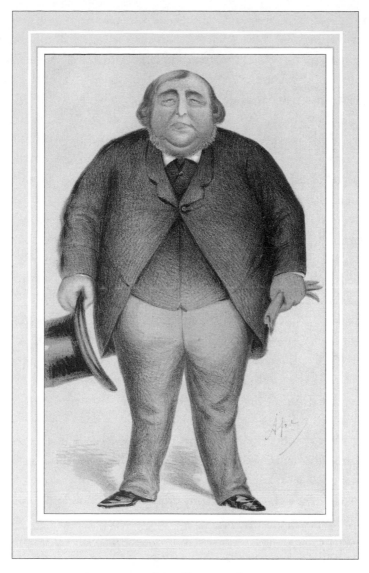

A caricature of the Claimant in his prime.
From *Vanity Fair*, June 10, 1871.

better than a degenerate halfwit, always untidy and unwashed, and addicted to vice, alcohol, and tobacco. The Stonyhurst fathers had ruined whatever good there was left in his character; they had tolerated his excessive smoking, enticed him to read immoral literature like the novels of Paul de Kock, and encouraged homosexuality through their vile private theatricals in which the boys acted the parts of women. "These are dreadful things, Dr. Kenealy," said the astonished lord chief justice after the last-mentioned wild accusation. After the court had been cleared of women, Kenealy read out some chapters from the naughty novels of Paul de Kock, to convince the jury of their corrupting influence. In the army, Roger Tichborne was ridiculed by officers and men alike. After traveling across South America in a drunken daze, he was carried on board the *Bella* to depart from Rio. Poor Roger had no worthwhile existence to return to; the brooding, depressed youth despised his own family and the wastrel he himself had become. After being rescued from the shipwreck, he preferred to stay in the glorious freedom of the Australian outback, which made him a man at last. He took up butchery because the wicked Jesuits at Stonyhurst had allowed him to dissect dead birds and cats; this was the only useful knowledge he possessed. The reason the Claimant remembered so little of his childhood and youth, Kenealy said, was that in Australia, he had deliberately tried to cleanse his mind of his unhappy boyhood and the debasing experiences at Stonyhurst.

Dr. Kenealy then spent the next two months calling more than three hundred witnesses in behalf of the Claimant. Among the old witnesses, Baigent and Dr. Lipscomb refused to testify, since they had been so badly blackguarded during cross-examination in the first trial, but a good many new witnesses had been recruited through the notoriety of the case. The Claimant was supported by two members of Parliament, Guildford Onslow and G. H. Whalley, both proper Tichborne fanatics, ready to believe any cock-and-bull story when it appeared to favor their friend. A great number of the Wapping witnesses gave rambling and sometimes contradictory accounts of Arthur Orton's youth and physical marks. Several new Australian witnesses testified that Orton and Tichborne were two different people. A Captain James Brown was produced as a surprise witness. He testified that he had met Roger Tichborne in Rio and helped him on board the *Bella* in a state of great intoxication; he ended by confidently identifying the Claimant as Tichborne. During the cross-examination, however, it turned out that the captain's mariner's certificate indicated that he had been nowhere near Rio in 1854. The captain's evidence was completely discredited, and he was later sentenced to three years in prison for perjury. Whalley, an enthusiastic amateur detective, had found another last-minute sensation witness, a man of mystery who called himself Jean Luie. This shady individual declared that he had actually been on board the *Osprey* and remembered rescuing Roger Tichborne from a lifeboat. But Luie was exposed as a Swede named Lundgren, alias Sorensen, a convicted swindler and bigamist, who had been in Hull and Cardiff at the time he claimed to have performed his heroic sea rescue. Lundgren received seven years in prison for perjury.

The double blow resulting from the antics of these two corrupt witnesses would have floored a lesser man, but Dr. Kenealy countered with another monthlong tirade on his pet subjects. In contrast, the prosecuting counsel for the crown, Sir Henry Hawkins, closed his case in a succinct and elegant manner, pointing out that the major evidence against the Claimant from the first trial remained largely unchallenged.[10] The lord chief justice himself ended the proceedings with another monthlong speech. Cockburn censured Kenealy for his "unceasing torrent of invective and foul slander": he had bullied and browbeaten the opposition witnesses, made vile accusations against respectable people like the Stonyhurst fathers, and likened the lord chief justice himself to the notorious Judge Jeffreys. Cockburn then presented a masterly overview of the entire case, topic by topic. It was clear to Kenealy that the edge of his arguments was always against the Claimant and that Cockburn feared that some of the jurors might have been swayed by Kenealy's eloquence and the great popular support for the Claimant, and wanted to avoid a unanimous verdict. But the jury decided unanimously against the Claimant, who was sentenced to fourteen years in prison for "crimes as black and foul as Justice ever raised her sword to strike," as Cockburn put it. Before he was led out of court, Kenealy shook the Claimant's hand, saying, "Good-bye, Sir Roger, I am sorry for you!"

## THE END OF THE STORY

To Westminster and Wapping now
I must bid a long adieu,
I'll think of you Kenealy,
In the land I'm going to.

When the Jury said I was not Roger
Oh! How they made me stagger.
The pretty girls they'll always think,
Of poor Roger's Wagga-Wagga.

—"Poor Roger Tichborne's Lamentation"

THE CLAIMANT WAS sent to Millbank Prison, where he was registered as convict Castro, since he stubbornly refused to be called Arthur Orton. He was ordered to clean his cell with a broom, but objected that his huge belly prevented him from using this implement. The unfeeling prison authorities then provided him with a broom with an extra-long handle and set him to work. Nor could he use the normal sleeping arrangements in the prison, as a street poem eloquently expressed it:[11]

They call him Wagga-Wagga, which isn't quite a treat,
They say he's fed in Newgate, upon Australian meat;
The hammock they provided him, it could not hold his fat,
So they bought him a special bedstead, now what do you think of that?

The prison rations were small and the regime harsh; the poor Claimant wept bitterly, since he was always hungry and missed his liquors and cigars. He lost so much weight that he was often taking in his prison uniform to fit his shrinking frame; this frequent experience in needlework led to his being employed as the prison tailor. Dr. Kenealy painted a dark picture of the Claimant's early life in jail: he was starved, bullied, and surrounded by the dregs of humanity. To induce him to confess, Kenealy claimed in one of his flights of fancy, the poor prisoner was tortured in the most brutal manner. He was stripped naked, his genitals closely inspected, and galvanic batteries applied to his most delicate parts. When the bold doctor and some other supporters were finally allowed to see the Claimant after six months, they were aghast to see that the suffering prisoner had lost nine stone—one-third of his body weight. They were at a loss for words to describe this dreadful scene: the once jolly, rotund Claimant was a deathlike, waxen-faced invalid, with sunken eyes and a care-worn, despondent expression. Kenealy wrote that had Lady Radcliffe been present to see her former lover in this desperate plight, she would have screamed and confessed all.[12]

As the Claimant languished in prison, Dr. Kenealy continued the battle. Although the establishment newspapers greeted the verdict with great relief and satisfaction, the radical press fumed about the corrupt government and deceitful aristocracy swindling the poor honest Claimant out of his birthright. Kenealy's violent outbursts in court and open disrespect for the lord chief justice led to his becoming disbarred, but the doctor had other means of carrying on the fight. He founded a newspaper called the *Englishman*, which soon gained an enormous circulation. On Kenealy's expansive tours throughout England, Scotland, and Wales, he drew huge crowds. In a by-election in Stoke-on-Trent in early 1875, he stood for Parliament and was elected by an impressive majority. The bold doctor hoped to form a Tichborne party, to act for parliamentary reform and the prompt release of the Claimant. He bragged that in the next election there would be fifty candidates standing for this party, if every one of the estimated one million Tichborne supporters would provide sixpence each. His rabble-rousing activities continued ceaselessly, and a protest march from Hyde Park

to Trafalgar Square was attended by 100,000 Tichbornites. In spite of
his still considerable popular support, however, Dr. Kenealy's political
career was facing difficulties in the late 1870s: he lacked money and
was but feebly aided by the Claimant's friends. In April 1880, he failed
to be returned to Parliament, and then suddenly died a fortnight later.
The Claimant, who had never shared the belief, common among the
establishment lawyers, that Kenealy's eccentric defense had cost him
his chances in the second trial, grieved that his foremost champion
was gone. Guildford Onslow and some other diehard supporters went
on with the struggle, though, and the *Englishman* continued publication until 1886. It kept reporting a steady trickle of news in favor of
the Claimant, mainly about obscure Australians coming forth to testify that Tichborne and Orton were two different people, and that there
had really been a ship called the *Osprey*, which had saved some shipwrecked sailors back in 1854. The most promising lead was the discovery of William Cresswell, an inmate of Paramatta Asylum in New
South Wales. This man was incurably insane and himself had nothing to contribute to the debate, but several people testified that he had
been a friend of Arthur Orton. Others said that Cresswell had spoken
of his family in Wapping and practiced as a butcher; he had been a
robber and a bushranger, and his insanity was brought on by excessive
drinking. Cresswell's wife believed that he was really Arthur Orton
and that Castro must have been Tichborne. This greatly cheered
Guildford Onslow and the Claimant's other over-exuberant friends,
and they paid for Orton's sister and Cresswell's brother to go to
Australia to try to identify the lunatic, but without the desired result.
As late as the 1890s, there was still debate in Australia about Cresswell's identity.[13]

After his unhappy early days in Pentonville and Dartmoor, the
Claimant was eventually removed to Portsea Prison, where his health
recovered. Wholesome food, outdoor manual work, and enforced
abstinence from alcohol and tobacco made him a stronger and health-
ier man; at the time of his release in 1884, the Claimant was ready to
take the lead in the fight for justice.[14] He traveled the country at

length, addressing crowds that were still reasonably large, but the Tichborne movement had lost much of its momentum after Kenealy's death. The radicals had found other causes to support, and the ordinary workman on the street regarded the Tichborne business as yesterday's news. The Claimant battled on for several years, finally performing in circuses and music halls, where he was shown like a curiosity. In 1886, the year the *Englishman* ceased publication, he went to New York, where hope had been held out for funds to restart his campaign. But the Americans were uninterested in his grievances, and he was again forced to perform in saloons and music halls, and even to be exhibited in a sideshow. Once, he met another Tichborne Claimant, who had just arrived from Australia. Showing much less bonhomie than Naundorff when introduced to the English pretender Meves, he gruffly called out "Impostor!" After his unhappy spell in the United States, the Claimant went back to London, where he sank even lower, selling his autograph in public houses at twopence a time, and living in abject poverty. In 1895, the *People* newspaper offered him £4,000 for the full confession of his life and impostures, and he readily agreed. The confession was serialized in the newspaper, but the Claimant eventually withdrew it, possibly because the editor had cheated him; not having the wits to ask for a substantial payment in advance, he received only a few hundred pounds.[15] In 1898, the Tichborne Claimant was found dead in his tiny flat near Edgware Road. He had no assets, but the local undertaker buried him for free in Paddington Cemetery, which is situated off the Edgware Road. His coffin was marked with a plaque inscribed "Sir Roger Charles Doughty Tichborne," but his grave has no tombstone or monument.

## ANALYSIS OF THE HISTORICAL EVIDENCE

> So cheer up, Roger, you are a jolly brick,
> For if you are not Roger, then you are Old Nick.
> Keep up your blooming pecker, you're sure to win the day
> If the judge and jury see it out, and let you have fair play!
>
> —The chorus from "The Great Tichborne Trial"

THE MAIN EVIDENCE in favor of the Claimant would be that not only his alleged mother but also many other people recognized him as Roger Tichborne. There is no question that many of these witnesses were honest, upstanding people, who genuinely believed he was the right man. Moreover, the Claimant's impressive knowledge of the Tichborne estates, Hampshire hunting lore, and various incidents from Roger Tichborne's military career was remarked upon by many. Could an impostor really have mastered the minutiae of his subject in such detail? The question of whether there was a ship named *Osprey*, and whether this ship actually saved the shipwrecked sailors from the *Bella*, is by no means solved. Some evidence also suggests that Roger Tichborne actually reached Australia. Several witnesses testified that a thin, melancholy Englishman of superior breeding was in Melbourne at the right time period; others could recall Tichborne and Orton as two different people. In the best book on the Tichborne Claimant mystery, the journalist and historian Douglas Woodruff pointed out that the Claimant's behavior was not that of a typical impostor; he appeared uninterested in his own fortunes and made many avoidable mistakes. For example, he could easily have gone to Stonyhurst to observe the layout of the school and recapitulate what subjects were taught in the curriculum; the Claimant did neither. The letter to Melipilla, which was to cause him so much dismay, was also the Claimant's own initiative; would an impostor really have exposed his own precedents in such a manner? Nor was the Claimant particularly well served by his legal representatives. In the first trial, Ballantine was several times outmaneuvered by his clever opponents; in the second trial, the monomaniacal Dr. Kenealy mismanaged his case by using it to promote his own pet theories. It was particularly ill advised actually to try to prove that the Claimant was Roger Tichborne, instead of concentrating on the prosecution's arguments, some of them not all that impressive, that he was Arthur Orton. Sir Henry Hawkins, who represented the family in the first trial, privately said that he could have won the second trial for the Claimant by knocking over the prosecution's case that he was Arthur Orton; he may have been right. Of importance was also the question of money. Whereas the Tichborne family had a good supply of fighting funds, the Claimant, in spite of his Tichborne bonds, was on the verge of bankruptcy. It is clear, too, that the family used this advantage well; it briefed superior legal teams, used private detectives to gather intelligence, and hired agents abroad to look into the Australian and Chilean evidence. There is also evidence that Dr. Kenealy was not entirely wrong when he accused the family's solicitors and detectives of bribing witnesses; several of the Wapping witnesses, including Arthur Orton's own siblings, seem to have been "persuaded" by these means. The Seymour brothers, the solicitor Bowker, and the detective Whicher were all ruthless men with a strong interest in the Claimant's downfall. Charles Orton, Arthur's brother, later openly confessed that Whicher had bribed him to recognize the Claimant as Arthur. Mina Jury, one of the Tasmanian witnesses who had been instrumental in identifying the Claimant as Arthur Orton, also later alleged that she had been bribed, but that the family solicitors had never paid the money she had been promised.

The first of the heavyweight arguments against the Claimant is his abysmal ignorance about Roger Tichborne's youth and school days. It is not natural that even the most backward schoolboy should forget his entire education, particularly since the Claimant seems to have had considerable powers of memory, as evidenced by his mastery of Tichborne minutiae. A second strong argument is that the Claimant could not speak French, Roger Tichborne's first language, which he used almost exclusively until he was sixteen. As in the Naundorff case, this inability is not reasonable, since it is a person's first language that is most strongly imprinted in the memory. Thus, if the real Roger Tichborne had been struck by some degenerative brain disease, he would have been more likely to forget English rather than French. The Claimant's story of memory loss while suffering from sunstroke is not at all convincing, particularly since other aspects of his memory were not at all affected. It is also suspicious that he was actually able to speak some Spanish, a language Roger Tichborne never knew, but one that Arthur Orton would have had the opportunity to pick up while in Melipilla. Some very damning details are evident from the Claimant's early letters, written when he was still in Australia. He referred to his "mother" as Harriet Frances, when her real name was Henriette Felicité, and described her as a very tall, stout woman when she was in fact short and thin. He got the name of his old school wrong, and that of his regiment. In a will he wrote in June 1866, he bequeathed properties that did not exist and appointed executors who were wholly unknown to the Tichborne family.[17] Again, the Claimant's explanation—that he had invented the will while being the worse for drink—does not ring true. We then know of the Melipilla evidence and the Claimant's fateful visit to Wapping; both were strong arguments that he was Arthur Orton. The handwriting evidence should be interpreted with caution, but there is a strong resemblance between Orton's letters to his family when he was in Tasmania and the Claimant's later writings. Both contain the use of a lowercase *i* for the personal pronoun and such misspellings as "Elizaberth." Arthur Orton used an unusual hieroglyph following the signature in these family letters; it recurs in the Claimant's letters to the Orton sisters. Such a symbol is commonly used in the Spanish-speaking world; it is called a *rúbrica* and often done in red ink, for use as a symbol of recognition.[18] Many of the Claimant's spelling mistakes have their origins in nineteenth-century East End slang, unlike those of Roger Tichborne, which betrayed his French education.

As for the Australian evidence, if there had really been other survivors from the shipwreck of the *Bella*, one of them would surely have turned up to give evidence, since there was a strong financial incentive to do so. The case was so widely publicized that even the most obscure outback Australian newspaper contained reports of the Claimant's fortunes. Valuable later research by Professor Michael Roe, of the University of Tasmania, has added much evidence against the Claimant, mainly with regard to the skillful way he inserted incidents from Arthur Orton's life into his own story.[19] For example, the Claimant stated that, at his first landfall in Melbourne, he stayed in a public house called the Roxburgh Castle, Elizabeth Street. There has never been any such pub in Melbourne, but there is one on Elizabeth Street of Hobart, Tasmania. The Claimant gave the date of his (Sir Roger's) departure for South America as that of Arthur Orton for Tasmania. The name he gave to the Captain of the *Osprey* was Owen Lewis; this was the name of one of Orton's shipmates when he went to Tasmania. Another of Orton's shipmates was a certain John Peebles; the Claimant referred to this man as one of the sailors on the shipwrecked *Bella*. There is also the question of a notebook allegedly used by the Claimant in Wagga Wagga, which was found to contain several incriminating references, among them a note that Sir Roger arrived at Hobart on July 4, 1854. This could imply that he was originally planning to incorporate his Tasmanian life into Roger Tichborne's, but later decided against it. The same notebook contained a memorable quotation: "Some men has plenty money and no brains, and some men has plenty brains and no money. Surely men with plenty money and no brains were made for men with plenty brains and no money. R.C. Tichborne, Bart."[20] Professor Roe has also reviewed the Claimant's 1895 confession and found it to contain several references to obscure names and places in Hobart that can be verified as correct. This strongly suggests that the man who wrote the confession was the Arthur Orton who had been to Tasmania in the 1850s.

## ANALYSIS OF THE MEDICAL EVIDENCE

Some say that he was tattooed,
Some say that he was not,
And his head was thick and empty
As a forty shilling pot.

They said Roger was bled and blistered
From his head down to his toes,
He had leeches on his ankles,
And a fish-hook in his nose.

—"The Claimant's Defence"

IN PARALLEL WITH the fierce debate on almost every point of Roger Tichborne's short life, and the similarities of the Claimant's experiences with those of Arthur Orton, was a much more low-key discussion about the use of various physical marks to identify the Claimant as either Tichborne or Orton. Every medical journal in Britain took the side of the establishment; just like the *Times* and *Observer* newspapers, the *Lancet* and the *British Medical Journal* poured scorn on the dirty vulgar butcher who tried to pull off such an audacious deception.[21] In fact, not a single word of dissent from the medical profession was published in any medical journal of repute. The Claimant's supporters, some of whom were doctors or quacks, were tireless in publishing articles and pamphlets suggesting novel physical marks that would solve the mystery once and for all.

The only hint, except for fallible human memory, of what Roger Tichborne really looked like during life was in the two daguerreotypes done in 1853. These were well attested by quite a few people to be very good likenesses of Roger, and not even Dr. Kenealy dared to dispute their authenticity. He may well have wanted to, however, because the features depicted were completely unlike those of his

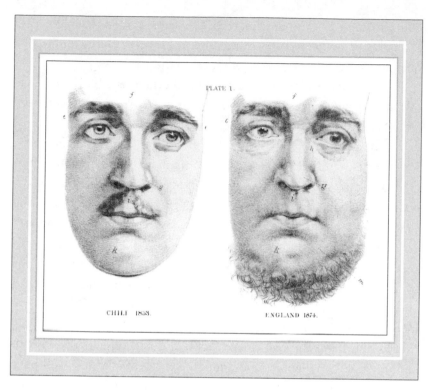

An anthropometric analysis of the portraits of Roger Tichborne and the Claimant.
From E. V. Kenealy, *Introduction to the Tichborne Trial* (London, 1875).

own client. The resourceful doctor countered this argument by claiming that the hard life in Australia had coarsened Roger's face as well as his demeanor; the accumulation of fat had done the rest. A journalist applied a specially designed gridwork over the 1853 daguerreotype and an 1873 photograph of the Claimant, and proved to his own satisfaction that the facial proportions were the same, but I do not share his conviction.[22] It is of particular importance that, in the daguerreotypes, Roger's ears are lobeless, while the Claimant's ears can be plainly seen to have large fleshy lobes. Dr. Kenealy quoted two doctors who claimed that lobes could actually grow from the ears in cases of mental disturbance, but he rightly doubted that this argument (which is, of course, completely erroneous) would find favor in court. Instead, he dropped hints that the daguerreotypes, which, after all, had been possessed only by members of the Tichborne family, had been doctored by an expert hand to erase the ear lobes.[23]

There is good evidence that Roger Tichborne was 5 feet 8½ inches tall at the age of twenty, according to his cornetcy examination records; Arthur Orton had been 5 feet 9½ inches tall at the age of eighteen and a half, according to his mariner's ticket. The Claimant, when measured in 1873, was 5 feet 9 inches. Since human beings gradually grow shorter with age, this would suggest that he was Orton, but the original difference in height is not an impressive one, and the routines for measuring people in those days certainly had a greater error margin than those in use today. Nor could it be ruled out with certainty that Roger Tichborne actually grew in height after he was twenty years old, as was pointed out by the Claimant's supporters. An obvious argument against the Claimant was, of course, his immense increase in weight from 1865 to 1870. Despite access to nourishing, calorie-rich food, the real Roger Tichborne had remained very lean and unwholesome looking; he drank a good deal and may well have suffered from delirium tremens. The Claimant weighed 187 pounds when weighed in Sydney in August 1866; he had increased in weight to 387 pounds when weighed at Crystal Palace in September 1870. Thus, after abandoning the healthy lifestyle he had enjoyed in Wagga Wagga, the Claimant had more than doubled his weight in four years. The Claimant was a heavy drinker, dispatching amazing amounts of beer, wine, and spirits, but, unlike Roger Tichborne, was seldom seen intoxicated, and there is no evidence of any serious physical ill effects of his addiction to the bottle.

Much effort went into researching possible physical marks on the bodies of Roger Tichborne and Arthur Orton.[24] The plan was then to have a team of four doctors make a medical examination of the Claimant to see which of the marks could be observed. As wittily expressed in the epigraph poem above, every incident in poor Roger's life that could have left a permanent mark somewhere on his body was looked into, and affidavits from witnesses secured. When he was a sickly young lad, Roger Tichborne had been frequently bled, from the arm, ankle, and temple. There is good evidence that his temporal vein was opened in Canterbury. Furthermore, according to a medical dogma obsolete even at the time, an "issue" was used on the poor boy's arm with a seton to produce a weeping wound, since the resulting inflammation was thought to have beneficial results for his weak constitution. When a young boy in France, Roger fell down, producing a scar on his head, and he later received a wound from a fishhook that got stuck in his eyelid. Scars from bloodletting are often very faint, however, and the evidence whether these scars could be seen at all was conflicting. It was also debated whether the other calamities had really left any permanent marks.

The evidence regarding Arthur Orton's physical marks was even more confusing. He was said by some witnesses to be pitted with smallpox, to have pierced ears, to have a scar on the cheek, from when a boy threw an oyster shell at him, a brown birthmark on his side, and a mark on the arm from the bite of a pony; other witnesses stoutly denied that he had any of these marks. On examination, the Claimant proved to have a scar on the back of the head, but no bloodletting scars, no mark from a seton, and no scar from a fishhook through his eyelid. It would have been reasonable to presume that at least the seton produced a visible scar. The doctors involved in the examination, even the celebrated Sir William Fergusson, were criticized in both the newspapers and the medical press for being overly cautious in their certificate.[25] One of them, Dr. Wilson, incurred further odium by testifying that although his three colleagues could not see the bloodletting scars, he himself could feel them by a special method, details of which he refused to reveal. There was much laughter in court when another unfortunate doctor stated that the Claimant's body had no signs of *vivisection*, a gaffe for venesection.

All four doctors agreed that there was a rather large brown birthmark on the Claimant's upper body, just beneath the ribs, as some claimed for Orton but others denied. The prosecution emphasized that Lady Tichborne did not acknowledge any such mark on her son, nor did several other witnesses who had seen him undressed as a youth. However, a former Tichborne servant named Elizabeth Kill later swore that young Roger really did have such a mark.[26] The doctors also noted that the Claimant's left thumbnail was somewhat deformed and thickened.[27] The perjurer Captain Brown (who had already sworn that Roger had the brown mark) was just as ready to swear to the thumb. Another witness rather hesitantly did the same, but put the deformed thumb on the wrong hand. The vacillating medical experts were again divided, but seemed to indicate that the Claimant's thickened thumbnail might have been artificially produced. The description of it, however, is very suggestive of a chronic fungal infection rather than a congenital deformity, depriving it of any value as evidence. Among Lady Tichborne's effects was a lock of the true Roger's hair, cut off in 1852. The Claimant's long hair was heavily greased, and probably artificially darkened, meaning that comparison would be difficult. There was another lock of hair, though, admitted by the Claimant to have been cut off his head by a lady in 1851 when he was in South America; when these two were contrasted in court, it was conceded they could not have originated from the same head. It was, of course, still possible for Kenealy to suggest that either lock of hair could easily have been substituted at any time, and not much was made of this evidence. The newspapers expressed disappointment that medical science had failed to condemn the hulking Antipodean impostor. A writer in the *Lancet* rightly concluded that although anthropometry and physical marks were usually valid methods in cases of disputed identity, they were largely useless in this extraordinary case, given the extremely conflicting evidence regarding which marks the two protagonists had possessed in the first place.[28]

Much more straightforward, and of vital importance for the outcome of the case, was the question of tattoo marks.[29] Lord Bellew, a contemporary of Roger's at Stonyhurst, testified that as a schoolboy, he had tattooed Roger with his initials R.C.T. on the left arm. Strangely enough, tattooing was quite fashionable among the lowbrow set at this distinguished public school, and a number of the boys sported tattoos. Lord Bellew further stated that, at the time, Roger was already tattooed with a cross, heart, and anchor on the same arm. Nine other witnesses had seen this tattoo and gave descriptions of it that largely agreed with Lord Bellew's. When asked whether the tattoo had been executed properly, the peer rolled up his sleeve to show that another tattoo, done by Roger at the same time and with the same equipment, was still perfectly legible. Lord Bellew and others had clearly seen the tattoo on Roger's arm five years later. Dr. Kenealy could not shake the peer's evidence; instead he chose to blackguard him as a scoundrel and adulterer whose word could not be accepted in a court of law. The doctor also managed to muster quite a few witnesses who asserted that they had seen Roger's arm and that he had no tattoo; his suggestion that the tattoo had been done in blue pen as a joke was pooh-poohed by the prosecution. In the medical examination, the Claimant had been found to have no tattoo marks whatsoever. There was a scarred area on one of the Claimant's arms, which corresponded suspiciously well to a small tattoo of A.O., which many witnesses had seen on Arthur Orton's arm, suggesting that it had been obliterated by some means.

The most remarkable medical evidence was the Tichborne malformation, as it soon became known. In the early days of his career, the Claimant had met Dr. Lipscomb, the Tichborne family doctor, who recognized him as Sir Roger. In due course, the same elderly medical man performed a physical examination of the Claimant. In a letter, he described a strange malformation of the Claimant's private parts, which the doctor had never before seen in a man of that age. The Claimant himself maintained that his mother had known about this malformation and that she had satisfied herself that he was her lost son by pulling down his trousers and grabbing him by the genitals! This scandalous evidence was touched upon only lightly in the first trial, out of delicacy, but Dr. Kenealy lacked these finer feelings. During the medical inspection of the Claimant, the aforementioned Dr. Wilson described what is today known as a retractile (or hidden) penis.[30] The organ in question was out of sight even when the

Claimant sat down to urinate, and could be pushed back toward the neck of the bladder like a sheath. Dr. Wilson had seen a thousand sets of male genitals, he said, but never anything similar to this. This malformation did not render the Claimant impotent, and there was no other structural defect. Dr. Kenealy first called witnesses who testified that Arthur Orton's private parts had nothing abnormal. He then summed up the evidence that Roger Tichborne had this malformation. Had he not been dressed as a girl as a child, had he not bathed dressed in trousers when at Stonyhurst, had he not been called "small cock" in the military, and had his fellow officers not teased him by putting prostitutes in his bed? Lady Tichborne had alluded to "a Malformation of Person, called His Seal or God's Mark," in a letter, now lost, and a doctor in Chile also referred to something extraordinary about Roger's genitals. Moreover, Dr. Kenealy knew about a married woman in Alresford who declared that she had an illegitimate child with Roger Tichborne and that she could identify him by the malformation. As soon as she was introduced to the Claimant, the big hulking fellow said, "What you, Topsy, come to see me?" The woman was very pleased that he had remembered his particular nickname for her! Her husband expressly forbade her to pull down the Claimant's trousers, however.[31] In his summing-up, Cockburn sternly reminded the jury that although there was no question the Claimant had the malformation, not a single person actually stood up in court and said Roger Tichborne had it; all Kenealy could muster on this subject was conjecture and idle gossip. Another witness claimed to have known Arthur Orton in Tasmania and spoke of his being like a hermaphrodite, although the same man also claimed that he had met Roger Tichborne and that he had the same malformation.[32] As for Lady Tichborne's alleged method of identifying her lost son, Cockburn had exclaimed, "A more shocking or revolting suggestion, involving the greatest indelicacy, I have never heard!"

Another part of the medical evidence was the question of Saint Vitus' dance. This imprecise denomination was widely used in the nineteenth century to cover a whole range of childhood and adult movement disorders. Most common of these is a neurological disorder that is today known as Sydenham's chorea, characterized by irregular, rapid involuntary movements of the muscles of the face, neck, trunk, and extremities. It occurs most frequently in children between five and fifteen years old, following acute rheumatic fever caused by a streptococcal infection. The symptoms of incoordination and involuntary movements are quite characteristic, and because the disease itself was much more common in the mid-nineteenth century, it is very likely that Arthur Orton's "Saint Vitus' dance," which interrupted his schooling, was really Sydenham's chorea. The same Wapping witnesses who were unable to agree about Arthur's physical marks were unanimous he had had the disease and that he had recovered to some degree, although he still suffered from nervousness and facial contortions eight years later. It is a damning fact that the Claimant, when writing from Australia to convince Lady Tichborne that he was Roger, stated that he had suffered from Saint Vitus' dance; this was verified by the solicitor Gibbes. Everyone agreed that Roger never had this disease. Here the debate ended in the 1870s, but today we know more about this type of movement disorder and can assay an explanation why the Claimant was so keen to point out that he had really suffered from this disagreeable malady. Although the involuntary movements themselves usually disappear with time, a fair proportion of untreated cases have other, more insidious late manifestations, like clumsiness and facial tics.[33] There is good evidence that the Claimant suffered from a kind of convulsive grimacing, descriptions of which are compatible with a late manifestation of Sydenham's chorea. This would be difficult to hide, and he was keen to point out a plausible explanation to his "mother."[34]

During and after the second trial, many medical scientists were dismayed that their own profession had cut such a sorry figure. One of them was the Scottish missionary Dr. Henry Faulds, who took a great interest in the Tichborne case. He applied his mind to the problem of distinguishing physical features, and after observing that potters had left their thumb prints on old Japanese pottery, he got the idea that fingerprints could be used in cases of disputed identity.[35] But even if fingerprint identification had been established at the time, it could not have been applied in the Tichborne case, since no previous prints from either Tichborne or Orton existed. A way to solve the mystery definitely would be the use of DNA technology, however. The Claimant had four children, two sons and two daughters. Neither daughter had issue. The sons both joined the army, possibly under assumed names to evade their father's notoriety; there is no evidence that either of them had children. Furthermore, the Claimant's good lady was not the most faithful of wives. Not only did she have an illegitimate child with another man already at the time of their marriage, but she deserted her husband soon after he was convicted, and later entered a workhouse accompanied by two more illegitimate children, born during her husband's incarceration. Thus, even if a descendant of the Claimant could be tracked down, there would be a fair possibility of illegitimacy. Exhumation of the Claimant's own remains would be possible, but there is a strong risk this unmarked gravesite has been used for other burials since; a similar uncertainty surrounds some of the Orton family members.

## A PSYCHOLOGICAL ANALYSIS OF THE CASE

> They say Lady Tichborne swore to him, by this thing and by that,
> She really ought to know him, in spite of all that fat;
> About the marks upon him, they have made a great to do,
> They say that he's tattooed upon his hoop de dooden do!
>
> —"Jolly Old Sir Roger"

FROM THE POINT of view of a cognitive psychologist, the Tichborne case is one of several interesting historical examples of the fallibility of person identification after an absence of several years.[36] A famous sixteenth-century instance is that of Martin Guerre. In 1558, a man returned from the wars after an absence of eight years, claim-

ing to be the respected villager Martin Guerre. He had forgotten the
Basque language, and his uncle repudiated him as an impostor; yet
Martin Guerre's wife and many other people believed him. Eventually
doubts as to his identity led to a full-scale trial, where more than 200
witnesses gave evidence. The man was convicted and later confessed
the imposture. The case of the Caille claimant in late seventeenth-
century France resembles the Tichborne mystery even more. In 1699,
a young man appeared claiming to be the young nobleman Philippe
de Caille, who was presumed to have expired three years earlier. He
was illiterate and did not even know his mother's Christian name, and
the wealthy Caille family opposed his claim. But teaming up with a
discarded family servant, he finally won the case in 1706. He was
installed in the family château and married a relation of the judge. But
then another young woman appeared and claimed him as her husband, the convict and former galley slave Pierre Mège. A second trial
ensued, with 110 witnesses swearing that the claimant was Caille and
182 swearing he was Mège; the latter included the doctor who had
treated the undoubted Caille and the undertaker who had buried him.
In 1712, the claimant was finally convicted as an impostor and
bigamist. Another French cause célèbre is that of the marquise de
Douhault, who was presumed to have died in 1788. But eighteen
months later, an inmate in a Paris madhouse claimed to be the marquise. Her wicked relatives had drugged her and inveigled her into
the asylum, she said. She appeared to be a lady of superior breeding
and was released from the asylum to start a relentless campaign to
recover her property. No member of her family recognized her, but
hundreds of villagers, servants, and former tenants did. The family
claimed that the soi-disante marquise was a certain Anne Buiret, a
local quack and charlatan, and again droves of witnesses testified
either way. In 1804, the alleged marquise was finally nonsuited, to the
family's relief. The family went on to prosecute her for fraudulent
impersonation, but the court agreed she was not Anne Buiret, and the
case fell through. The poor woman then appealed to the judge, asking that if she was not the marquise de Douhault and not Anne

Buiret, what name was she entitled to use? No answer was forth-coming from the legal dignitary, and the "Woman without a Name" kept up the struggle until 1817.[37]

A mid-nineteenth-century Indian case, concerning the lost heir of the rajah of Badwar, was almost a blueprint of the Tichborne case. The young rajah had died and been cremated many years earlier, but after the old rajah expired, a claimant appeared. He had just feigned illness, he said, since some priests had recommended that he go on a fourteen-year pilgrimage. He had faked his own death: after the last mourner had departed, he leaped from the funeral pyre into the Ganges. A disgruntled old retainer of the old rajah's helped and advised the claimant. When the case went to court, there was a mul-titude of witnesses for and against, and much discussion about bod-ily marks, habits of speech, and lapses of memory, before the claimant was finally convicted. Another Indian case, that of Bhowal Sannyasi, also involved the lost heir to a fortune, an interrupted cremation, and a disappearing corpse. It went on between 1930 and 1940, featuring 608 days of legal proceedings and 1,548 witnesses. The judge com-mented that while it had been the Tichborne Claimant's undoing that almost every member of the Tichborne family stood against him, the situation here was the direct opposite: most of the relations supported the claimant. Accordingly, the lost heir joined the exclusive few pre-tenders who actually managed to support and maintain his claim.

There are thus several historical cases in which many witnesses on either side were confident about the identity of a claimant who reap-peared after a lengthy absence. Such confidence is common in iden-tification cases, and it is not often well placed. The decision of the witness is not entirely based on the physiognomy of the claimant but also depends on the witness's own expectations and on the context of the confrontation. The shape of the human face changes with age, from infancy to adulthood, because of the growth of the facial skele-ton; thereafter, changes in facial features are due to changes in fat dis-tribution, loss of skin elasticity, and hair loss.[38] In the Tichborne case, the likelihood of an erroneous identification would thus have been increased even further by the Claimant's immense gain in weight, leading to gross changes in his facial profile. We know that the Tichborne Claimant used to impress the old soldiers and servants with his knowledge of local affairs, details he might well have learned from Bogle or from the soldiers who lodged at his house. In these instances, recognition seems to have depended very little on facial features, and more on social and contextual variables. It is also clear that the Claimant made the most of his popularity among the lower classes. Just like the French peasants who wanted to support the pretended marquise de Douhault against her wicked relatives, the Tichborne servants and old Carabineers were all predisposed in favor of jolly Sir Roger, who was coming back to recover his estates. People wanted to believe that the Claimant was the rightful heir, and this subconsciously led them to recognize him.

But surely, the reader might object, these misidentification farces are things of the past. At least the courts in the trials of Klaus Barbie and John Demjanjuk for World War II Nazi atrocities seem to have thought so, since the evidence against these two included witnesses who unhesitatingly identified them as war criminals after a period of more than forty years. A recent case, however, provides a chilling reminder that fallacies of facial identification are still very much with us.[39] The thirteen-year-old American schoolboy Nicholas Barclay disappeared without a trace in 1993. Three years and four months later, a boy turned up in Spain claiming to be him. He had been kidnapped by an international pedophile ring, he said, and had finally managed to escape after years of torture and abuse. His mother, sister, grandmother, cousins, and friends all recognized him as Nicholas and were delighted that he was back home with them again after his terrifying ordeal. A private detective investigating the case for a TV documentary soon suspected foul play, however. The boy's eyes were the wrong color, and his speech had a distinct French accent. When challenged, "Nicholas" retorted that the pedophiles had injected some substance into his eyes to make them change color, and that his lengthy residence in Spain had changed his accent. Although the detective was incredulous, the family accepted the story. "Nicholas" even passed a polygraph test, but his reluctance to provide a blood sample made the detective suspicious, even though the furious mother accused him of wanting to steal her son a second time. But after he had spent four months with the family, fingerprint evidence sent to the Interpol revealed that "Nicholas" was the twenty-three-year-old French con artist Frédéric Bourdin. This individual had been in trouble with the police all over Europe for trying to gain money and favors from various charitable institutions, by telling them cock-and-bull stories about pedophiles and child abuse. A clever, plausible young sociopath, he had seen Nicholas's name in a list of missing children, and his imagination had done the rest.

## SUMMING UP AND VERDICT

This is the Claimant's Ghost who each morn
Haunts the court to see how his case gets on,
For though the Judge has for years been dead,
And the Jury have all from the box long fled,
And the Usher his sombre robes has laid by,
And there's nought in the court but a bluebottle fly,
He hopes some day the case will end,
And then from his purgatory he may wend.

—From the leaflet "The Tichborne Trial as Told to Our Grandchildren"

THERE IS NO doubt that both historical evidence and medical evidence in this remarkable case point toward the Claimant's being an impostor. The data accumulated since the trials, concerning Orton's activities in Tasmania and the Claimant's use of incidents in Orton's past life in his version of events, add much weight to the prosecution evidence, as do the medical arguments I have delineated above. The psychological analysis of the case makes it easier to accept the number of people identifying the Claimant as Tichborne. Granted that the

Claimant was an impostor, and that he was most likely Arthur Orton, it remains to analyze his motives and explain why he was so successful in impersonating a man with whom he had practically nothing in common. One theory is that Arthur Orton was really an illegitimate child of Sir James Tichborne, and thus Roger's half brother. Not only is the evidence for this liaison very unsatisfactory, but such a relationship still does not explain how Arthur Orton obtained so much knowledge about Roger Tichborne's life.[40] A more plausible theory assumes that Roger Tichborne really made it to Australia and that he met Arthur Orton when they worked together as cowboys, as some of the Australian witnesses suggested. Orton then killed him and stole his papers, later using this information to impersonate Roger when he saw Lady Tichborne's advertisement. But there is no evidence that Roger Tichborne had any papers with him that might have been useful for an impostor. The only thing he might have had was a diary of his travels. Yet, although the Claimant had detailed knowledge of old incidents when Roger was at Tichborne Park, he knew nothing about Roger's travels in South America. Nor would this theory explain why Orton went along with the claim although he was so very unlike Roger physically. Yet another version brings the lunatic Cresswell into the story. Orton and Cresswell befriended Tichborne and learned about his origin. But Roger was ill fitted for survival in the Australian bush; he knew no useful trade and was feeble of mind and body. After obtaining all the information they could from this aristocratic misfit, the two conspirators either killed him or allowed him to drink himself to death. The plan was then that Cresswell should impersonate Tichborne, but instead he went insane.[41] Disappointed, Orton withdrew to Wagga Wagga. When his life reached a low ebb there, he decided to become the Claimant himself, if only to obtain a free passage away from Australia. On board ship on his way from Sydney to New York (for further passage to London), a young woman was employed as the nursemaid of his child.[42] She much later deposed that the Claimant had tried to seduce her, suggesting that they should jump ship in Panama and settle there together, leaving the Claimant's family stranded.

Another theory is that Bogle, not the Claimant, was the mastermind of the imposture. Although he showed both cunning and composure in the witness-box, and in fact performed much better than educated witnesses like Baigent, contemporary writers and later historians alike have treated Bogle as a figure of fun. The reason for this is mainly the color of his skin. During the first trial, Sir Henry Hawkins likened the tall, thin Bogle with his shock of curly white hair to an ebony cane with an ivory knob. During the second trial, the lord chief justice himself remarked on Bogle's simplicity and apparent honesty, drawing a parallel to the loyal, uncomplaining slave depicted in *Uncle Tom's Cabin*. There is good evidence, however, that Bogle must have played a vital role in the plot. We know that when the Claimant was in Sydney, his knowledge of the Tichborne family was fairly poor: he did not even know the Christian name of his "mother." When he was canvassing in Hampshire, by contrast, his knowledge of family affairs was very impressive. Bogle was the only person who could have briefed him on these matters and coached him for his confrontation with Lady Tichborne. Little is known about Andrew Bogle's antecedents except that he met Sir Edward Tichborne in Jamaica and was taken into his service in 1818. It had been Sir Edward's intention to leave him behind, but the enterprising young Bogle was found stowing away on the ship that brought him home in 1826. Bogle then served Sir Edward for many years as a trusted personal valet.[43] Although some people seem to have been taken aback by his swarthy appearance, he soon became a popular and respected figure locally. He married two English women—first the Tichborne governess and then the local schoolmistress—and had several children. There is evidence that Bogle and Roger Tichborne were good friends: for years, they used to smoke and talk together. Bogle also knew the Tichborne family history and the local lore and geography very well. The circumstances of Bogle's departure after serving the family for twenty-eight years remain unclear. There appears to have been a quarrel after one of Bogle's sons was suspected of dishonesty, and the death of Sir Edward Tichborne in 1853 was used as a pretext to pension him off with £50 a year. Bogle was in his late forties at the time and would have expected to serve the family for several years to come; it was also the custom then to provide a trusted servant with some small cottage on the family estate after retiring. Thus Bogle had a motive to dislike the Tichborne family, for instead of living comfortably at Tichborne Park, he had been left with such a small pension that he had decided to go to Australia. During his many years as a servant, Bogle had ample time to practice the part of the simple, honest, uncomplaining blackamoor who was devoted to his master whatever happened. In court, he played the same part with considerable success; he escaped without the slightest censoring, and the lord chief justice even called him "a very fine specimen of the Negro race."

Like Naundorff and Kaspar Hauser, the Claimant had all the romance of the returned heir; like them, he was supported by adherents who were little less than fanatics. It is natural to liken the fierce pamphlet wars between the pro- and anti-Naundorffists in France and between the Hauserians and anti-Hauserians in Germany to the counterattack waged by Dr. Kenealy and his friends at the *Englishman* after the second trial. The case was like a stage drama, and its bulky hero an impersonation of John Bull returning from abroad to fight the wicked aristocratic usurpers who had stolen his property. There was a strong host of supporting characters: Baigent the muddleheaded academic, Bogle the faithful Uncle Tom, Lady Radcliffe the wicked Jezebel, and Dr. Kenealy the hero's forthright Irish defender. It is not surprising there were three competing London stage plays about the case, as well as many pantomimes and Christmas plays.[44] The novelist Charles Reade was the first to exploit the case in a literary work; he was followed by several later writers, and there is even a recent film.[45] The Tichborne case led to a revival of the old London tradition of catchpenny balladry, where the rhymes were sung to popular tunes. There were china figures and clay pipes in the image of the Claimant, and even a set of plaster figurines of all the major players in the case. In 1871, a huge wax model of the Claimant, dressed in a suit of his own clothes, was uncovered at Madame Tussaud's.

The reason the Tichborne case never really became a national enigma like those of Louis XVII and Kaspar Hauser appears to be twofold. First, there was a reasonably convincing case against the Claimant at the time, and later discoveries strengthened this case further. There were simply not enough educated people who believed in the claim. Second, the Tichbornites were closely allied with political radicalism, but this movement gradually lost interest in the cause during the 1880s. No present-day radical would be expected to get all fired up by the thought of Sir Roger's losing his family mansion and £2,000 a year.

# 6

---

## *The Duke of Baker Street*

THE GREAT DRUCE-PORTLAND mystery is today a rather forgotten piece of British history, quite undeservedly so, since it was as famous in its day as the Tichborne case, and kept the law courts busy for thirteen years, from 1896 until 1908. Its principal actors were a duke who liked solitude, a shopkeeper who liked large bushy beards, a lady who liked beating people up with her umbrella, a homeopathic doctor who liked to imitate a performing bear, and an Australian carpenter who liked money. A clever private detective was employed to resolve the question that was consuming all of England with curiosity: was the shopkeeper really a duke in a false beard?

### AN ODD DUKE

THE DUKEDOM OF PORTLAND, one of the most distinguished noble houses of England, originated with the courtier and diplomat

William Bentinck, who was high in the favor of William of Orange; he was made earl of Portland in 1689, and his son became the first duke of Portland in 1716. William Henry Cavendish-Bentinck, the third duke of Portland, was a leading eighteenth-century politician, and twice prime minister. William John Cavendish-Bentinck-Scott, the future fifth duke of Portland, inherited little of the stamina and intellectual qualities shown by his illustrious forebears, however. Born in 1800, he was never sent to public school but educated at home because of delicate health. His brief army career was cut short by "lethargy." After his elder brother died, in 1824, William John became marquis of Titchfield and heir to the title. He also became a member of Parliament for King's Lynn, a seat traditionally held by younger members of his family, since many of the electorate were their tenants or dependents. After just two years in Parliament, mostly as a spectator, he resigned the seat to his younger brother Lord George Bentinck. A melancholy figure, always complaining of ill health although doctors found little wrong with him, the young marquis was never seen at court and very seldom seen in society. However, he was a patron of the opera and fell madly in love with the celebrated young opera singer Adelaide Kemble. One day, out of the blue, he asked her to marry him. She jilted him in no uncertain terms, and the marquis was mortified. Many people in society were amazed that she turned down this wealthy and noble suitor, but the explanation is very likely to be found in his appearance and personal mannerisms. He was a nervous, shy, reclusive character, and by no means a ladies' man. Some mysterious skin disease gave his features a scabious, unwholesome look. The marquis was desperately afraid of catching cold and used to wear three pairs of socks and three frock coats, one on top of the other, and often one or two overcoats or a thick fur coat as well. His trouser legs were tied to his ankles with strings to keep out the drafts. No matter how hot the weather was, he never went outdoors without having an extra overcoat slung over his arm and carrying a large, old-fashioned umbrella. His head was covered by an unfashionable, overly large brown wig, upon which rested a tall hat two feet in height.[1]

In March 1854, William John succeeded his father and became the fifth duke of Portland. He did not attend his father's funeral. He was now the owner of many London houses and vast country estates, the foremost of which was stately Welbeck Abbey, the family seat. But as the years went by, the duke's behavior became increasingly eccentric. He developed a mania for reclusiveness and could hardly bring himself to leave his rooms at Welbeck Abbey during daylight hours. None of his hundreds of servants were allowed to speak to him or even to acknowledge his existence in any way, on pain of instant dismissal; they were to walk by him as if he were a tree. The duke had a special carriage built, outfitted with heavy curtains to shield him from observation. At his main London residence, Harcourt House in Cavendish Square, he had a high stained-glass wall erected to prevent neighbors from peeping in at him. In spite of his eccentricities, the duke was a good landlord and a competent manager of his vast estates; he was charitable to the poor and sick among his numerous tenants. He developed a passion for building and had a new servants' wing and many new lodges and workmen's cottages constructed. In Welbeck Abbey itself, an army of plumbers installed water closets in every bathroom, and in many of the main rooms as well. The duke frequently changed his mind while planning his building projects. In 1860, he wanted to pull down the servants' wing that had been constructed just a few years earlier, since it was in the way of an elaborate glass corridor that was to connect his new museum and chapel with the main buildings at Welbeck. Planning the welfare of his many dependents, be they two- or four-legged, with the randomness of a child building houses with bricks in a playpen, he next abandoned this project and instead built a grandiose dog kennel and a no less splendid set of stables. Even more over the top was the duke's immense indoor riding ring, 396 feet long and 108 feet wide, and lit by four thousand gas jets.

But worse was to come. In the caves and catacombs under Welbeck Abbey, the duke employed a thousand workmen for twenty-five years to create a second, underground palace. Every room was painted pink,

Welbeck Abbey. From the Hallward Library, University of Nottingham, reproduced by permission.

including the great hall, 160 feet long and 63 feet wide. At night, the duke emerged from his bedroom and could be seen walking through the corridors of his underground palace, which extended for miles and were surrounded with ballrooms, galleries, and museums.[2] A tunnel over 1,000 yards in length stretched from the underground palace to the riding house; a second, more roughly constructed tunnel, running parallel, was used by the workmen so that the duke never risked meeting anyone. Every day, the duke's covered carriage was driven through an immense tunnel leading from the Welbeck catacombs to the Worksop railway station, where it was loaded onto a special truck that took it to London. Here another troop of the duke's servants harnessed a new team of horses onto the cloaked vehicle and drove it to Harcourt House, down another underground tunnel, where they left it, not knowing whether the duke had been traveling in the carriage. Sometimes a weird, hooded figure could be seen to emerge from it, sometimes not.

By the late 1870s, the duke appears to have lost whatever grasp of reality he may once have possessed. His building projects became weirder and weirder. Several large lakes were emptied of water and their bottoms concreted to make them easier to manage, but the concrete cracked, so this plan came to nothing. Equally scatterbrained was his underground library with a floor of waterproof concrete, and the underground chapel with seating for 162 people. This chapel was finished, but never consecrated. The duke's health gradually deteriorated, and he died in December 1879. He had shown no interest in the female sex after Adelaide Kemble rebuffed him, and thus had no direct heir. His sisters, Lady Howard de Walden and Lady Ossington, inherited some of the estates, but the title was inherited by his second cousin William John Arthur Cavendish-Bentinck, who became the sixth duke of Portland. The new duke was aghast to see the state of Welbeck Abbey brought on by his predecessor's peculiar building projects.[3] Toward the end of his life, the old duke had shut himself up in a suite of five rooms in the west wing of Welbeck Abbey, and the remainder of the palace had been allowed to fall into disrepair. All his rooms were painted pink, and all had a water closet in the corner. His only means of communicating with his servants was letter boxes, one for outgoing and one for incoming messages, on all the doors. The duke's bedstead had large folding doors to exclude the drafts and to make it impossible to tell whether the bed was occupied. The dressing room was lined with large cupboards filled with green boxes, containing the duke's collection of wigs. Other cupboards held his fine silk shirts, with high collars and inordinately long sleeves and frills, and dozens of handkerchiefs and socks.

## AN ODD SHOPKEEPER

ALREADY DURING THE lifetime of the fifth duke of Portland, there had been much gossip about his secretive habits and strange behavior. An article in the *World* magazine of 1878 said that the nobleman "has only himself to thank for the mass of legend which has already crystallised around his name. Queer stories of Harcourt House and of Welbeck are muttered with bated breath." It was said that the high glass wall at Harcourt House had been erected to conceal that a dead body had been hidden on the premises; these rumors became so widely believed that a sanitary official paid a formal visit to investigate, but without finding anything untoward.[4] According to another story, the duke had a great fear of being buried alive by mistake and ordered that his mortal remains be kept in a glass coffin, in a glass-encased dome, on the roof of another of his London houses, at 13 Hyde Park Gardens. This story was later improved upon: the duke's ghost was said to rise from the glass coffin, haunting the house. It could be seen walking down stairs from the glass dome on the house's roof. Hundreds of people had seen the "Paddington Ghost," and there was much public uproar, but the story found a perfectly natural explanation: the glass dome was intended as an observatory and not as a mausoleum, and the caretaker's daughter liked to walk up there to admire the London skyline.[5]

These idle tales were nothing compared with the wild accusations from Mrs. Anna Maria Druce, however. She was the widow of an upholsterer named Walter Thomas Druce, who had died in 1880 aged twenty-eight.[6] He was the son of Thomas Charles Druce, a wealthy cabinetmaker who was the owner of the Baker Street Bazaar, one of London's largest and most successful shops for fine furniture. He had been partially intestate at the time of his death in 1864, and in the early 1890s there was still litigation over how his fortune should be divided among his six children and their families. In particular, Anna Maria Druce, who had not been left much by her husband after his untimely death, was in desperate need of money. It annoyed her that her husband had obtained so little of Thomas Charles Druce's considerable fortune. She made frequent visits to Mr. Alexander Young, the solicitor who served as Thomas Charles Druce's executor, to accuse him of fraudulently keeping her lawful inheritance from her. The solicitor was embarrassed by her histrionics, which were often staged in front of his other clients, and used to give her small sums of money to keep her away. In June 1894, she was arrested by the police for issuing worthless checks and brought before the Bow Street magistrates. She shrilly accused the executor Young of withholding her money, but he denied all responsibility.[7] In September of the same year, she again appeared before the Bow Street magistrates, charged with assaulting her landlady and threatening to dash her brains out with a large bottle, and later going on a rampage through the house and breaking thirty-five window panes and a china footbath.[8]

Mrs. Druce's next newsworthy action was that she appealed to the home secretary to obtain permission to open the vault of her father-in-law, Thomas Charles Druce, at Highgate Cemetery. When asked why she wanted to do so, she told a fantastic story: the fifth duke of Bedford and Thomas Charles Druce had been one and the same person! In middle age, the duke had obtained a liking for ordinary family life and deserted his underground palace for years on end to work as a shopkeeper and live in a cosy little house with his wife and children. Mrs. Druce claimed that Thomas Charles Druce's coffin was empty and that the duke had faked Druce's death after growing tired of life as a commoner, before returning to Welbeck Abbey and living there for several years under his own name. The home secretary turned a deaf ear to this remarkable appeal, as did the cemetery authorities and the Bow Street police; after all, Mrs. Druce was well known in the police courts for her unbalanced behavior. She then boldly appealed to the House of Lords to have the sixth duke of Portland ejected in favor of her son, but again without success. In March 1898, the persistent lady finally succeeded in obtaining a receptive audience for her remarkable claim; by appealing to the bishop of London that there had been a false burial and that the grounds of Highgate Cemetery had been desecrated, she was referred to a sitting of the venerable Consistory Court of London.

At the meeting of the Consistory Court, held in solemn form in St. Paul's Cathedral, Mrs. Druce piled sensation upon sensation.[9] She claimed that during the lifetime of his father the fourth duke, the marquis of Titchfield (as the fifth duke then was) had fallen deeply in love with Annie May, the illegitimate daughter of the earl of Berkeley. His younger brother Lord George Bentinck was his fiercest rival, and the old duke favored Lord George's suit, ridiculing his eldest son for his revolting appearance. The brothers confronted each other at Welbeck one day in September 1848; afterward, Lord George's lifeless body was found not far from Welbeck Abbey. There were rumors that the marquis had struck his brother a mighty blow, but these were hushed down, and the cause of death given as "a spasm of the heart." After this fatal encounter, the fratricide marquis felt bitter remorse and the most abject terror; convinced that justice would one day catch up with him, he took steps accordingly. His first idea was to begin the vast excavations at Welbeck Abbey, to serve as a refuge. The fearful noble-man's second plan was to change his identity: he invented the persona of Thomas Charles Druce and transferred considerable sums of money to this fictitious individual, before setting up business at the Baker Street Bazaar. Just as at Welbeck, he had a vast network of tun-nels constructed underneath the Bazaar, to allow him means for a hasty escape in the face of retribution. As Druce, the nobleman led a highly immoral life: he kept many mistresses and rented rooms to prostitutes in exchange for "favors."

The faithful Annie May, who apparently did not mind becoming a shopkeeper's wife instead of a duchess, still wanted to marry the duke, but he had tired of her and often beat and kicked her brutally, even when she was pregnant. It was not until she threatened to expose his double life to the authorities that he finally relented and took her to the altar. This unpromising start to their married life did not prevent the couple from having several children. After running the bazaar for thirteen years with considerable success, the duke had enough of life as a shopkeeper. Apparently, he also had enough of his wife and chil-dren, since he covertly faked his own death in 1864 and returned to Welbeck Abbey as the duke of Portland, leaving poor Annie May and her young almost destitute. But in spite of his labyrinthine under-ground tunnels, and his collection of six hundred wigs and countless sets of false beards, whiskers, and mustaches with which to disguise his appearance, the fratricide duke did not feel safe. He contacted the leading alienist Dr. Forbes Winslow, posing as an insane homeopathist named Dr. Harmer. By "conducting himself in the most extravagant manner," the duke soon convinced Dr. Winslow that he was a madman. After spending a year at Winslow's private asylum at Hammersmith, the duke suddenly "recovered" and went back to Welbeck. Far from dying in 1879, the duke actually returned to the asylum, spending many years there in the guise of Dr. Harmer before finally expiring sometime in the 1890s. Mrs. Druce presented an affidavit from Dr. Winslow stating that he himself and a faithful old retainer named George New had both seen a photograph of Druce and identified it with the individual they knew as Dr. Harmer. This homeopathic doctor had labored under the delusion of being a performing bear, and could often be seen dancing clumsily in the grounds of the asylum.[10]

The Consistory Court was amazed at this fantastic story of a duke transforming into a shopkeeper and then back into a duke, before finally ending up as a homeopathist dancing bear. But Mrs. Druce went through the cross-examination unscathed, as did her leading witness, an elderly lady named Mrs. Margaret Hamilton, who swore that she had seen Thomas Charles Druce twice after his alleged death in 1864. The court reluctantly decided that the best way of resolving this extraordinary case was to issue a permit for the vault to be opened. Mrs. Druce thus won a surprising victory. Her relations with the newspaper press had initially been tempestuous, particularly after she beat up an impudent journalist with her umbrella after he had teased her; as a result, her cranky ideas had been derided in almost every newspaper. After her victory in the Consistory Court, though, she was in a position to grant interviews to the assembled gentlemen of the press, exulting in the prospect that the vault would be found empty, as she had predicted. She was described as a forceful-looking woman in her forties, with a sallow complexion, a prominent jaw, and a fierce look in her eyes. If one of the journalists forgot his manner, she tightened her grip on the handle of her umbrella and reminded him that she was the duchess of Portland still. If they were well behaved, she invited them to the grand banquet she planned to arrange once the sixth duke had been ousted and her son installed at Welbeck in his place.[11] Soon, several large London newspapers, the *Daily Mail* in particular, were actively pro-Druce.[12] Much invigorated by the support from the press, Mrs. Druce lost no time in producing a pamphlet entitled *The Great Druce-Portland Mystery*, in which the claim was elaborated upon in every ludicrous detail. It ended with an appeal to the men and women of England to buy her Druce bonds, which gave the purchaser a share of the Portland fortune, and by the sale of which she hoped to finance her future litigation.[13]

By 1898, the sixth duke of Portland and his solicitors were well aware of Mrs. Druce's accusations. In his memoirs, written many years later, the duke wrote that he treated the entire business with supreme contempt.[14] Yet there is considerable evidence that the padded nobleman was actually quite alarmed by Mrs. Druce's claims and worried that there might be something in them after all. He had himself not known his secretive predecessor—no one had—and he could well remember the unusual "redecorations" at Welbeck Abbey, and the many rumors concerning the old duke's eccentric activities. The sixth duke had to admit that a man who wasted £60,000 a year on his scatterbrained building projects, wore three exquisitely tailored frock coats one over the other, and collected six hundred brown wigs could be capable of at least some of the weird actions listed by Mrs. Druce. The ducal solicitors were briefed and after many consultations made a plan. The appeal to open the Druce vault should be firmly opposed by Mr. Herbert Druce, the eldest son of Thomas Charles, and by the executor Young; both these men were willing pawns for the ducal cause. By bringing action after action to delay the opening of the vault, the solicitors would gain time carefully to investigate the background of Thomas Charles Druce and the movements of the fifth duke of Portland. Some support came from Mrs. Harmer, the wife of the homeopathist turned dancing bear, who wrote to the newspapers denying that her husband, who had had a large practice in Richmond before he lost his reason, had anything to do with Druce and the duke. Mrs. Druce airily replied that there had been two insane homeopathists named Harmer in Forbes Winslow's asylum. She was much dismayed and frustrated by the legal obstructionism of her wily opponents, however, and told the newspapers that Herbert Druce was a bastard (in every sense of the word); Thomas Charles Druce, alias the duke, had not been married to Annie May by the time Herbert was conceived. She also complained that mysterious men were following her about; this was put down to her usual paranoia and histrionics. She feared that the sixth duke would arrange to have Druce's coffin clandestinely removed from the vault, and went on a daily pilgrimage to Highgate Cemetery to check that there were no covert attempts to tunnel into the vault. These proceedings attracted even more newspaper interest, and there was a good deal of sympathy for the underdog: why, if Mrs. Druce was just a deluded madwoman, were Herbert Druce and his sinister forces so intent on preventing her from exhuming Druce's coffin?

## DETECTIVE LITTLECHILD'S INVESTIGATION

THE SIXTH DUKE's solicitors suggested that a clever and ruthless private detective could find out much about the motivations of Mrs. Druce and her witnesses, and they knew the right man for the job. Detective Chief Inspector John George Littlechild was one of the leading Scotland Yard detectives of the 1870s and 1880s. He was part of the section investigating foreign criminals and terrorists and in 1883 became head of the Special Irish Branch. Later, he took a hand in the search for the elusive Jack the Ripper.[15] After retiring from the Yard in 1895, at the age of forty-five, he set up a large and successful private detective agency in London. He had numerous assistant detectives and a wide network of informants in the criminal underworld. One of Littlechild's first big cases was to collect information about Oscar Wilde's sexual habits for the trial that was to lead to his downfall.

In mid-1898, Littlechild was briefed by the sixth duke's solicitors about Mrs. Druce's action. They told him that the sixth duke had suggested that the former Welbeck servants be closely interrogated, so that it might be possible to state unequivocally that the duke was at Welbeck at some time that Druce could be pinned down as having stayed in London. But the servants were old and infirm, and their doddering testimony could not rule out that the duke had been larking about in London for years on end. In spite of a lengthy search of the rambling rooms and catacombs at Welbeck, no photographs of the fifth duke could be found. Two busts of him had been made during his lifetime, but neither was particularly like him.[16] Littlechild was amazed that so little was known about the fifth duke, and advertised in the newspapers for information concerning him, but the result was similarly dismal, since the only responses came from the "lunatic fringe."[17] One woman wrote that the duke had been hideously disfigured by venereal disease; another suggested that he had entered the sultan's harem as a young man, and afterward built his underground passages because he was ashamed to show his disgraced face before decent English people.

One of Littlechild's first ideas was to have Mrs. Druce followed almost around the clock; her "delusion" that strange men were following her about was thus nothing but reality![18] He could soon report to the duke's solicitors that she was "mixing herself up with a queer lot of City men," some of whom were known criminals. Another clever move of Littlechild's was to contact some old servants of Thomas Charles Druce and his sons, to find out more about the Druce family and about Mrs. Druce's background. A man named Stoward, who had been underbutler in Thomas Charles Druce's household, told him that he believed that his master's family had come from the eastern counties. Stoward obviously had little liking for Mrs. Druce and said that far from being a member of the country gentry, as she herself had claimed in her newspaper interviews, she was the daughter of an impecunious London paperhanger. She had come into the Druce household as a governess, afterward seducing and marrying the weak-

Two photographs alleged to portray the fifth duke of Portland
(without beard) and Thomas Charles Druce (with beard).
From the Hallward Library, University of Nottingham,
reproduced by permission.

minded young Walter Thomas Druce, who was powerless against her
feminine wiles. These revelations interested Littlechild enough for
him to employ Stoward as a spy, with instructions to attend the sessions at the Consistory Court and to make notes of participants
known to him. After one of the sessions, Stoward sat next to a bicy-
cle inventor named Mr. Marler, who told him that he was Mrs.
Druce's landlord and that she had lived there for nine months without paying any rent. He would probably have made further revelations, had not Mrs. Druce herself seen the old butler lurking in the
courtroom. She advanced upon the two men, a steely glare in her
eyes, and lashed out at Marler with her umbrella, asking how he
dared to have any conversation with such an infernal scoundrel as
Stoward. Poor Marler fell off his seat and begged for mercy. Stoward
beat a hasty retreat and afterward found it advisable to decline any
further undercover work in the duke's service.[19]

Stoward's talk about the Druce family's being from the east of England prompted Littlechild to send his assistants to various churches in Essex and Cambridgeshire, but they never found any trace of them in the parish records.[20] A few months later, a Mr. Trewinard contacted him and offered to deliver some important information about the Druce family in exchange for a large sum of money; he would not say exactly what it was but promised that Littlechild would not be disappointed. By a clever ruse, the detective instead managed to find Trewinard's source: it was Mr. Izard, the husband of Thomas Charles Druce's granddaughter from his first marriage. Littlechild went to see the Izards, and they volunteered much valuable information without asking a penny for it.[21] In 1816, when Thomas Charles Druce was twenty-one, he had married Miss Elizabeth Crickmer at Bury St. Edmunds. They had at least five children, all of whom were suspected to be dead at the present time; the only daughter, Elizabeth Druce, was Mrs. Izard's mother. The eldest son, Harry, had become a sailor and drowned at an early age; two other sons, named Charles and George, had gone to Australia. It was thought that Charles and George Druce had both fathered children, at least one of whom was still living, as a tailor in Sydney. Littlechild brought this highly encouraging information before the duke's solicitors; if they could find the eldest son of Thomas Charles Druce, he or his descendants would be rightful heir to the Druce estate, whether it consisted only of the Baker Street Bazaar or extended to the fortune of the dukes of Portland, and Mrs. Druce's claim would be crushed. The solicitors were a little concerned about actually searching for the Australian Druces, however—might not a young, active man be a more dangerous adversary than Mrs. Druce? They instead leaked the information to the press. On February 26, 1899, the *Weekly Dispatch* newspaper could announce all the details about Thomas Charles's first marriage. The duke's solicitors hoped that Mrs. Druce would give up her quest for the truth, but she did nothing of the sort. First she denied the existence of the marriage and then, after Littlechild actually found the marriage certificate in Bury St. Edmunds, stated that all the children were nevertheless illegitimate. The solicitors understood that unless they were actually able to drag one of the Australian Druces out of the bush, they had no chance of defeating her. Mrs. Druce had won again.

Detective Littlechild next focused on the antecedents of Mrs. Hamilton, Mrs. Druce's star witness in the Consistory Court. She had looked like a benign matron in her neat black dress and frilled cap when she testified about her meetings with the long-dead Druce, but Littlechild described her to the solicitors as "a very crafty old woman, and I have no doubt money-making is her motive." Through his agents in Liverpool and Leeds, he found out that her father's name was Atkinson but that he called himself Stuart; Mrs. Hamilton called herself Miss Stuart, even after her alleged marriage to Captain Hamilton. Her sister was in an asylum, and she herself was described as "very peculiar" since an early age; this did not prevent her from earning a living, for quite a few years, as a hotel housekeeper. Littlechild found out that Mrs. Hamilton's daughter lived in Norwich, and went there to see her. The moment he saw the daughter's husband, who called himself Edward Bower, he knew he had come onto a good thing. Littlechild knew Mr. Bower under his real name, Giuseppe Mussibini, and had probably made his acquaintance during the years Littlechild was in charge of criminal foreigners at Scotland Yard.[22] It is not known what misdeeds Mussibini committed in London, or exactly why he changed his name and went to Norwich, but it is certain that he had enough to hide for Littlechild to make him his spy and informant, by the threat of blackmail. Mussibini was to write to Mrs. Hamilton and inform her that unless she desisted from appearing in court, he and his wife would both be facing "horrible ruin." The crafty crone, who obviously had little liking for the Italian crook who had married her daughter, first made a defiant reply but, unwisely in doing so, gave away her hotel address in London. Littlechild used this information to intercept and steal her mail, including at least one letter from Mrs. Druce. He later sent Mussibini to London, and this time the Italian managed to persuade his mother-in-law to withdraw from the case. Littlechild himself may well have been present to intimidate Mrs. Hamilton further and to point out that her lies about her own past would be exposed during the trial, thus rendering her testimony useless.[23]

Mrs. Hamilton's defection happened at an unfortunate time for Mrs. Druce. In 1901, she was finally able to pin the opposition down and fix a date for her case to be reheard in the Probate Division. In addition to Mrs. Hamilton, five witnesses had made prior depositions on her behalf. Most startling were statements from several witnesses that they had seen Druce wandering in the tunnels underneath the Baker Street Bazaar *after his death*; they had all believed him to be a ghost, and it was somberly testified that the manager Thomas Stewart and the housekeeper Johnson, among others, had lost their reason as a consequence.[24] The forewoman Mrs. Pledger had gone stark raving mad after meeting Druce in one of the tunnels, and later died in an asylum, screaming, "I see him now! The dead man!" But at the trial, all Mrs. Druce's witnesses had withdrawn, some of them certainly coerced by Littlechild, others sensing that the case was lost after Mrs. Hamilton's defection. Poor Mrs. Druce was equally confused and furious. Throughout the trial, she behaved most obstreperously, in spite of being repeatedly cautioned by the judge.[25] She blasted the executor Young as a swindler, and her first question to the eldest son, Herbert Druce, an awkward-looking character with a huge bushy beard, was "You are an illegitimate son of Thomas Charles Druce?" The duke's solicitors had found old Druce's doctors, who testified that he had really died in 1864, after suffering from anal abscesses. Operations had been in vain, and poor Druce's posterior slowly and painfully putrefied away. A nurse named Catherine Bayly corroborated this testimony, but she was shamefully blackguarded by Mrs. Druce. When the meek old woman said that she had locked Druce's room up after his demise, Mrs. Druce screamed, "Why did you lock up the room— to keep out the devil? What was in there—a corpse? A skeleton? What was in this wonderful Bluebeard's chamber—an effigy, ha! ha! a wax figure, ha! ha! a face, or what!" Mrs. Druce then went on to assert that the dastardly duke had ordered a wax effigy of Druce at Madame Tussaud's establishment to deceive Catherine Bayly. The outcome of the trial could be only one: Mrs. Druce was nonsuited, and the Druce vault would remain undisturbed. Furious at the behavior of her witnesses, she wrote an angry letter to Mrs. Hamilton, but the sly crone had withdrawn to Mussibini's house in Norwich to be out of reach of her erstwhile friend's lethal umbrella. Anyway, the letter was stolen by Littlechild's agents, and the duke's solicitors must have had great fun reading this vituperative missive.[26]

## THE DRUCE-PORTLAND COMPANY

FOR TWO YEARS, peace was restored to Welbeck Abbey, and the sixth duke of Portland could live quietly without having to listen to implausible tales about coffins full of lead, false beards, and dancing homeopaths. Although Mrs. Druce was still active in the law courts, her strength had been broken by the setback in 1901, and her appearances in court became increasingly pathetic. Her precious Druce bonds had never brought in much money and were now completely worthless. But the troubled duke was not to enjoy his carefree life for long. In 1903, the newspapers announced that another claimant to the dukedom of Portland had come to London—the Australian George Hollamby Druce. Very little is known about the antecedents of this obscure individual, except that he was born in 1855, the son of Thomas Charles Druce's son George, who had gone to Australia to seek gold, and that he was a carpenter in Sydney for many years. Unlike his impetuous kinswoman Anna Maria Druce, he was a cagey person, who believed in careful planning. He consulted a clever Australian solicitor named Thomas Coburn, and they spent several years drawing up a plan of attack on the Portland millions. First, they bribed George Hollamby Druce's cousin Charles Edgar, who was actually the main claimant, to sign over his rights and then to keep a low profile. They must have read about their notorious countryman the Tichborne Claimant and approved of the Claimant's clever ruse of issuing Tichborne bonds to raise money for his cause; an issue of Druce-Portland bonds took place in Australia in 1903, to pay for Druce and Coburn to establish themselves in London. They found it more than a little precarious personally to issue a lawsuit against Herbert Druce and his backers. The establishment, headed by the powerful duke of Portland and his associates, would stand ready to prosecute him if the claim failed and he was branded an impostor, just as the Tichborne Claimant had been crushed in 1872. But Druce and Coburn thought of a way out. They founded a series of limited liability companies— among them G. H. Druce Ltd., the Druce-Portland Company Ltd., and the New Druce-Portland Company Ltd.—purportedly associations of interested shareholders who believed in Druce's claim, and arranged that all court actions were to be made by these parties.

Druce and Coburn had to put a new spin on the old story for it to fully suit their ends. They did so in two pamphlets entitled *The Druce-Portland Case* and *Claim to the Portland Millions: Was Druce the Duke?*, both published in 1905 by the *Idler*, a popular pro-Druce magazine.[27] Adroitly, they reinterpreted the known facts about Thomas Charles Druce's early marriage: it had indeed been the dashing sixteen-year-old William John Cavendish-Bentinck, the future fifth duke of Portland, who had come galloping from Welbeck to Bury St. Edmunds to win the heart of the twenty-one-year-old Elizabeth Crickmer. The teenage nobleman married her in 1816 under his assumed identity of Thomas Charles Druce, and they lived together for five years and had as many children. William John then basely deserted his wife and children, choosing to return to his old life of opulence at Welbeck, little caring what happened to his destitute wife and starving children. This was the reason why the young Druce sons grew up in such squalor, and why they left for Australia as soon as they could. In 1835, the duke again put on his false beard and assumed the identity of Druce. He opened the Baker Street Bazaar with funds he had previously transferred from the Portland bank accounts. The treacherous nobleman did not tell his poor wife about this latest development, but at least had the decency to make his reemergence known to his two favorite children—the young seaman George and his sister Frances. They lived with his two mistresses—Mrs. Demaine and the Frenchwoman Madame Elise. Their lecherous, bushy-bearded father also introduced them to other elegant lady friends of his, all of whom they were instructed to call "aunt." In 1846, the duke started to prepare his excavations at Welbeck; in 1851, he married Annie May as Thomas Charles Druce; in 1864, he deserted his second wife and family and went back to Welbeck; he finally died in 1879.

George Hollamby Druce and Thomas Coburn also abstracted Mrs. Hamilton's evidence, which she had amended considerably since her 1898 and 1901 depositions. She now claimed that her father, the wealthy gentleman Robert Lennox Stuart, had known Thomas Charles Druce for many years, knew all about his double life, and had once heard him confess that he had killed his brother. Mrs. Hamilton had also known Druce well from 1849 onward and sometimes visited him at Welbeck, although her father, familiar with Druce's lecherous tendencies, strictly forbade her to go out in a coach alone with her bushy-bearded admirer. Mrs. Hamilton and two other people claimed to have seen Druce after his alleged death in 1864. Detective Littlechild was dismayed by the reemergence of Mrs. Hamilton; the explanation was that Mussibini had died in the intervening years and that the crafty old woman felt free to add her undoubted talents to those of the Australian contingent. Mrs. Hamilton was living at a London hotel under an assumed name, but Littlechild's men found her after staking out her daughter's house. Littlechild was waiting for her one evening and promised that he would see her ruined if she appeared in court, but the tough crone was defiant.[28]

Druce and Coburn claimed that Thomas Charles Druce and the fifth duke of Portland were of very similar build and appearance; they supported this by comparing a photograph they said portrayed the clean-shaven, cadaverous-looking duke with two others of Druce, an odd-looking fellow with an enormous beard. In one of the photos, where he is holding up the (false?) beard in front of him, it looks as if he were swallowing a Pekingese dog. Druce and the duke had very similar habits, the

pamphlets claimed—the same haughty, unapproachable manner, the
same loathsome skin disease, and the same abstemious diet.

George Hollamby Druce valued the sixth duke's fortune at £16 million. He decided to put £1.6 million up for grabs and invited shareholders to buy his Druce bonds, which would pay the holder sixty-four
times the investment if he managed to oust the nobleman from Welbeck and usurp his title and fortune.[29] One of the takers was John
George Littlechild, who had been alerted by the sixth duke's solicitors
about the emergence of the Australian claimant. He sent one of his
assistants to the office of the Druce-Portland Company, where this individual was offered to buy shares at £4 each; he drove a hard bargain
and finally bought four shares for £10. Littlechild's men were actively
following the main shareholders of the Druce-Portland Company,
among them a certain Captain Whitsun and "a most obnoxious and
undesirable person" named John Thomas Wyatt. It was feared that
scoundrels of this kind would not stop short of breaking into the Druce
tomb and stealing the body, and Littlechild arranged to have the tomb
discreetly watched. Druce's agents were spreading rumors that the duke
was offering to settle the case for a very high sum, and this improved
the sale of the Druce bonds considerably.[30] They also obtained support from the popular press, and in 1907 the Australian claimant and
his wily legal adviser had a capital of £30,000, largely derived from the
sale of their bonds. Just like the Tichborne case thirty-five years earlier, the Druce-Portland affair caught the public fancy by its reversal
of the Victorian class barriers: a duke becoming a shopkeeper was just
as astonishing as a butcher becoming a baronet. Again, the sale of the
bonds was greatly enhanced by Druce's and Coburn's appeal to the English sporting spirit, and the traditional support for the underdog, the
honest Australian who had come to challenge the wealthy duke.

## THE SECOND TRIAL

IN OCTOBER 1907, Druce and Coburn were finally ready for battle
in court. Shrewdly, they chose to attack Herbert Druce, whom they

prosecuted since he had sworn, during Mrs. Druce's 1901 trial, that he had seen his father immediately after his death and later in his coffin. If Thomas Charles Druce had not died, Herbert Druce was guilty of perjury. Druce and Coburn invested part of their capital in employing a first-rate legal team; their prosecutor was the well-known barrister Atherley Jones.[31] In his opening before the Marylebone Police Court, the eloquent Jones presented three main witnesses. Mrs. Hamilton would testify that she and her father knew all about the duke's other identity and that he was alive after his presumed death in 1864. Miss Mary Robinson, the daughter of a wealthy American plantation owner, would testify that she had been very close to Thomas Charles Druce, alias the fifth duke of Portland. This had come about in a singular manner. Apparently, Charles Dickens had been acting as the duke's pimp in between writing novels, charged with procuring innocent young females for the nobleman's amusement. Jones did not dwell on the details, but claimed that, during her "girlish intimacy" with Druce, Miss Robinson had had ample opportunity to observe his second identity as the duke of Portland. There was also a surprise witness, who had just arrived from the United States: the seventy-one-year-old Irish-American Robert Caldwell of Staten Island, who was actually the first to appear in the witness-box. Caldwell testified that from an early age he had been afflicted by a particularly disagreeable disease known as a bubulous nose, meaning that his nose was full of small eruptions and abscesses. After touring the world to find a cure, he finally met a British officer named Captain Joyce in India, and purchased from him a secret medicine that finally cured his deformed, aching nose. Not long thereafter, Caldwell was contacted by the fifth duke of Portland, who also had a bubulous nose. For the price of £5,000, he cured the duke and was afterward rewarded by presents worth nearly £10,000. The duke had enough confidence in his favorite quack doctor to confide in him fully about his secret identity as Thomas Charles Druce; he even introduced him to his wife and children. When the time came to fake Druce's death in 1864, Caldwell had personally purchased a coffin and weighted it with lead, before conducting the mock funeral with hearse and mourning coaches.

But when cross-examined by Herbert Druce's barrister, Horace Avory, Caldwell cut a sorry figure. Asked whether he had seen himself described as "the Great American Affidavit-Maker," he answered, "Yes!" Moreover, he could not deny that he had told many lies under oath in an American court case involving the will of a Mr. Stewart. The

A drawing of the dramatic scene when Caldwell gives evidence.
From the *Illustrated London News*, November 11, 1907.

distinguished surgeon Sir Morell Mackenzie, whom Caldwell claimed to have consulted for his nose, was just seventeen in the year the American had given for the consultation. Caldwell replied that if he had known his age at the time, he would have quarreled about the doctor's fee! Captain Joyce, the officer who cured him, was in Dublin, and not in India, at the time. When asked about the building works at Welbeck, during the second day of questioning, Caldwell was also snared into a number of contradictions. John George Littlechild had received information from Ireland, and Avory asked a series of pointed questions about the criminal activities of a certain Robert Caldwell, who had defrauded many people. Caldwell replied that this was his brother William, who often called himself Robert. This brother looked, wrote, and talked very much like himself, and had moved to the United States at the same time! "Was he as truthful as you or more so?" asked Avory icily. Still, Caldwell's native wit had not abandoned him. He said that the duke had once asked whether he knew any honest lawyer who could draw up his will, but Caldwell had replied that he did not know a single honest member of the legal profession! When asked about a man he had treated for a nose condition, Caldwell refused to state his former patient's name. "He is not a duke, I suppose?" asked Avory. "No, he is a reputable gentleman!" replied Caldwell amid loud laughter in court. When asked what exactly he had done to treat the duke's bubulous nose, Caldwell answered, "Ah, you would like to get at that! You would go into business yourself if you could!" When the sneering, sarcastic Avory asked whether the duke had had the good taste at least to wear black false whiskers for his own funeral, Caldwell replied, "No, they were gray!" At this stage, poor Atherley Jones, not to mention George Hollamby Druce and Thomas Coburn, must have heartily regretted that they had allowed this transatlantic buffoon to appear in court.

Next to give evidence was the fifty-six-year-old Mary Robinson. She created an instant sensation in court when she complained that a valuable diary, which gave all the details about her relationship with the duke, had been stolen. When she was walking in Hammersmith

Broadway, a mysterious man called out that there was a spider on her coat, and Miss Robinson screamed and waved the diary about, rendering it easy for the stranger to snatch it.[32] Jones asked whether a copy made before the theft could be admitted as evidence, but Avory objected strongly to this. Miss Robinson said that she had first met Thomas Charles Druce at a London children's party in 1862, where he acted the part of the grandmother in Little Red Riding Hood; she did not mention whether he removed his bushy facial adornment before adopting this role. In 1868, her friend Charles Dickens introduced the seventeen-year-old girl to Thomas Charles Druce at Welbeck Abbey; she did not know that he was the duke, but promptly agreed to live nearby under the name Madame Tussaud and act as his secretary when required. She used to take long romantic walks with her elderly admirer in the park at Welbeck, where tame foxes were running about at will. Although her testimony was extraordinary, and her behavior in court somewhat histrionic, Miss Robinson was well briefed and gave guarded answers when Avory tried to lure her into contradictions. The only time she seemed put out was when she reluctantly had to let the judge examine a brooch that she claimed had cost the duke £300; he commented that it looked more like a cheap trinket.

Mrs. Hamilton was next in the witness-box and repeated her entire testimony without contradictions. An expert photographer then testified that he had photographed Thomas Charles Druce in 1855, and that he was certain his beard and whiskers were false. These photos, and another of a beardless man alleged to be the duke, were put before the court. There were several minor witnesses, mainly old Welbeck servants who thought the photograph resembled the duke, and London tradesmen who had thought Thomas Charles Druce's beard looked false or seen the duke's carriage parked at the Baker Street Bazaar. There were also some individuals who claimed they had seen Druce after his death in 1864, but Avory was able to shake their testimony considerably. The appearance of the old servants was equally counterproductive, because some of them willingly testified, at Avory's prompting, that the duke had never had any deformity of the nose and that they had never heard of any Miss Robinson (or Madame Tussaud) at Welbeck.

Before the opening of the defense, Atherley Jones again stood up. Having had time to consider Caldwell's disastrous testimony, he chose to disown the American as a witness, since it was not proper to rely upon his evidence. Avory, of course, stood crowing at length about Caldwell's various shortcomings before releasing the bombshell that the American was now a fugitive from justice, heading for his native country on board a fast transatlantic liner!

It was now time for Avory to make his case for the defense. Poor Herbert Druce had suffered much odium as a result of this vile charge of perjury by his own nephew, and Avory promised that he would not rest until his client was vindicated. He deplored that Druce and Coburn had deliberately waited until all of Thomas Charles Druce's doctors were dead or unable to give evidence. The old nurse Catherine Bayly was still alive, however, and stalwartly testified that Druce had really died in 1864. Avory blasted Miss Robinson's evidence. Thomas Charles Druce had been operated on for a serious complaint in 1862 and was in no condition to lark about at children's parties. It was equally shocking to hear the revered name of Charles Dickens mentioned in connection with such a miserable intrigue. Mrs. Hamilton was the worst of the perjurers: "a very crafty, cunning, and deceiving old woman," she had altered her story considerably since her 1898 testimony. After the defense rested, most people probably expected that the judge, Chichele Plowden, would decide in favor of Herbert Druce. Instead, he emphasized that every doubt should be eradicated, in case the decision was called in question sometime in the future, and ordered the Druce tomb to be opened. On the morning of December 30, 1907, over ten years after Anna Maria Druce had started her campaign, the grave was finally opened. Electricians, gravediggers, clergymen, and forensic specialists attended, and the press was there in force. A sturdy oak coffin bearing Thomas Charles Druce's name was hoisted to the surface, and when the lead inner coffin was pried open, the shrouded remains of an elderly, bearded man could be seen. Mr. Thackrah, a former business partner at the

Baker Street Bazaar, positively identified the corpse as that of Thomas Charles Druce.

The sixth duke of Portland wanted to crush his opponents once and for all, to teach them a hard lesson, and to keep any other Australian Druce claimants from trying their luck. But his solicitors reported that Druce and Coburn had been too clever for them; there was no case against either of these two slippery gentlemen. The nobleman next wanted to take vengeance on Atherley Jones, some of whose comments in court had annoyed him, by alleging that his actions as prosecutor in the Druce case made him unworthy to hold his honorary legal position as recorder.[33] The solicitors replied that they thought this a little *unsporting*, given that Jones had only been doing his job. The three perjurers were thus the only people left to face the full brunt of the duke's wrath. John George Littlechild had investigated the antecedents of Miss Robinson and found that she had never set foot in the United States, but was the daughter of a police sergeant in Mortlake. She had later married an impecunious shepherd named Robinson and moved to New Zealand with him.[34] She was sentenced to four years of penal servitude, while Mrs. Hamilton escaped with a sentence of eighteen months, mitigated by her age (she was seventy-eight). As for Robert Caldwell, they retained a warrant against him for perjury. As soon as the ship he had fled on anchored at Hoboken, he was arrested at the request of the British authorities. But Caldwell was not yet beaten. He claimed to be desperately ill and was released on bail to seek medical attention. A doctor reported that he was not expected to live more than a few days, and the request for extradition was adjourned indefinitely. But the British authorities, egged on by the duke of Portland's solicitors, were incredulous. They knew what a scoundrel Caldwell was, with a long career as a professional con man in Ireland and the United States. In addition, having seen nothing wrong with his health during his stay in London, they suspected that he had made plans beforehand with his doctor accomplice in case his appearance in court backfired. They attempted to force Caldwell to be examined by an independent doctor, but the cunning perjurer kept one step ahead of them:

he was admitted to a lunatic asylum at his own request. One of the psychiatrists told the press that Caldwell was suffering from what specialists described as "a twist in the brain" and that he could not be extradited, on medical grounds. Caldwell thus escaped extradition and could live in relative comfort in the private wing of the Ward Island Asylum for the Insane. He was reported to have died there in 1911.[35]

## THE END OF THE STORY

IT IS CLEAR that the Druce-Portland affair originated in the mind of Anna Maria Druce. The instigator of the entire business, she herself fully believed every ludicrous detail of her story. It is equally clear that she was not quite sane, possibly a paranoid schizophrenic with delusions of grandeur, just like some of the false dauphins. Her tenacity and single-mindedness deserved a better cause, and she demonstrated her cleverness by the way she kept her opponents at bay during the 1898 trial. She had many other obvious delusions of grandeur. She claimed that she was a Miss Butler and that her father was a member of the gentry and agent to Lord Pembroke, but this was mere fantasy, similar to her idea that Thomas Charles Druce's wife, Annie May, was the daughter of the earl of Berkeley and that old Mrs. Hamilton was really the dowager duchess of Abercorn.[36] It is interesting that a newspaper account from 1895 mentions that Mrs. Druce was characteristically agitated in an appearance in court in June 1895, before the Bow Street magistrate Sir John Bridge, claiming that her son was the rightful duke of Somerset.[37] She shortly afterward altered her claim to that of the dukedom of Portland, very likely because Thomas Charles Druce was one of the duke's London tenants, whose name was mentioned on old lease documents for the Baker Street Bazaar. Had Mrs. Druce chosen any other nobleman or magnate, her claim would have had scant success, but the fifth duke of Portland was unique; in spite of his noble title and enormous wealth, he had no wife or children and no friends or business associates, and lived in near-total isolation from his fellow humans. Such behavior gave rise to rumor and speculation that he was hiding some hideous secret. In reality, he seems to have been suffering from abnormal shyness since an early age, particularly with regard to women; over the years, this shyness turned into bitterness, hypochondria, and egotism. Mrs. Druce was actually in a stronger position than she knew in 1901, and it may well be true that she refused an offer from the sixth duke to settle the case.[38] So very little was known about the fifth duke's doings that even John George Littlechild was baffled and resorted to his disreputable scheme of blackmailing Mrs. Hamilton. Mrs. Druce was reported to have been in a lunatic asylum in 1903, but, according to Littlechild, she was living in opulence in a London hotel in 1907, being handsomely paid off by the Australian contingent. She died in 1911.[39]

But what about the second claimant, George Hollamby Druce? It has been stated by several authors on the case that he was an honest, sincere man, who really believed the entire ludicrous story. His solicitor Coburn did everything he could to project this image: when the sixth duke of Portland gloatingly referred to Druce as an impostor in a speech, Coburn had the effrontery to write to him to complain about this insult to his client.[40] But there is good evidence that both Druce and Coburn were ruthless swindlers. Mrs. Robinson wrote a confession while in prison, detailing how Druce had recruited her to the cause after she had written him a letter about the fifth duke; it had been his idea that she should fabricate a false diary about her friendship with the duke.[41] John George Littlechild did not for one moment doubt that both Druce and Coburn were out-and-out crooks.[42] Much more clever and worldly-wise than Mrs. Druce, they milked the favorable press coverage and the populist feelings of the time for all they were worth. The cunning ruse to spread rumors that the duke was going to settle for a large sum lured many an unwary investor into the net of the two antipodean con men. They earned huge amounts from the sale of their bonds and are unlikely to have spent all of this money on their amusements. After the trial, Druce and Coburn claimed they were bankrupt and dissolved all their companies, but Littlechild suspected that they had hidden funds and ordered his agents to follow them day and night.[43] The two Australians and their families gave no hint, however, where they had stashed their takings, and quietly slipped back to their native continent. In 1913, Druce tried to revive his claim, but without success.

The dukedom of Portland became extinct after the death of the ninth duke, a distinguished diplomat, and Welbeck Abbey is today an army college.[44] The garden and some of the underground rooms are at times open to the public, and two architectural historians who were allowed to see them in the 1990s were much awed by the extent of the tunnels and excavations.[45] The duke's underground ballroom is today the gymnasium of the military college, proving that even the weirdest and most romantic flight of fancy will eventually become bogged down by common utilitarianism.

# 7

## *A World of Mysteries*

THE BEST-KNOWN claimant to royalty in the twentieth century was
Anna Anderson, the alleged Grand Duchess Anastasia of Russia. Her
career as a pseudo-royal is one of the longest in history. In 1920, two
years after the murder of the last tsar and his family, a confused
woman was pulled out of a canal in Berlin. She claimed that she was
Grand Duchess Anastasia, the daughter of Nicholas II (and the great-
great-grandniece of Alexander I, alias Feodor Kuzmich). She played
dead when her parents and siblings were shot, she said, and evaded
the Bolshevik patrols with the help of a loyal soldier. She married this
soldier and had a child by him, but he died during street fighting in
Bucharest. Anna then escaped to Germany and, after her rescue from
the canal, made her true identity known. Some German nobles and
Russian émigrés felt pity for her and let her stay in their houses to be
confronted by various people who had known the real grand duchess.
Several servants and old soldiers, and also the tsar's doctor Gleb Bodkin, recognized her, and became her core supporters. Grand Duchess

Olga, the sister of Nicholas II, who had no doubt that Feodor Kuzmich was really Alexander I, was much more skeptical when facing her alleged niece; she proclaimed that Anna was an impostor.

Like the Tichborne Claimant, Anna cleverly learned details from Bodkin and her other friends, to be able to impress other witnesses with her knowledge of various odd details of life at the tsar's court. To her considerable detriment, though, she did not share the Claimant's jovial and easygoing temperament. Throughout her long and troubled life, Anna remained a quarrelsome, difficult character, who fell out with her friends and broke with her well-wishers. But just as Naundorff had persistently claimed to be the Lost Dauphin, she stubbornly maintained that she was really the lost Anastasia, although she shared the French pretender's linguistic backwardness; when asked to speak Russian, she always declined to do so. Already in middle age, Anna Anderson looked more like a fairy-tale witch than a fairy-tale princess, for she had lost all her teeth and preferred to dress in old tattered garments.

After the German legal system failed to uphold her claim in a lengthy series of trials, Anna went to the United States, where she married the eccentric American Jack Manahan in 1968 and set up headquarters in his large house in Charlottesville, Virginia. Manahan took care of his nervous and frail wife as well as he could, before he himself became an invalid owing to diabetes and some kind of dementia. The Manahans had thirty cats and the same number of large fierce dogs; the latter guarded the growing piles of garbage outside their house and chased mailmen and delivery boys away. In 1983, Anna was finally taken to a mental hospital, and she died the year after in a hospital in Virginia.[1]

In 1991, Russian scientists announced that some of the skeletons of the murdered Tsar Nicholas and his family had been found. The dental evidence, and also comparison with mitochondrial DNA of present-day Romanov descendants, later verified this finding.[2] Since the bones of the tsarevitch and one daughter were missing, it was impossible to say whether Anastasia's bones were among those found.[3]

The Romanov mitochondrial DNA did not match that from a hair sample and an intestinal biopsy taken from Anna Anderson during life. In the 1920s and 1930s, there had been speculation that Anna was in fact a Polish factory worker named Franziska Schanzkowska. One of Schanzkowska's sisters had claimed Anna as her kinswoman, but Anna had regally dismissed her. It turned out, however, that mitochondrial DNA from a tissue sample from one of Schanzkowska's family members matched that of Anna Anderson.[4] Thus it can be concluded that, like Naundorff, Anna Anderson was an impostor. But the books and films about the pseudo-Anastasia have made her famous, and people still want to believe her story. They speculate that the KGB faked the tsar's remains or that the CIA switched biopsies in the hospital, and some Internet homepages still uphold her claim.

The reader remembering the false dauphins will not be surprised that there was more than one Anastasia claimant. In the years after the Russian revolution, bogus grand duchesses and tsarevitches appeared in every Siberian town. Since World War II, there have been at least ten Anastasias: three in Britain, one in Tokyo, one in Russia, and one in Montreal. One American claimant appeared in Rhode Island in the 1960s; another ran the Anastasia Beauty Salon in Illinois. The only one of them to achieve even a small fraction of Anna Anderson's fame was Eugenia Smith, who wrote her memoirs in 1963 and passed a lie detector test arranged by *Life* magazine. Her story was unconvincing however, and when asked to provide a DNA sample in the mid-1990s, she refused. The ten Anastasias had no shortage of sisters to choose from; there were at least three claimants for each of the titles of Grand Duchesses Olga, Maria, and Tatiana.[5]

And these bogus grand duchesses were not lacking in brothers. Of the eight men claiming to be Tsarevitch Alexis, the most prominent was the Polish secret service officer Colonel Michael Goleniewski, who defected in 1960 and went to the United States. A brazen impostor, he claimed that his father the tsar had lived on in Poland until 1952 and that three of his sisters were still living there. Eugenia Smith, the bogus Anastasia, was his fourth sister, he claimed, and they had a touching reunion, only to denounce each other a few weeks later. Goleniewski died in New York in 1993, sharing his "sister" Eugenia Smith's distrust of DNA testing to the last. Another Alexis claimant was active in Australia, where he sold noble titles to the highest bidder. In the 1990s, there were two claimants by proxy, each of whom proposed his deceased father as the tsarevitsch and himself as the heir to the throne.[6] A powerful argument against these pseudo-Alexises is that they were reasonably healthy and fit, and lived to a respectable age. The undoubted Alexis suffered from severe hemophilia coupled with arthritis of the knees; had he reached adulthood, he would have become crippled by secondary knee osteoarthritis. Anna Anderson's biographer James Blair Lovell aptly summarized the situation with regard to these ubiquitous Romanov claimants; when working on his book, he was continually pestered by sane or insane women who said they were Anastasia's daughter or granddaughter from a secret marriage, or claiming descent from one of the last tsar's other children.

## LOST HEIRS, SECRET MARRIAGES, AND IMMORTAL KINGS

THESE SURVIVAL LEGENDS concerning the Russian imperial family are examples of the "lost heir" historical mystery. An heir or heiress to a royal title and/or vast fortune disappears under tragic and mysterious circumstances that allow the possibility of survival, and after a certain period of time pretenders start to appear. As we know, there were more than a hundred false dauphins and enough pretended children of Tsar Nicholas II to repopulate the imperial family several times over.

Some early lost heirs were the products of political intrigue, like Lambert Simnel and Perkin Warbeck, who appeared after the "Princes in the Tower," the two young sons of King Edward IV, had disappeared in the 1480s.[7] A very similar story is that of the three false

Dmitris of Russia, who pretended to be the lost son of Tsar Ivan the Terrible, who had died under mysterious circumstances in 1591.[8] The first of them actually managed to usurp the throne in 1605 and became very popular, since he tried to protect the people from the tyranny of the aristocracy. But the false Dmitri reigned little more than a year before he was murdered in a riot. Later historians have speculated that he was really a monk named Yuri Otrepyev.

A well-known twentieth-century lost heir is the infant son of Colonel Charles Lindbergh, kidnapped for ransom in 1932. What was purported to be his dead body was later found and identified by the family. The carpenter Bruno Hauptmann was convicted for the kidnapping and murder and executed in the electric chair. Although strong forensic evidence links Hauptmann with the crime, some people have continued to doubt his guilt. Conspiracy theories have abounded: had the baby been kidnapped and murdered by the Mafia, by the gang of Al Capone, by his aunt Elizabeth Morrow, or even by Charles Lindbergh himself? More audacious still is the suggestion that Charles Lindbergh Jr. was not killed at all. It has been claimed that a gang of bootleggers from New York used to ship their liquor on the back roads near the area searched by the police looking for the Lindbergh baby. Fed up with being stopped and searched by the police, they prepared a baby's corpse and planted it in the woods to get the police off their tracks and enable them to ply their trade as usual.

In the 1970s and 1980s, several claimants surfaced, attracted by the Lindbergh millions; they had implausible tales to tell. The factory worker Kenneth Kerwin claimed to have recalled being kidnapped as a child in a session of hypnotic regression; he could also describe the Lindbergh nursery in some detail. But his adopted father told the journalists that Kerwin was certainly not a Lindbergh. His claim was not aided by the fact that whereas he had brown hair and dark eyes, Charles Lindbergh Jr. had been blond and blue-eyed. The fellow claimant Lorne Huxted also "remembered" his true identity during a hypnosis session and even passed a lie detector test. Following Naundorff's precedent, he had his name legally changed to Charles Augustus Lindbergh Jr. In the 1990s, he was still pursuing his claim.

The best-known Lindbergh claimant is the Connecticut business-man Harold Olson. His story was that Colonel Lindbergh had been a leading crime fighter in the Prohibition era. The imaginative Olson claimed that Lindbergh used to fly his airplane over New Jersey to mark the coordinates of any plume of smoke that would indicate an illicit distillery for moonshine whisky and then called in the police. Some of the bootleggers decided to get back at Lindbergh by kidnapping his son. Framing Hauptmann as the kidnapper was part of the plot. They then used the Lindbergh baby in a blackmailing scheme to spring Al Capone from prison, but Lindbergh chose to sacrifice his son rather than to be responsible for this notorious gangster's being set at large. The ending of this preposterous story is that after their plot had failed, the gangsters no longer had any use for their hostage. With uncharacteristic clemency, they did not kill him, but instead were kind enough to hand him over to caring foster parents. Both Olson and Kerwin were still active in 2002, along with at least five other pretenders, one of them a black woman from Oklahoma, who told the journalists a wild story of skin dyes and sex-change operations. The pretenders demand DNA testing, but the Lindbergh family has ignored them.[9]

———

MOST ROYAL FAMILIES have had their fair share of bastard children. In Britain, King Charles II was notorious for his many amours with various ladies at his merry court; more than a few noble families can boast royal blood as a result of the king's attentions to their forebears. As we have seen, George III's brothers and sons also sowed their wild oats freely. A bastard child of a royal personage can claim neither title nor inheritance, but the situation changes completely if it can be proved that the king or duke secretly married the mother. The legend of Hannah Lightfoot is the most famous example of this. Although there was a preexisting London tradition about the prince and the fair quaker, it is clear that much of the publicity about the case in the 1820s was due to the activities of Princess Olive, who herself claimed royal descent from another secret marriage.

Another curious example of a "secret marriage" mystery comes from nineteenth-century Sweden. King Gustaf IV Adolf of Sweden, who reigned from 1792 until 1809, was a feeble creature—wrong-headed, incompetent, and bigoted. The only redeeming elements in his character were his heartfelt religiosity and high moral values. His disastrous foreign policy ran the country into war with Russia, resulting in the loss of the province of Finland to the armies of Tsar Alexander I. Not long thereafter, the king was dethroned and exiled to Germany. There he underwent a complete personality change; he divorced the queen, drank and reveled to excess, slept with many prostitutes, and left a trail of illegitimate little princes and princesses all over Germany. In the meantime, the French marshal Jean Baptiste Bernadotte was elected king of Sweden; after his death, the throne was inherited by his son Oscar I. But at this time a strange woman with aristocratic looks and demeanor appeared in Stockholm. She called herself Helga de la Brache and claimed to be the legitimate daughter of Gustaf IV Adolf and Queen Fredrika, who she alleged had briefly reconciled and secretly remarried during the exiled king's travels in Germany. Queen Fredrika was a princess of Baden, and this would have made Helga de la Brache the cousin of Kaspar Hauser, if both their claims had been genuine. Many upper-class people in Stockholm accepted Helga de la Brache as a princess of the old Vasa dynasty, and King Oscar himself gave her a pension and paid off her debts. She was called the Ghost of the Kingdom of Sweden, since it was believed that she had dangerous knowledge that might even enable her to claim the throne. A gloomy, hypochondriacal character, this Scandinavian pretender wholly lacked the dash and vivacity of Princess Olive. In the 1870s, a clergyman looked into the Ghost's past and exposed her as Aurora Magnusson, the daughter of a poor, drunken customs constable. The king stopped her pension, and the Ghost died impoverished in 1885. Later research has supported the conclusion that she was an impostor.[10]

The "Sickert legend," well known to students of Jack the Ripper and his crimes, is yet another variation on the "secret marriage" theme. Since the 1970s, the artist Joseph Sickert claimed that the duke of

Clarence, the grandson of Queen Victoria and the heir to the throne, had secretly married a lower-class woman named Annie Elizabeth Crook. They had a daughter named Alice Margaret, who reached adulthood; she had an affair with the artist Walter Sickert that produced Joseph himself, born in 1925 and the sole descendant of the duke of Clarence. But the story does not end there. According to a fanciful author whom Sickert had fed with information in 1975, both the duke and Annie Elizabeth were kidnapped by Queen Victoria's agents, and she was operated on by the sinister physician Sir William Gull to render her a lunatic for life. But five East End prostitutes knew the truth about the duke's secret marriage and resorted to blackmail. The queen then dispatched Sir William Gull, Walter Sickert, and a coachman named John Netley to murder all five women; this was the plot behind the Jack the Ripper killings in 1888. This audacious theory attracted much newspaper publicity, but it suffered a drawback in 1978, when Joseph Sickert confessed that his tale of Gull as the Ripper was a complete invention. He still maintained that he himself had royal blood. In 1991, Sickert was up to his old tricks again. He told an amateur historian another spicy story: the Ripper commando had been led not by Gull but by Lord Randolph Churchill, the father of Winston. More competent authorities on the Ripper crimes have tended to disregard the Sickert legend altogether, and parts of it have been proven to be false.[11]

———

A THIRD TYPE of legend is that of a wealthy, powerful individual who decides to "disappear" and plots to make people believe that he or she has really died. The motive for this can be world-weariness, a love affair with an unsuitable partner, or a desire to seek obscurity. In the case of the fifth duke of Portland, it was purported to have been a desire for seclusion. In the legend of Alexander I, alias Feodor Kuzmich, it was a sense of guilt; as a penance for having plotted to kill his own father, the tsar had to humble himself as a hermit in Siberia. This interpretation of the legend had a symbolic meaning to many

Russians, since several similar tales were current at the time. One told that Alexander's wife, Empress Elizabeth, did not die in 1826; rather, she also faked her death and lived on for more than a decade as Vera the Silent, a humble nun in Siberia.

Charles XII, Sweden's famous warrior king, was shot dead, quite possibly by his own men, in 1718. But many Swedes refused to believe that he was really dead. There were tales that the king was walking the countryside, disguised as a tramp, to find out whether the people still supported him after eighteen years of war and carnage. In 1721, a claimant appeared in Dalecarlia and managed to convince quite a few people he was Charles XII. When arrested by the authorities for inciting rebellion, he confessed that he was an apprentice goldsmith named Benjamin Dyster.[12]

Another allegedly immortal Swedish royal was Prince Gustaf, the son of the aforementioned Oscar I, who supported Helga de la Brache. He was very popular, and there was much consternation when he suddenly died in 1852, at the age of just twenty-five, having been healthy and fit. Rumors soon spread in Sweden that the prince had faked his death, since he had fallen madly in love with a Russian countess, whom his family had forbidden him to marry. There were even alleged sightings of the prince, living abroad with his new wife. In reality, there is little doubt about Prince Gustaf's death.[13]

More mysterious is the death of Archduke Johann Salvator of Austria, presumed to have been lost at sea in 1890. A feckless, dissatisfied character, he had changed his name to Johann Orth, married an opera dancer, and denounced his noble titles the year before. He aspired to become a merchant mariner, purchased a large sailing ship, and took it for a lengthy cruise to South America. The impetuous archduke was last seen in La Plata, where he dismissed the ship's captain, took command himself, and left for Valparaiso. He never arrived, and no trace of his ship was ever found. His mother refused to believe that he was dead. Rumors had it that he had faked his own death to escape into obscurity, and he was sighted as a monk in Spain, a lumberjack in Uruguay, a playboy in Biarritz, and a polar explorer on his way to the Antarctic.[14]

Marshal Michel Ney was one of Napoleon's leading military commanders. The emperor used to call him "the Bravest of the Brave." After Napoleon's abdication and fall, Ney swore allegiance to the dismal Bourbon monarch Louis XVIII. When the emperor returned from Elba in 1814, Ney was sent at the head of an army to capture him. But most of France joined Napoleon's uprising, and so did Ney and his entire army. Napoleon's glorious Hundred Days ended at Waterloo, where the valiant Ney led the last charge of the Old Guard. After Waterloo, there was a general amnesty for Napoleon's supporters, but Ney was not included. In spite of objections from the duke of Wellington, Ney was led out for execution. According to eyewitnesses, he was killed instantly by the firing squad. But it was rumored that Ney had been saved by Wellington, who had thought it unsporting to have his old adversary executed, or that the French soldiers had loaded their rifles with blanks and smuggled Ney away after this mock execution. In 1819, a schoolmaster named Philip Stuart Ney turned up in Georgetown, South Carolina. He looked like Marshal Ney, was an expert swordsman, and had intimate knowledge of the Napoleonic Wars. Some of the anecdotes about him have an uncanny resemblance to those told about Feodor Kuzmich. Once, an old French soldier fell to his knees when he recognized the schoolmaster as his former commander. Another time, he was visited by a mysterious stranger, whose identity he refused to divulge; it later emerged that one of the marshal's sons, Count Eugene Ney, had visited America at this time. When Napoleon's death at St. Helena was announced, Philip Stuart Ney fainted and fell to the floor. But unlike the Siberian hermit, Ney the schoolmaster freely claimed to be the marshal; the soldiers in the firing squad had been aiming high at the orders of the duke of Wellington, he said, and he had placed a sack of red liquid on his chest to give the appearance of blood. Although some historians have accepted Philip Stuart Ney's story, most biographers of the marshal have been unconvinced, rightly pointing out that there is no hard evidence supporting his claim. Ney the schoolmaster knew Latin, Greek, and Hebrew, languages Ney the marshal had never studied.

Furthermore, the marshal's young wife was still living in France, yet Philip Stuart Ney never contacted her.[15]

The United States has no kings, queens, and nobles to spin legends around, but the "immortal king" legend nevertheless makes its appearance in American culture. Probably the best-known example is the case of John Wilkes Booth, the assassin of Abraham Lincoln. Conventional history states that Booth was shot dead at Garratts Farm, Virginia, on April 26, 1865, twelve days after killing Lincoln at Ford's Theatre, in Washington. But speculation has been rife that the assassin managed to escape or that the body of another man was given out to be that of Booth as part of a larger conspiracy. There were also rumors that Booth was alive long after 1857. One had it that he became an actor in San Francisco, another that he kept a saloon in Granbury, Texas, and a third that he went to Bombay, where he was last heard of in 1879. In 1903, in Enid, Oklahoma, a man named David George confessed on his deathbed that he was really John Wilkes Booth. Although some people objected that he was much taller than Booth and had blue eyes whereas Booth's were black, the Memphis lawyer Finis L. Bates bought the corpse, had it mummified, and set out to exhibit it in the circus. Bates wrote a book to prove his mummy was really that of John Wilkes Booth, but he was much ridiculed and died penniless in 1923. The later career of the mummy was as adventurous as that of the heart of the Temple Child: it was bought and sold, seized for debt, chased out of town for not having a license, and at least once kidnapped for ransom. It remained a steady earner throughout its long sideshow career. In the 1930s, it was x-rayed in an attempt to prove it was really Booth's, but results were inconclusive. Many Texans saw the Booth mummy on the carnival circuit during the 1930s and 1940s; it was exhibited as late as 1972, but its present whereabouts are unknown.[16]

Booth is not the only notorious American to be credited with amazing powers of survival. As a part of the glorification of nineteenth-century gunslingers and twentieth-century gangsters, legends of immortality have cropped up about quite a few of them. Jesse James was not killed in 1882, but lived on in Granbury, Texas, until his death in 1951, at the ripe old age of 103. Billy the Kid lived nearby and attended Jesse's 102nd birthday party in 1949. Butch Cassidy and the Sundance Kid did not die in Bolivia, but went back to the United States and led a comfortable life for many years. The notorious outlaw and gunslinger Wild Bill Longley cheated the hangman in 1878 and lived on for forty-five more years as the quiet family man John Calhoun Brown in Iberville Parish, Louisiana. It was not the gangster John Dillinger who was killed in Chicago in 1934 but his double, and the real Dillinger lived on into the 1960s. Professional historians have marveled at these legends, which have very little foundation in fact, but this has not kept them from gaining a fanatical following among various enthusiasts.[17] Longley's execution was witnessed by four thousand people, three doctors declared him dead, and the sheriff personally nailed the coffin shut. Yet the interest in proving that Wild Bill had survived was such that an exhumation of the gunslinger's skeleton was made in 2001. Its DNA matched that of one of Longley's descendants.[18] Science has also disproved the ridiculous myth about the centenarian Jesse James: the 1882 remains were exhumed, and its mitochondrial DNA matched that of two of Jesse's descendants.[19]

There are several twentieth-century examples of the unexpected death of a famous public character triggering the creation of a similar myth. When Lord Kitchener, the secretary of state for war, was lost at sea in 1916, rumors spread that he lived on as a captive, having been taken to Germany in a U-boat, or that he had become a hermit living on an isolated island. When Amelia Earhart, the celebrated aviator, disappeared in 1937, rumors started to fly that she had been captured by the Japanese or that she had faked her own death to escape from the public eye, finally ending up in a New Jersey retirement home in the 1970s.[20] The case of Elvis Presley has many of the typical components of the "immortal king" legend. It has been alleged that, like Alexander I of Russia, the king had become tired of fame and riches and wanted to withdraw from the world. As the duke of Portland was presumed to have done, he had a wax effigy made, complete with large bushy sideburns, to persuade the many fans attending his lying in state in Memphis that he was really dead. The coffin was also presumed to contain portable refrigeration equipment to prevent the wax dummy from melting in the hot weather; the result was that the ten pallbearers were groaning under its weight as they struggled to carry it to the grave.[21] The madcap speculation that J. F. Kennedy and Marilyn Monroe are still alive, or that Jim Morrison (of the Doors) and John Lennon faked their deaths to escape into obscurity, is in the same vein as the tale of the immortal Elvis.

The best-known example of an "immortal" modern celebrity is Diana, Princess of Wales. Her tragic death in Paris stunned the world, and it did not take long for urban legends to grow about what really happened in the tunnel underneath the Seine where the Mercedes carrying the princess and her entourage crashed in 1997. Conspiracy theories have abounded. Had she been murdered by the British secret service for wanting to marry her "unsuitable" lover Dodi al-Fayed, the son of Mohammad al-Fayed, the owner of the famous Harrods department store in London? Or had the queen and the duke of Edinburgh decided that she had to be killed, for Prince Charles to be able to marry his longtime paramour Camilla Parker Bowles? Another conspiracy theory was that the princess had decided to fake her own death. Like Alexander I of Russia and Elvis Presley, she was supposed to have tired of being chased by the media, and decided to retire to a quiet life with young al-Fayed. There have been alleged sightings of Diana in Hong Kong and Japan, and conspiracy theorists have presumed that she lives with al-Fayed in an Asian island paradise. This leaves unexplained why she has not contacted her two sons, but there has been speculation on the Internet that she visited them incognito in the guise of a royal nanny, after having undergone extensive plastic surgery to change her appearance.

———

A FOURTH TYPE of legend is that of the mysterious simpleton—a child or young adult who suddenly appears out of nowhere, unable to explain his or her history and origins. The mysterious simpleton is taken care of by the kindly local people, but there is soon speculation that he or she must be someone of very high birth, who has been rendered unable to enjoy the privileges of nobility by accident or by stratagem. The mystery of Kaspar Hauser is the most famous example of this type of legend, but by no means the only one.

In 1776, a young woman was begging in the villages near Bristol. A beautiful, fragile-looking creature, she was obviously of superior breeding. She refused to live in a house, preferring to sleep in a haystack just outside the village of Bourton. This singular habit made "Louisa, the Lady of the Haystack," a well-known local curiosity.[22] She could speak good English, although it was noted that she was obviously of foreign birth. Louisa's friends advertised widely in German, Austrian, and French newspapers to find out whether any well-bred young lady had been lost in either of these countries, but they received no replies of interest. Louisa's mind became increasingly feeble and clouded, and she was finally incarcerated in a lunatic asylum. But in the 1780s a pamphlet appeared in the French language, describing how a certain Count Cobenzel, the Austrian minister at Brussels, had been charged with taking care of a mysterious young lady. She had been brought up by two old women in an isolated house, but was sometimes visited by a handsome officer who showed her much kindness. Once, in the Austrian embassy, she fainted dead away when she recognized her benefactor in a large portrait—a painting of the late Emperor Francis of Austria.

After traveling on to Bordeaux, our heroine became known as Mademoiselle La Frülen and received generous financial support from wealthy noblemen. Her great likeness to the late emperor was remarked upon by Count Cobenzel and others, and caused much gossip in town. Suddenly, her benefactors withdrew their support, and she was arrested for debt and taken to the count's house. The dowager empress made public her belief that Mademoiselle La Frülen was an impostor claiming to be a natural daughter of the late emperor. The pamphlet leaves it unstated what means were taken to dispose of Mademoiselle La Frülen. Louisa's friends in Bristol at once suspected that she had lost her reason as a result of her sufferings and been set at liberty in the English countryside, where her enemies thought no one would recognize her. Thus the Lady of the Haystacks was none other than the daughter of Francis I, emperor of Austria. Poor Louisa's clouded mind gave few clues as to her identity, although her friends questioned her as closely as Feuerbach and others had interrogated Kaspar Hauser in trying to uncover his true identity. It was considered significant that she laughed merrily whenever anyone spoke German and that she said, "That is papa's own country!," when Bohemia was mentioned in the conversation. It is obvious, however, that Louisa's claim suffers from a similar lack of hard evidence and surfeit of sentimental speculation as the myth of Kaspar's Baden princedom.

There are hints of the mysterious simpleton also in the strange tale of Princess Caraboo.[23] In April 1817, a mysterious young girl appeared in the village of Almondbury, in Gloucestershire. Lost and penniless, she appeared to speak no European language. She kept repeating the word "Caraboo," and it was presumed this was her name. The kind people gave her food and shelter and put much effort into finding out who this mysterious simpleton might be. She dressed in strange Oriental garb, armed herself with a bow and arrows, and performed wild, dervish-like dances. When the vicar showed her some Chinese prints, she appeared to recognize them. Several experts came to see her to find out which language she spoke, but the great linguists were confounded by her strange gibberish. To trick Caraboo, a witty cleric sneaked up behind her and whispered "You are the most beautiful creature I ever beheld! You are an angel!" When she did not show any sign of feminine modesty, it was concluded that she was no impostor. Finally, a Portuguese gentleman delighted everybody when he declared that he understood every word she said. She was Princess Caraboo, a native of a small island near Sumatra, who had been kidnapped by pirates and sold into slavery, before escaping and swimming ashore when the ship was sheltering from a storm. Princess Caraboo lived in comfort at the local manor house and then moved on to Bath, where she found new admirers. A certain Dr. Wilkinson showed great interest and persistence in deciphering her strange language and wrote a series of articles about her in the local newspapers. One of these had the unexpected result that a landlady named Mrs. Neale appeared, saying that the information given made her certain the princess was the servant girl Mary Baker, who had previously lodged in her house. Caraboo confessed that this was indeed the case. She had been tramping around the countryside with some Gypsies and picked up their language, which she enjoyed using to confound the linguists. She had sworn the Portuguese man into her joke, with excellent effect. It was never divulged what had prompted this remarkable imposture in the first place.

## THE LEGACY OF THE GREAT PRETENDERS

THUS WE HAVE seen that many of these historical legends and mysteries of disputed identity fit into a set of type legends, some of which have very ancient origins. The legend of the lost heir has echoes of the long absence of Ulysses and his return as a claimant. The legend of the mysterious simpleton who turns out to be a prince dates back to medieval folk tales. The legend of the immortal king has more than passing similarity to the medieval tradition of Emperor Barbarossa, who would rise again when his kingdom was in peril, or of King Sebastian of Portugal. In particular, there was a strong tradition in Russia, predating the false Dmitris, about the pious young tsar, the protector of the common people against the aristocracy, who rises from the dead in imitation of Christ.

The liking for mystifications and conundrums in nineteenth-century romantic history built on these ancient legends. It also interacted with the prevailing literary taste of the early nineteenth century. As Professor Richard D. Altick has convincingly argued, there was a symbiosis between the reporting of Victorian crime in newspapers and magazines and the fictional representation of crime and criminals in the sensa-tion novel.[24] In a similar manner, the nineteenth-century writer on his-torical mysteries presented his subject matter within the boundaries set by the traditional gothic novel. In these books, heirs to vast for-tunes are lost, secret marriages entered into, ancient castles haunted, and noble titles usurped. Elusive criminals are at large, enigmatic her-mits appear with cryptic prophecies, and mysterious prisoners are hid-den away in dark, inhospitable dungeons. The nineteenth-century reader had a liking for kings and lords, and as the typical gothic novel had an all-aristocrat cast, the historical mysteries took place in high circles of society. There was a fascination with royalty, wealth, and priv-ilege, coupled with disgust at the depravity and perfidy of those in power. Had there not been a conspiracy against blameless young Han-nah Lightfoot, who had been so cruelly treated by her false husband George III and the despicable Queen Charlotte? Had not Louis XVIII engineered a diabolical cover-up to keep the truth about the martyr king Louis XVII from becoming known, even going to the lengths of kidnapping his tragic sister Marie Thérèse and keeping her captive to prevent the truth from becoming known? The perfidy of the house of Baden in keeping the Christlike Kaspar Hauser away from his proper inheritance was a major tenet in mid-nineteenth-century German rad-ical propaganda. The Tichborne Claimant cleverly used the radical antiestablishment and anti-Catholic feelings, and also the traditional British liking for the jovial aristocrat and tendency to back the under-dog. Druce and Coburn played a similar game, but the time was no longer right, and they had much less success.

In terms of psychology, the legend of the king who faked his death seems to have arisen from the despair over the death of a public fig-ure that is so sudden and inopportune as to seem a perversion of fate's intentions. This was true for the battle-hardened king Charles XII, who was widely believed to be immortal, unless shot with a silver bul-let or with a button out of his own coat. Similar shock and alarm greeted the sudden death of popular young Tsar Alexander I, who had saved Russia from Napoleon's invasion. The refusal to accept a tragic, unexpected, and unnecessary death is apparent also in the modern cases of Elvis Presley and Diana, Princess of Wales.

With Louis XVII and other lost heirs, the anomaly is instead a historical one. After the Bourbon monarchy had been restored, many Frenchmen were horrified that their civilized nation could have committed such vile crimes against a defenseless young boy. This national remorse made many people unconsciously want Louis XVII to be alive, and allowed rumors of an escape from the Temple to grow like wildfire and the false dauphins to find many friends. That Marshal Ney, the bravest of the brave, had been executed as a common criminal by his own countrymen was another historical anomaly, which could be expunged by rumors that Ney was still alive. There was similar horror, remorse, and disgust at the wholesale murder of the Russian imperial family, particularly the ailing young son and blameless teenage daughters; the stage was set for people wanting to believe that at least one of these martyred grand duchesses survived the Bolshevik fusillade. In 1930s America, the kidnapping of Charles Lindbergh Jr. was a much publicized incident, and every decent American hoped the infant son of the great aviator would be rescued from the kidnappers. The murder of the Lindbergh baby was a particularly vile crime, only partially expunged by the execution of Bruno Hauptmann; the way was prepared for rumors that the child had not really died.

———

TO MANY PEOPLE, an impostor or "pretender" is a twentieth-century con artist like Stanley Weyman or Ferdinand Waldo Demara. Weyman had a liking for uniforms and often acted the part of a U.S. navy officer. During World War I, he pretended to be the Romanian consul general and once inspected a U.S. battleship before treating the officers to dinner at the Astor Hotel and having the bill sent to the Romanian consulate. On then finding out that Princess Fatima of Afghanistan was visiting the United States, he played the part of a state official and took her to Washington. A photograph of Weyman and the princess chatting to President Warren G. Harding on the White House lawn still exists. Later Weyman became a fashionable quack, and personal physician to the actress Pola Negri and her lover Rudolph Valentino.

Similarly, from an early age, Ferdinand Waldo Demara had an obsession to try out various academic professions. Although lacking any higher education, he successfully worked as a schoolmaster, a university lecturer, a zoologist, a vicar, and a cancer researcher. He received an award from the state of Texas for his valuable work as deputy governor for a large prison and was equally successful as faculty dean at a Pennsylvania university. By moving between states and frequently changing his name and alias, he kept one step ahead of the police. During the Korean War, Demara worked as a ship's doctor on a destroyer and was instrumental in saving some shipwrecked, wounded soldiers; this, ironically, led to his being discovered by the authorities. It is no coincidence that both Weyman and Demara acted as doctors at some stage in their careers; the field of medicine remained a particular magnet for the psychopathic impostor. Bogus doctors, some of them working for years before being seen through, are at large throughout the Western world.[25]

There are several parallels between these twentieth-century con artists and the great pretenders of history: they are intelligent, gifted, ruthless, and worldly and have superior verbal ability. Not driven solely by the quest for money, they take a perverse delight in deceiving people. But while Weyman, Demara, and others of that ilk have flitted from impersonating one prominent character to another, the likes of Olive Serres, Naundorff, and Anna Anderson have developed a fixed idea that they are a certain historical personage. A historical mystery is created if one of these talented impostors comes across a remarkable story. For example, Naundorff would have made little stir if he had claimed to be a lost plumber, nor would Anna Anderson had she insisted she was the daughter of a washerwoman; by plugging into two versions of the legend of the lost heir, they became immortal claimants to royalty, adding their own embellishments to the type legend as they went along.

---

ANOTHER RECURRING THEME in this book is the clash between conventional academic history and the romantic version of history spread by amateurs and conspiracy theorists. Today an insurmountable chasm separates the Oxford history professor writing scholarly papers on medieval agriculture, or pontificating on the intricacies of French law at the time of Louis XI, and the Internet conspiracy theorist trying to make a case that William Gladstone was Jack the Ripper or that Adolf Hitler escaped the Berlin bunker and lived to a ripe old age. But in the nineteenth century the gap between conventional and romantic history was much narrower. Widely read, eccentric dilettantes devoted their lives to solving great historical mysteries and sifted through vast quantities of contradictory evidence; both Naundorff and Kaspar Hauser recruited some of their warmest supporters from their ranks. Not until the 1950s could a clear and growing impatience with the survivalist rumors be noted among French academic historians, although their books on Louis XVII did little to put the national myth of the lost dauphin to sleep. In Germany, the Hauserians maintained the upper hand even longer. Hermann Pies and Johannes Mayer, whose herculean efforts to prove that Kaspar was the prince of Baden were reviewed earlier, were both private scholars. The rationalist German academics who wanted to point out the many shortcomings of the Hauserian propaganda had difficulties even getting their works into print. In some of the other historical cases of disputed identity, where the amount of conflicting evidence was much less, modern historians have succeeded in refuting the claims of some nineteenth-century great pretenders. The claim of Olive Serres was crushed by the 1930s, and that of Helga de la Brache by the 1970s. In addition, the arguments presented by Professor Roe, and reinforced by myself in this book, clearly refute the notion that the Tichborne Claimant was Roger Tichborne.

## THE END OF THE GREAT PRETENDERS?

AS WE HAVE seen, developments in medical science have reduced the ability of pretenders to come forward with claims, and have helped solve some of the great nineteenth-century mysteries. Since the early 1990s, DNA analysis has become a commonly accepted tool for investigating historical questions of disputed identity. Indeed, any skeleton in the royal closet, past or present, appears to be fair game for scientific testing. For example, there has long been a rumor among London journalists that eighteen-year-old Prince Harry, the son of Diana, Princess of Wales, was fathered not by Prince Charles but by her lover James Hewitt. To investigate this matter, some unscrupulous newsmen enlisted a pretty young lady to embrace the dashing Prince Harry in a nightclub—and secretly snip off some of his hair so that its DNA could be compared with Hewitt's.[26] It has to be kept in mind, however, that the results achieved by any DNA analysis in a case of disputed identity can be compromised by shortcomings in the method used or by questions concerning the authenticity of the material tested.

The genetic matter of the normal human being is arranged into forty-six chromosomes. Of these, twenty-two autosomes and one sex chromosome are inherited from each parent: the male is XY and the female XX. The use of autosomal DNA requires a close relationship between the individuals tested, as in the much publicized case of the Nazi doctor Josef Mengele, whose remains were compared with a DNA sample donated by his son, to prove he was truly dead.[27] But after several generations very little nuclear DNA is shared between the living relatives and their historical forebear. One way out is to study the Y chromosome, if there are descendants in the male line. A major drawback of this method is the risk of illegitimacy, prevalent in both high and low circles of society. If a handsome mailman has inserted his Y chromosome in place of that of a duke or prince, it would have dire consequences for a claimant's alleging descent from a common forebear. This should be taken into account when evaluating the aforementioned investigation of Hannah Lightfoot's putative descendants, which used comparison with Y chromosome DNA from the earl of Munster, a descendant from George III in unbroken male line. The better and more solid technique used most frequently is that of analyzing mitochondrial DNA. The mitochondria, subcellular organelles with their own DNA, are inherited in the female line, and thus this method would be confounded only by a secret adoption or substitution of children.

In most instances of DNA analysis of historical material, the method used is wholly appropriate, although the authenticity of the material tested is sometimes dubious. For example, it has long been alleged that King Charles XII of Sweden was killed by his own men, shot by a button cut out of his own coat. A candidate button was later found and has been in a Swedish museum since the 1920s. In 2001, it was determined that DNA from this button matched blood from Charles XII's gloves. But this button may well have been cleaned at the museum, and it has been handled by many people, resulting in deposit of body fluid of some description on the button; there is no method of establishing whether the genetic matter tested really originated from blood.[28] Neither a positive nor a negative match would have much significance.

For a more blatant misuse of DNA technology in the service of pseudo-history one needs to look no further than Patricia Cornwell's recent book that claims to close the case on the elusive Jack the Ripper. Since the 1970s, a theory had been stewing about that Walter Sickert, the eminent Victorian painter claimed as father by Joseph the fantasist, was somehow involved in the murder. The arguments for this were feeble, even by ripperology standards; he was fascinated by the Whitechapel murders and often discussed them, and it has been speculated that he had painted clues to the murders into his paintings, although art historians do not agree. Competent experts on the Ripper crimes have always found Sickert an unlikely suspect: he is not recorded to have committed any violent crime, he had no motive to murder prostitutes, and there is no evidence he was even in London at the time of the murders. In 1888 and 1889, the London police received many letters from people claiming to be Jack the Ripper. Around six hundred of these are still kept today; most, if not all, are considered the work of hoaxers. Sickert was cremated, but Cornwell devoted much energy to securing samples of mitochondrial DNA from a number of letters written by him, as well as from the Ripper letters kept at the Public Record Office. A DNA sequence found on some Sickert letters matched one of the Ripper letters, the so-called Openshaw letter, one long considered to have been a hoax. It is curious, however, that the sequence in question was found on letters from both Sickert himself and from his wife, Ellen, suggesting that they may have licked each other's stamps or used the same sponge to dampen the gum. It has been calculated that the DNA sequence in question would occur in approximately 1 percent of the population, meaning that 400,000 people in Victorian Britain would share it. All of those people would have to be ruled out to get merely close to proving that Sickert sent the letter. Thus what the book really achieves is to render it possible that Sickert had written a hoaxing Ripper letter, although even this assumption is based on slender evidence indeed.[29]

If the Cornwell Ripper investigation is basically flawed because of the doubtful authenticity of the material used, the opposite can be said for the investigation of the bones of the Russian imperial family, which is a model of its kind. Anthropological evidence and sex testing of the skeletons rendered it likely that the bones were the right ones. This was verified by comparison of mitochondrial DNA from the bones of the empress with that from a blood sample from Philip duke of Edinburgh, her grandnephew of unbroken maternal descent, as well as by comparison of that from the bones of the tsar with that from two living relatives of the same matrilineage. It was curious that the tsar had what is known as a heteroplasmy, namely that the individual's mitochondrial DNA has both matching and nonmatching sequences at one particular position; the authenticity of the bones was established when it was discovered that he shared this abnormality with his brother Grand Duke Georgij Romanov. Similarly, it is impossible to level any criticism against the clear and telling identification of Anna Anderson as Franziska Schanzkowska.

The investigation of Kaspar Hauser's claim to be the crown prince of Baden is valid only as long as the bloodstain on his coat is accepted as genuine. The bloodstain is definitely human blood, from an individual unrelated to Grand Duchess Stephanie of Baden. If someone had tried to "improve" it by using his or her own blood, one would have thought this would have become apparent during testing, unless the same individual had not taken pains to completely wash out the original bloodstain. But when this book was already in press, I discovered that in December 2002 a German TV documentary had reported some unexpected findings. Investigators had extracted mitochondrial DNA from Kaspar Hauser's sweat-stained hat and socks, and from some hair samples from him that had been taken by von Feuerbach. All these sources of DNA would on their own have appeared rather dubious, the hair samples in particular, but the result was actually that all six samples coincided, adding strength to the conclusion that these were really samples from Kaspar Hauser. They did not match the bloodstain from the underpants.[30] This would raise the suspicion that just as people had been gossiping in Ansbach, someone had "improved on" the bloodstain on Kaspar's underpants using human blood. The enterprising German TV journalists went on to compare these new DNA samples from Kaspar Hauser with one from a descendant of Grand Duchess Stephanie, no doubt hoping to prove the prince legend. To their chagrin, it did not match the DNA from the house of Baden. Nevertheless, these findings serve to demonstrate the potential fallacies of using DNA technology in investigating historical questions of disputed identity. The people who demanded an exhumation of Kaspar Hauser's skeleton before the DNA results could be accepted have belatedly been vindicated. Unless the Hauserians were right in their mutterings about grave-robbing commandos from the dastardly house of Baden, an exhumation would be the only way to obtain an undoubted DNA sample from Kaspar Hauser, in order to finally disprove the legend of Prince Kaspar. In my opinion, the weight of the medical and historical arguments against the prince theory is so overwhelming as to close the case, however.

The investigation of the mystery of the Lost Dauphin is also technically flawless. There is no doubt that the hair and bone originated from Naundorff, and his exposure as an impostor agrees well with the available historical evidence. The study of the dauphin's heart has the benefit of a positive match, indicating that it comes from a matrilineal descendant of Empress Maria Theresia, the mother of Marie Antoinette. But in this case the available historical and medical evidence is much less clear than in that of Kaspar Hauser; there are numerous puzzling circumstances indicating the possibility of a substitution of children, although not an escape. The impact of the DNA evidence is reduced by the fact that the heart several times shared a repository with other Habsburg hearts, and possibly also with the heart of the first dauphin, Louis Joseph, but this may just be my wish to believe that at least one proper historical mystery of disputed identity remains for future generations to ponder.

# Notes

CHAPTER 1: THE LOST DAUPHIN

1. Many thousands of books and articles have been written about the riddle of the Lost Dauphin. L. Parois, *Essai de bibliographie sur Louis XVII* (Paris, 1992), lists 1,192 items, but still claims only to summarize the most important literature on the subject. The nineteenth-century standard works are J. Eckard, *Mémoires historiques sur Louis XVII* (Paris, 1818), A. de Beauchesne, *Louis XVII* (Paris, 1852), translated as *Louis XVII* (New York, 1855), and R. Chantelauze, *Louis XVII* (Paris, 1884). Important twentieth-century contributions include G. Bord, *Autour du temple* (Paris, 1912), G. Lenôtre, *Le roi Louis XVII et l'énigme du Temple* (Paris, 1920), translated as *The Dauphin* (London, 1921), E. Muraise, *Du roy perdu à Louis XVII* (Paris, 1967) and *Les treize portes du Temple* (Paris, 1980), M. Garçon, *Louis XVII ou la fausse énigme* (Paris, 1968), A. Castelot, *Louis XVII* (Paris, 1971), R. Ambelain, "Capet, lève-toi . . ." (Paris, 1987), P. Conrad, *Louis XVII* (Geneva, 1993), P. Delorme, *L'affaire Louis XVII* (Paris, 1995), G. Bordonove, *Louis XVII et l'énigme du Temple* (Paris, 1995), P. E. Blanrue, *Le "Mystère du Temple"* (Paris, 1996),

and M. Lecoeur, *Louis XVII, dernier duc de Normandie* (Condé-sur-Noireau, 1998). Three worthwhile English-language sources are J. G. Lockhart, *Here Are Mysteries* (London, 1927), pp. 65–128, J. B. Morton, *The Dauphin* (London, 1937), and H. G. Francq, *Louis XVII: The Unsolved Mystery* (Leiden, 1970). D. Cadbury, *The Lost King of France* (London, 2002), gives an up-to-date review of the life and death of Louis XVII; a descriptive rather than an analytical work, it takes the solution of the mystery for granted.

2. On Baron de Batz, see G. Lenôtre, *A Gascon Royalist in Revolutionary Paris: The Baron de Batz* (London, 1910); on Mrs. Atkyns, see F. Barbey, *A Friend of Marie Antoinette* (London, 1906), and E. E. P. Tisdall, *Mrs. Pimpernel Atkyns* (London, 1965).

3. This quotation is from K. Prescott Wormeley, *The Ruin of a Princess* (London n.d.), p. 270.

4. Quoted in much detail, from the memoirs of Barras, by Lenôtre, *Dauphin*, pp. 192–98.

5. Harmand's account was originally published in the obscure collection *Anecdotes relatives à plusieurs événements remarquables de la révolution* (Paris, 1814), quoted extensively by Chantelauze, *Louis XVII*, pp. 301–10.

6. Lenôtre, *Dauphin*, pp. 243–44.

7. Desault's distinguished career has been described by C. J. Prat, *Un chirurgien au XVIIIe siècle: J.-P. Desault* (Paris, 1929), by B. Barker Beeson in *Annals of Medical History*, n.s., 5(1933): 342–48, and by the comtesse d'Armaille in *Hippocrate* 4(1936): 65–73. On the story of the niece, see H. Madol, *The Shadow-King* (Boston, 1930), p. 70.

8. Lenôtre, *Dauphin*, p. 246. On Pelletan's biography, see the article by J. Sonolet and J. Poulet in *Semaine des Hôpitaux de Paris* 48(1972): 3513–20. A. Decaux, *Louis XVII retrouvé* (Paris, 1947), pp. 104–8, lists a series of dubious sources said to show that Pelletan, Dumangin, and Jeanroy were all aware that a substitution of children had occurred.

9. The last days of the Temple Child have been described by de Beauchesne, *Louis XVII*, 2:301–37, and by Chantelauze, *Louis XVII*, pp. 386–423.

10. The autopsy report is given by O. Friedrichs and Dr. Cabanès in *La Chronique Médicale* 4(1897): 404–9, 472–73. Some authors, including the otherwise reliable Francq, in *Louis XVII*, pp. 91–93, have advanced the theory that he was poisoned, but there is no direct evidence for this, and the death is well explained by the autopsy findings. Equally dubiously, P. Sipriot, *Louis XVII et les mystères du temple* (Paris, 1994), p. 127, speculates that the death of the Temple Child was due to a particularly virulent worm infestation.

11. The identification procedure is thoroughly described by Chantelauze, *Louis XVII*, pp. 386–409, and by Lenôtre, *Dauphin*, pp. 254–74.

12. The debate about the grave of the Temple Child is reviewed by Chantelauze, *Louis XVII*, pp. 424–42, and by Francq, *Louis XVII*, pp. 94–107.

13. An admirable work on false dauphins in general is R. Le Conte, *Louis XVII et les faux Dauphins* (Paris, 1924); it is brought up to date by Delorme, *L'affaire Louis XVII*, pp. 129–51. Hervagault was described by A. de Beauchamp, *Le faux Dauphin actuellement en France* (Paris, 1818), and A. Vast, *Un faux Dauphin* (Paris, 1929).

14. On Bruneau, see A. de Beauchamp, *Histoire des deux faux Dauphins* (Paris, 1818), J. de Saint-Léger, *Louis XVII dit Charles de Navarre* (Paris, 1916), and V. Fourreau, *Le duc de Normandie, Charles de Navarre* (Paris, 1980).

15. On Richemont and his supporters, see J.-V. Claravali, *Vie de Mgr le duc de Normandie* (Paris, 1850), and J. de Bonnefon, *Le dossier du Roi* (Paris, 1908).

16. Naundorff's memoirs were published as *Abrégé de l'histoire des infortunes du Dauphin* (London, 1836), translated in M. Vitrac and A. Galopin, *The King Who Never Reigned* (London, 1908), pp. 173–270.

17. The Naundorffist point of view is ably summarized by M. Gruau de la Barre, *La branche aînée des Bourbons* (Haarlem, 1871), and O. Friedrichs, *Un crime politique* (Brussels, 1884); in English by P. Allen, *The Last Legitimate King of France* (London, 1912), and Madol, *Shadow-King*. E. Dupland, *Naundorff l'imposteur* (Paris, 1990), is fiercely anti-Naundorffist.

18. This is actually a historical mystery in its own right. There are still people who believe that Marie Thérèse was kidnapped and ended her days in Germany as the "Dark Countess of Hildburgshausen." A slightly more credible version of the story tells that Marie Thérèse became pregnant in 1795, probably after being raped in the Temple, and that she decided to withdraw from the world. Her half sister Ernestine de Lambriquet, an illegitimate daughter of Louis XVI, accepted to play her part and to marry the duke of Angoulême. But if the duchess of Angoulême was an impostor, she must have been among the most successful ever, since she played her role with consummate skill for more than fifty years. See O. V. Maeckel, *The Dunkelgraf Mystery* (London, 1929), and Prinz Friedrich Ernst von Sachsen-Altenburg, *Die Rätsel der Madame Royale* (Hildburgshausen, 1991), as well as the three articles by H. Rühle von Lilienstern in *Jahrbuch des hennebergisch-fränkischen Geschichtsverein* (1995): 137–202, (1997): 57–94, and (1999): 139–76. The story of the "Dark Countess" has many supporters both in France and in Germany, and in July 2002 plans were being made to exhume her skeleton for DNA testing against Marie Antoinette. See *Der Spiegel*, no. 29(2002): 52, and *Daily Telegraph*, July 28, 2002. There is also an excellent German Internet homepage about the mystery, www.madame-royale.de.

19. On Meves, see the book by his son "Auguste de Bourbon," *The Dauphin—Louis XVII* (London, 1876).

20. On these American candidates for Louis XVII, see Delorme, *L'affaire Louis XVII*, pp. 129–51. On Audubon, see A. J. Tyler, *"I Who Should Command All"—Audubon (Louis XVII)* (New York ,1942).

21. E. E. Evans, *The Story of Louis XVII of France* (London, 1893). Another curious source on the strange life of Eleazar Williams is P. V. Lawson, *Prince or Creole* (Menasha, Wis., 1905). Williams was not the only Native American pretender. The empress of the Washitaw tribe, an alleged descendant of Louis XVII who fled to the United States and married a squaw, claims that her tribe is the rightful owner of the Louisiana Territory, fraudulently claimed by the U.S. government in 1803.

22. On these two individuals, see Delorme, *L'affaire Louis XVII*, p. 150, and C. Jordan, *Louis XVII a-t-il été guillotiné?* (Paris, 1950).

23. On Madame Simon and her story, see Lenôtre, *Dauphin*, pp. 364–73, and also the second volume of his *Vielles maisons, vieux papiers* (Paris, 1908).

24. Variations on the theme of the Swiss Louis XVII are given by M. Minnigerode, *The Son of Marie Antionette* (London, 1935), and L. de La Chapelle, *Louis XVII* (Paris, 1995).

25. L. M. A. d'Andigné, *Mémoires* (Paris, 1901), 2:45–48. The Temple tower was demolished in 1810. See also A. Crosnier, *Le général d'Andigné* (Angers, 1893), pp. 59–61.

26. See Francq, *Louis XVII*, pp. 220–21; Bordonove, *Louis XVII*, pp. 345–53; L. A. Pitou, *L'urne des Stuarts et des Bourbons* (Paris, 1815), p. 351.

27. L. Hastier, *Le double mort de Louis XVII* (Paris, 1951) and *Nouvelles révélations sur Louis XVII* (Paris, 1954). Louis Hastier's ingenious theory has received support from a very logical and well-written book by E. Dupland, *Vie et mort du Louis XVII* (Paris, 1987), and a more whimsical study by P. Sipriot, *Louis XVII et les mystères du temple*. M. Grey, *Enquête sur le mort de Louis XVII* (Paris, 1988), has a more audacious theory, namely that Louis XVII caught typhoid from Desault, died on June 4, and was buried near the Temple.

28. See, in particular, the analysis by Francq, *Louis XVII*, pp. 211–23, 234–36.

29. J. Turquan, *Du nouveau sur Louis XVII* (Paris, 1908), translated in Vitrac and Galopin, *King Who Never Reigned*, pp. 271–359.

30. Two standard works for the rationalists are Garçon, *Louis XVII*, and Blanrue, *Le mystère*. On the arguments given here, see Lenôtre, *Dauphin*, pp. 260–63, and Morton, *Dauphin*, pp. 193–94. But Bellanger may have misdated his account; see Dupland, *Vie et mort*, pp. 284–85.

31. These stories are given by de Beauchesne, *Louis XVII*, 2:245, 260, 279, 293, 319, 321.

32. In particular, the erudite historian Georges Lenôtre was led badly astray. He proposed a daring rescue from the Temple and a link between the Lost Dauphin and the murder of the Petitval family in 1795, all on the basis of documentary material of very dubious origin.

33. Francq, *Louis XVII*, pp. 67–68; Madol, *Shadow-King*, p. 81. See also Decaux, *Louis XVII retrouvé*, pp. 52–65.

34. Dr. Stuyt in *Histoire de la Médicine* 6(1956): 31–44, and E. Dupland, *Naundorff*, pp. 372–78.

35. These portraits have been reproduced by Lenôtre, *Dauphin*, and Castelot, *Louis XVII*, among others.

36. Francq, *Louis XVII*, p. 95.

37. Lenôtre, *Dauphin*, pp. 360–62.

38. F. de Backer, *Louis XVII au cimetière Sainte-Marguerite* (Paris, 1894); see also Francq, *Louis XVII*, pp. 100–15, 171–83. A more critical view is that of Delorme, *L'affaire Louis XVII*, pp. 177–85, and P. L. Thillaud in *Cahiers de la Rotonde* 6(1983): 81–90.

39. On these excavations, see the articles by P. Pascal-Sol in *La Science Historique* 55(1976): 17–21, and P. L. Thillaud in *Cahiers de la Rotonde* 6(1983): 91–97.

40. Castelot, *Louis XVII*. The original papers were published in *La Gerbe*, Dec. 9, 1943, and *Le Figaro Littéraire*, June 16, 1951. The forensic scientist P.-F. Puech, in *International Journal of Legal Medicine* 107(1995): 209–12, used another approach—a computerized facial reconstruction based on the 1846 skull, which did not agree with the authentic portraits of Louis Charles. The studies of Castelot and Puech add further weight to the evidence that the bones in the Sainte-Marguerite cemetery were not those of Louis XVII.

41. Many of the older writers, including the otherwise reliable Chantelauze, in *Louis XVII*, pp. 248–55, are completely out of their depth when commenting on the medical aspects. More adequate discussions on the disease of Louis XVII and the Temple Child are given by A. Corlieu in *Gazette des Hôpitaux de Paris* 49(1876): 1062–63, 1070–71, 1077–78, Dr. Cabanès in *Journal de Médecine de Paris*, 2d ser., 3(1891): 435–37, and 5(1893): 257–60, O. Friedrichs and Dr. Cabanès in *La Chronique Médicale* 4(1897): 404–9, 472–73, L. Picard in *Gazette Médicale de Paris* 4(1904): 349–51, 361–63, and Prof. Dauwe in *Le Scalpel* 111(1958): 1002–15. Of particular value are the articles by L. Hastier in *Histoire de la Médicine* 3(1953):

45–60, and P. L. Thillaud in *Cahiers de la Rotonde* 6(1983): 72–80.

42. P. L. Thillaud in *Cahiers de la Rotonde* 6(1983): 72–80, and Delorme, *L'affaire Louis XVII*, pp. 123–24. These two authors are also wrong in claiming that a hernia would have been seen at autopsy—surely not, since it may well have been repositioned; anyway, the autopsy report was rudimentary, to say the least.

43. On tuberculous orchitis and epididymitis, see the articles by J. C. Ross et al. in *British Journal of Surgery* 48(1961): 663–66, B. G. Ferrie and J. S. H. Rundle in *British Journal of Urology* 55(1983): 437–39, D. A. Cabral et al. in *Pediatric Infectious Disease* 4(1985): 59–62, and N. D. Heaton et al. in *British Journal of Urology* 64(1989): 305–9.

44. On the "timetable of tuberculosis," see the articles by A. Wallgren in *Tubercle* 29(1948): 245–51, and M. Jubilar et al. in *Respiratory Medicine* 88(1994): 481–82; see also F. J. W. Miller et al., *Tuberculosis in Children* (London, 1970), pp. 73–78.

45. All available information on the heart and its strange odyssey has been collected, with copious notes, by P. Delorme, *Louis XVII: La vérité* (Paris, 2000). Contemporary medical articles on the heart include those by Dr. Arnaud in *La Révolution Française* 3(1882): 340–43, Dr. Cabanès in *La Chronique Médicale* 1–2(1895): 641–48, and Dr. Jouin, ibid., 3(1896): 25–27.

46. See the article by E. Jehaes et al. in *European Journal of Human Genetics* 6(1998): 383–95.

47. P. A. Boiry, *Louis XVII–Naundorff avant l'A.D.N.* (Paris, 1998), *On tue encore Louis XVII* (Paris, 2000), and *Le dossier Louis XVII* (Paris, 2000); see also C.-L.-E. de Bourbon, *La survivance de Louis XVII: Les preuves* (Paris, 2000).

48. See the articles by E. Jehaes et al. in *International Journal of Legal Medicine* 115(2001): 135–41, and in *European Journal of Human Genetics* 9(2001): 185–90.

49. L. de la Chapelle in *Les Cahiers Louis XVII* 20(2000): 9–17; see also homepage www.museelouisxvii.com.

50. Boiry, *Le dossier Louis XVII*, p. 101.

51. J.-N. Gannal, *History of Embalming* (Philadelphia, 1840), pp. 113–17; Delorme, *Louis XVII*, pp. 174–75. On the autopsy of Louis Joseph, see Chantelauze, *Louis XVII*, pp. 252–53, and R. Secker and Y. Murat, *Un prince méconnu* (Paris, 1998), pp. 202–3. For an opposing argument, quoting a specialist who claims that the heart analyzed might well have been prepared according to Gannal's elaborate embalming protocol, see Boiry, *Le dossier Louis XVII*, pp. 198–200.

52. Boiry, *On tue encore Louis XVII*, pp. 156–65, and *Le dossier Louis XVII*, pp. 181–93. In another version, two artists purchased the desiccated hearts, pulverized them, and used them to make a brown pigment for their paintings. See A. Petri, *Den forsvundne franske tronfølger* (Copenhagen, 1977), pp. 92–95.

53. Boiry, *Le dossier Louis XVII*, p. 114.

54. These important documents, including the 2003 pamphlet *Les deux cœurs de Louis XVII* by L. de la Chapelle, are on homepage www.museelouisxvii.com. See also Philippe Delorme's homepage www.chez.com/louis17 and the debate on histoforums.free.fr.

CHAPTER 2: THE MYSTERY OF KASPAR HAUSER

1. It should be noted that the historic part of Nuremberg was almost completely destroyed in World War II.

2. All sources on Kaspar Hauser's early days in Nuremberg have been collected by H. Pies, *Die Wahrheit über Kaspar Hausers Auftauchen und erste nürnberger Zeit* (Stuttgart, 1985).

3. The depositions of Weickmann, Merk, Wessenig, Wüst, Hiltel, and other eyewitnesses are given by Pies, *Die Wahrheit*, pp. 55–66, 210–36. See also H. Pies, *Kaspar Hauser: Eine Dokumentation* (Ansbach, 1966), pp. 9–42.

4. I have slightly abbreviated the text. The original letters are reproduced by P. Tradowsky and J. Meyer, *Kaspar Hauser: Das Kind von Europa* (Stuttgart, 1984), pp. 308–11.

5. The findings are reproduced in P. Tradowsky, ed., *Kaspar Hauser: Arzt-berichte* (Dornach, 1985), pp. 16–45.

6. Feuerbach's early impressions are in his *Kaspar Hauser: Beispiel eines Ver-brechens am Seelenleben des Menschen* (Ansbach, 1832), translated as *Caspar Hauser* (London, 1834); a superior translation is given by J. M. Masson, *Lost Prince* (New York, 1996), pp. 73–156.

7. The story in Kaspar's own words is given in full by H. Pies, *Kaspar Hauser: Augenzeugenberichte und Selbstzeugnisse* (Stuttgart, 1925; new ed., 1985), pp. 419–48; a partial translation is given by Masson, *Lost Prince*, pp. 187–95.

8. Binder's proclamation is reproduced by Pies, *Augenzeugenberichte*, pp. 456–68, and translated by Masson, *Lost Prince*, pp. 161–72.

9. Daumer's biography is given by K. Kluncker, *Georg Friedrich Daumer* (Bonn, 1984), and in *Castrum Peregrini* 164(1984): 41–58.

10. Many unflattering contemporary opinions on Daumer's mental stability are collated by W. Schriebmüller in *Genealogisches Jahrbuch* 31(1991): 45.

11. The results of these experiments were given at length by P. S. Preu in *Archiv für die homöopatische Heilkunst* 11(1832): 1–40, and by G. F. Daumer, *Mitteilungen über Kaspar Hauser* (Nuremberg, 1832); the lat-ter work is reproduced by Pies, *Augenzeugenberichte*, pp. 115–205. See also the article by P. Portwich in *Medizinhistorisches Journal* 31(1996): 89–119.

12. Daumer's early observations of Kaspar are in Pies, *Augenzeugenberichte*, pp. 115–205, and in J. Mayer and J. M. Masson eds., *Kaspar Hauser* (Frankfurt am Main, 1995), pp. 111–267.

13. See Feuerbach, *Caspar Hauser*, pp. 98–99, 135, and G. F. Daumer, *Oplysninger om Kaspar Hauser* (Copenhagen, 1859), pp. 63–64. P. H. Earl Stanhope, *Tracts relating to Caspar Hauser* (London, 1834), p. 23, quoted a newspaper report where the riding master Rumpler said that Kaspar was a talented and courageous rider.

14. In *Allgemeine Zeitung*, Feb. 6, 1834. Daumer had expressed similar sen-timents in a letter reproduced by Tradowsky and Mayer, *Kaspar Hauser*,

p. 337. It is curious to speculate how much of his later enthusiasm for Kaspar Hauser was due to a sense of guilt for "deserting" him in 1829.

15. The available sources for the 1829 assault are given by Pies, *Dokumentation*, pp. 57–76, and *Augenzeugenberichte*, pp. 469–97.

16. Investigations would hint that the Wallfisch (The Whale-Fish) was a tavern just outside Erlangen. An avenue insufficiently pursued at the time was the question what Kaspar had been doing there, and *whom he had met*.

17. On Kaspar's life with Biberbach and von Tucher, see Pies, *Dokumentation*, pp. 77–100.

18. According to Daumer's high-strung attack on the "She-Devil of Nuremberg" in his *Kaspar Hauser, sein Wesen, seine Unschuld* (Dornach, 1984), pp. 334–37, this wicked woman eventually committed suicide by leaping out of a window. Her low opinion of Kaspar is evident from a letter reproduced by Pies, *Dokumentation*, pp. 85–87. A daguerreotype in Tradowsky and Mayer, *Kaspar Hauser*, p. 392, shows no femme fatale, but a very ordinary-looking German woman.

19. This incident was reported as an accident by the police at the time; see Tradowsky and Mayer, *Kaspar Hauser*, p. 405, for the original document. Some later commentators have suspected that Kaspar tried to fake another attack on himself, but without speculating how he imagined this invented assailant was supposed to have entered the house and gotten past the armed guards.

20. J. Mayer, *Philip Henry Lord Stanhope* (Stuttgart, 1988).

21. Duchess of Cleveland, *The True Story of Caspar Hauser, from Authentic Records* (London, 1893), pp. 28–29.

22. On Kaspar's knowledge of the Hungarian tongue, see Pies, *Dokumentation*, pp. 77–84, and Daumer, *Kaspar Hauser*, pp. 166–70.

23. Stanhope, *Tracts*, pp. 3–10, and Duchess of Cleveland, *True Story*, pp. 38–40.

24. Meyer's own observations of Kaspar are reproduced by Pies, *Augenzeugenberichte*, pp. 239–344. More critical accounts of him are in Daumer, *Kaspar Hauser*, pp. 323–34, and in Pies, *Dokumentation*, pp. 101–32.

25. Feuerbach, *Kaspar Hauser*. Feuerbach went further in a memorial to the queen of Bavaria reproduced by Mayer and Masson, *Kaspar Hauser*, pp. 97–109, and directly proclaimed Kaspar the prince of Baden in unpublished notes reproduced by Tradowsky and Mayer, *Kaspar Hauser*, pp. 408–11.

26. The available material on the death of Kaspar Hauser has been collected by H. Pies, *Die amtlichen Aktenstücke über Kaspar Hausers Verwundung und Tod* (Bonn, 1928); a shorter and more accessible account is in Pies, *Dokumentation*, pp. 133–234. A good review is that by M. Kitchen, *Kaspar Hauser, Europe's Child* (London, 2001), pp. 112–32. The original purse and note are reproduced by Tradowsky and Mayer, *Kaspar Hauser*, pp. 623–33.

27. The often cited "fact" that only one set of footsteps, Kaspar's own, was found at the site is a complete invention. See H. Pies, *Kaspar Hauser: Fälschungen, Falschmeldungen und Tendenzberichte* (Ansbach, 1973), p. 291. Some German commentators have pointed out that M.L.Ö. might be an abbreviation for the name Möller. Similarly questionable is the suggestion that M.L.Ö. might stand for "Mi leckt's ölle," that is, "Kiss my ass" in the Franconian dialect. See Kitchen, *Kaspar Hauser*, p. 118.

28. See Pies, *Dokumentation*, pp. 209–10.

29. The reports of Albert, Heidenreich, and Horlacher have been reproduced in Tradowsky, *Kaspar Hauser: Arztberichte*; in addition, Heidenreich published an article in the *Journal für Chirurgie und Augenheilkunde* 21(1834): 91–123. These sources have been intelligently commented on by P. J. Keuler, *Der Findling Kaspar Hauser als medizinisches Phenomen* (Bochum, 1997), pp. 2–41. The arguments in favor of murder have been summarized by Pies, *Dokumentation*, pp. 133–60, and those in favor of suicide by W. Schriebmüller in *Genealogisches Jahrbuch* 31(1991): 43–84. The newspaper press of the time was largely in favor of murder: see *Frankfurter Journal*, Dec. 31, 1833, *Der Komet*, no. 1 (1834): 7, and *Der Komet-Beilage*, no. 7 (1834): 51–53.

30. Daumer is not a particularly reliable source, but his reference to Feuerbach's son adds credibility to his account. See Daumer, *Oplysninger*, pp. 99–101.

31. W. Schriebmüller in *Genealogisches Jahrbuch* 31(1991): 71, 73.

32. See the articles by I. West in *Medicine, Science and the Law* 21(1981):
    198–201, and R. D. Start et al. in *Forensic Science International* 56(1992):
    89–94, and in particular the review by T. Karlsson, ibid., 93(1998): 21–32.

33. On suicidal stabbing through clothing, see the articles by H. Shiono and
    Y. Takaesu in *American Journal of Forensic and Medical Pathology* 7(1986):
    72–73, B. Madea and P. Schmidt in *Archiv für Kriminologie* 192(1993):
    138–47, and M. Bohnert et al., ibid., 200(1997): 31–38.

34. See Pies, *Dokumentation*, p. 88.

35. The newspaper *Der Komet*, no. 7 (1834): 56, mentions two actors appre-
    hended in Augsburg, but this may have been a canard. Another press clip-
    ping from an unnamed newspaper, mentions an actor and two other
    individuals arrested in Würzburg. A Nuremberg newspaper instead sus-
    pected a Bohemian merchant who had left Ansbach just after the mur-
    der. See the archives of the Stadtbibliothek Nürnberg (2524.2170). In
    1853, a criminal former Ansbach innkeeper named Dorfinger actually
    confessed to having aided in the assassination, but was not believed by
    the police. See Schriebmüller in *Genealogisches Jahrbuch* 31(1991): 48.

36. Reproduced by Tradowsky and Mayer, *Kaspar Hauser*, pp. 684–85.

37. See Schriebmüller in *Genealogisches Jahrbuch* 31(1991): 71, 73.

38. Lord Stanhope's books were *Tracts relating to Caspar Hauser* and *Mate-
    rialien zur Geschichte Kaspar Hausers* (Heidelberg, 1835).

39. This quotation is in Masson, *Lost Prince*, p. 35.

40. W. C. Gräfin von Albersdorf, *Kaspar Hauser*, 2 vols. (Munich, 1839), and
    F. S. Seiler, *Kaspar Hauser, der Thronerbe von Baden* (Paris, 1840).
    According to a press-clipping in the archives of the Stadtbibliothek
    Nürnberg (2524.2170), Seiler was shot and wounded on the Paris bar-
    ricades in 1848. He later went to the United States and ended up as a
    lawyer in New Orleans.

41. D. Eschricht, *Kaspar Hauser* (Copenhagen, 1850).

42. Daumer, *Oplysninger*, pp. 153–54, 158–59, 162.

43. J. Meyer, *Autentische Mitteilungen über Caspar Hauser* (Ansbach, 1872).
    This work has been severely criticized by Pies, *Falschmeldungen*, pp.

247–75. Even some anti-Hauserians had to admit that young Meyer's editorial work was far from praiseworthy; see the article by I. Striedinger in *Zeitschrift für bayerische Landesgeschichte* 6(1933): 415–84.

44. Daumer, *Kaspar Hauser*. The assassination attempt is mentioned by J. Wassermann, *Lebensdienst* (Leipzig, 1928), p. 142.

45. J. Hickel, *Caspar Hauser: Hinterlassenes Manuscript* (Ansbach, 1881). This very dubious source contradicts the known facts on many points, particularly on Kaspar's death. Pies, *Falschmeldungen*, pp. 277–316, provides good evidence it is a forgery, probably by the fanatical anti-Hauserian Julius Meyer.

46. A. von der Linde, *Kaspar Hauser: Eine neugeschichtliche Legende*, 2 vols. (Wiesbaden, 1887).

47. See the article by W. Bates in *Notes & Queries*, 5th ser., 1(1874): 69–71, and the anonymous articles in the *New Monthly Magazine* 120(1860): 484–93, and the *Quarterly Review* 166(1888): 469–95, as well as the article by A. Lang in *Cornhill Magazine*, n.s. 16(1904): 104–17. J. G. Lockhart, *Here Are Mysteries* (London, 1927), pp. 193–223, has a typically dismissive chapter, uncritically accepting the arguments of Stanhope. On the debate about Kaspar Hauser in Britain, see the article by P. A. MacKenzie in *German Life and Letters* 35(1982): 118–37.

48. E. H. Evans, *The Story of Kaspar Hauser from Authentic Records* (London, 1892). This book is very much indebted to a scurrilous German work, Alexander von Artin's *Kaspar Hauser: Des Rätsels Lösung* (Zürich, 1892).

49. Duchess of Cleveland, *True Story*.

50. H. Peitler and H. Ley, *Kaspar Hauser: Über tausend bibliographische Nachweise* (Ansbach, 1927), lists more than 1,000 sources; the current figure is given by Schriebmüller in *Genealogisches Jahrbuch* 31(1991): 43.

51. When Hermann Pies expired in 1983, at the age of ninety-five, he had worked for more than seventy years to solve the mystery. His most valuable books are *Kaspar Hauser: Augenzeugenberichte und Selbstzeugnisse* (Stuttgart, 1925; new ed. 1985), *Die Wahrheit über Kaspar Hausers Auftauchen und erste nürnberger Zeit* (Saarbrücken, 1956; new ed., Stuttgart,

1985), *Kaspar Hauser: Eine Dokumentation* (Ansbach, 1966), *Kaspar Hauser: Fälschungen, Falschmeldungen und Tendenzberichte* (Ansbach, 1973), and *Die amtlichen Aktenstücke über Kaspar Hausers Verwundung und Tod* (Bonn, 1928).

52. K. Heyer, *Kaspar Hauser und das Schicksal Mitteleuropas* (Ravensburg, 1958).

53. P. Tradowsky, *Kaspar Hauser* (Dornach, 1980). An English translation was published in London in 1997. For other cranky theories, see K. Jauch, *Kosmische Geometrie im Leben Kaspar Hausers* (Schaffhausen, 1998).

54. Tradowsky and Mayer, *Kaspar Hauser*; the pictures and Mayer's often astute comments are of particular value.

55. J. Mayer, *Philip Henry Lord Stanhope*.

56. See K. Kramer, *Kaspar Hauser: Kein Rätsel unserer Zeit* (Ansbach, 1978), U. Leonhardt, *Prinz von Baden genannt Kaspar Hauser* (Reinbeck, 1987), and F. Mehle, *Der Kriminalfall Kaspar Hauser* (Kehl, 1994).

57. Examples are the valuable critical works of I. Striedinger in *Lebensläufe aus Franken III: Veröffentlichaft der Gesellschaft für fränkische Geschichte* 7th ser., 3(1927): 199–215, and *Zeitschrift für bayerische Landesgeschichte* 6(1933): 415–84, and W. Schriebmüller in *Neue juristische Wochenschrift* 43(1990): 1966–69, and *Genealogisches Jahrbuch* 31(1991): 43–84, and the thesis by Keuler, *Der Findling Kaspar Hauser*.

58. Masson, *Lost Prince*. A critical review of this book by B. J. Landau is in the *Psychoanalytic Quarterly* 67(1998): 333–35.

59. Many of these points have been reviewed by W. Schriebmüller in *Genealogisches Jahrbuch* 3(1991): 56–61, and by M. Dietenberger, *Land zwischen Hochrhein und Südschwarzwald: Beiträge zur Geschichte des Landkreises Waldshut,* special issue, 1(1997): 115–83.

60. Photographs of this alleged dungeon are reproduced by Tradowsky and Mayer, *Kaspar Hauser*, pp. 772–79. See also the article in *Fränkischer Kurier*, Oct. 11, 1924, pp. 18–19, and the article by U. Rach in *NN/RHV*, Dec. 7–8, 1996, p. 13.

61. Mayer, *Stanhope*, pp. 498–99.

62. H. Lakies and G. Lakies-Wild, *Das Phänomen* (Ansbach, 1978).

63. For examples of this, see the articles by E. Nau and D. Cabanis in *Münchener medizinische Wochenschrift* 108(1966): 929–31, and W. Hirsch and H. Gerhartz in *Fortschritte der Medizin* 91(1973): 299–301.

64. Articles in *Fränkische Landeszeitung*, April 24 and 26, 1996, in the Kaspar Hauser-Archiv of the Ansbach Markgrafenmuseum.

65. See the article by M. Blendinger in *NN/RHV*, Aug. 15, 1996, p. 9, and various press clippings from the Kaspar Hauser-Archiv of the Markgrafenmuseum of Ansbach.

66. *Der Spiegel*, no. 48 (1996): 254–71. The full scientific report was published by G. M. Weichold et al. in *International Journal of Legal Medicine* 111(1998): 287–91.

67. Articles in *Fränkische Landeszeitung*, Nov. 25, 1996, and in *FAZ*, Jan. 22, 1997, both in the Kaspar Hauser-Archiv of the Markgrafenmuseum of Ansbach.

68. *Die Zeit*, Nov. 29, 1996, and *Fränkische Landeszeitung*, Dec. 3, 1996.

69. H. Kühnert in *Die Zeit*, Nov. 29, 1996, p. 48; see also the article by M. Hummel in *Süddeutsche Zeitung*, 1996.

70. From an article in the *Fränkische Landeszeitung*, Dec. 17, 1998, in the Kaspar Hauser-Archiv of the Markgrafenmuseum of Ansbach.

71. H. Sendler in *Neue juristische Wochenschrift* 50(1997): 1133.

72. *Fränkische Landeszeitung*, Aug. 12–13, 2000. Dr. Biedermann has published *Kaspar Hauser: Neue Forschung und Aspekte* (Offenbach am Main, 1998).

73. K. Leonhard in *Confinia Psychiatrica* 13(1970): 213–229.

74. On cases of pseudologia fantastica, see the articles by J. A. Korkeila et al. in *Nordic Journal of Psychiatry* 49(1995): 367–71, H. Akimoto in *Psychiatry and Clinical Neurosciences* 51(1997): 185–95, T. J. Hardie and A. Reed in *Medicine, Science and the Law* 38(1998): 198–201, and N. Newmark et al. in *Comprehensive Psychiatry* 40(1999): 89–95.

75. On the dagger, see Tradowsky and Mayer, *Kaspar Hauser*, p. 634, and

the article by K. Kramer in *Fränkische Landeszeitung*, Dec. 16, 1999.

76. Ritter von Lang's article was in the *Blätter für literarische Unterhaltung* 4(1834): 13–14.

77. I. Striedinger in *Lebensläufe aus Franken III: Veröffentlichungen der Gesellschaft für fränkische Geschichte*, 7th ser., 3(1927): 199–215, and *Zeitschrift für bayerische Landesgeschichte* 6(1933): 415–84.

78. Dr. Hesse has published many articles on Kaspar Hauser, in *Münchener medizinische Wochenschrift* 109(1967): 156–63, *Deutsches Ärzteblatt* 81C(1984): 365–68, *Neue juristische Wochenschrift* 42(1989): 365–67, and *Genealogisches Jahrbuch* 31(1991): 87–93. He has been criticized by H. Boxler in *Land zwischen Hochrhein und Südschwarzwald: Beiträge zur Geschichte des Landkreises Waldshut*, special issue, no. 1(1997): 41–48. It is notable that Kitchen, *Kaspar Hauser*, the most recent English-language book on the mystery, accepts Dr. Hesse's hypothesis. Disregarding the bulk of evidence to the contrary, some of which he quite correctly reviewed earlier in the book, Kitchen concludes that Kaspar Hauser was just an epileptic idiot whom the Tirolese dumped on the Bavarians to rid themselves of a tiresome burden.

79. On epidermolysis bullosa, see the review by H. M. Horn and M. J. Tidman in *British Journal of Dermatology* 146(2002): 267–74.

80. Most recently M. Newton, *Savage Girls and Wild Boys* (London, 2002).

81. J. Money, *The Kaspar Hauser Syndrome of "Psychosocial Dwarfism"* (New York, 1992). See also the articles by P. Stumpft in *Praxis der Kinderpsychologie und Kinderpsychiatrie* 18(1969): 292–99, and N. Simon in *Journal of Autism and Childhood Schizophrenia* 8(1978): 209–17.

82. On Kaspar Hauser in literature, see the articles by A. F. Bance in *German Life and Letters* 28(1974–75): 199–210, and R. D. Theisz *German Quarterly* 49(1976): 168–80, and the books by U. Sampath, *Kaspar Hauser: A Modern Metaphor* (Columbia, S.C., 1991), U. Struwe, *Der Findling: Kaspar Hauser in der Literatur* (Stuttgart, 1992), and Kitchen, *Kaspar Hauser*, pp. 175–88.

83. On early American interest in Kaspar Hauser, see the article by P. A. MacKenzie in *German Life and Letters* 49(1996): 438–58.

84. J. Wassermann, *Caspar Hauser, oder Die Trägheit des Herzens* (Zürich, 1908), translated as *Caspar Hauser* (New York, 1992). On Stanhope's threat, see Wassermann, *Lebensdienst*, p. 146.

CHAPTER 3: THE EMPEROR AND THE HERMIT

1. The classic nineteenth-century biographies of Alexander I are those of N. K. Schilder, *"Imperator Aleksandr Pervij,"* 4 vols. (St. Petersburg, 1904–5), and Grand Duke Nicholas Mikhailovitch, *"Imperator Aleksandr Pervij,"* 2 vols. (St. Petersburg, 1912). Schilder's work has never been translated, but Grand Duke Nicholas's biography has been published in French: *L'empereur Alexandre I*, 2 vols. (St. Petersburg, 1912). F. Gribble, *Emperor and Mystic* (New York, 1931), is well researched but lacking in academic credentials; M. Paleologue, *Alexandre I* (Paris, 1937), is a whimsical account that presents no source material even for the wildest assumptions; L. Strakhovsky, *Alexander I of Russia* (London, 1949), contains much interesting material from Russian sources. The best modern biographies are A. Palmer, *Alexander I* (London, 1974), and H. Troyat, *Alexander of Russia* (New York, 1982).

2. There is a massive literature on the question of the identity of Alexander I and Feodor Kuzmich. Books in Russian include G. Vasilich, *Imperator Aleksandr I y Starets Feodor Kuzmich* (Moscow, 1910), L. D. Liubimov, *Tayna Imperatora Alexandra I* (Paris, 1938), and V. V. Nikolaev, *Aleksandr I—Starets Feodor Kuzmich* (San Francisco, 1984). The first European-language contribution was V. V. Bariatinsky, *Le mystère d'Alexandre I* (Paris, 1925), an admirable work that concisely sums up the arguments in favor of the legend. Next appeared, in Swedish, E. Rydelius and A. Belbodoroff, *Alexander I, en Gåtfull Tsar* (Stockholm, 1934); but although purportedly based on independent archival research, this book had little new to offer. Then came M. Winkler, *Zarenlegende* (Berlin, 1941), a valuable critical work attempting to debunk the old tale. The most recent full-length work is A. Troubetzkoy, *Imperial Legend* (New York, 2002), providing much new data and reviewing the case with a bias toward accepting the legend. Grand Duke Nicholas Mikhailovitch published an important article in *Beiträge zur russischen Geschichte: Theodor Schiemann Zum 60. Geburtstag* (Berlin, 1907), pp. 1–26. The later arti-

cles by J. Hessen in *Finsk Tidskrift* 117(1934), 298–317, 389–403, A. Törngren, ibid., 124(1938): 113–24, 180–98, and H. Müller-Dietz in *Sydsvenska Medicinhistoriska Sällskapets Årsskrift* 24(1987): 99–115, are all valuable contributions.

3. On Wylie, see the articles by H. Müller-Dietz in *Clio Medica* 4(1969): 99–107, A. A. Novik et al. in *Scottish Medical Journal* 41(1996): 116–20, and A. Shabunin and P. d'A. Semple in *Proceedings of the Royal College of Physicians of Edinburgh* 29(1999): 76–82.

4. R. Lee, *The Last Days of Alexander I and the First Days of Nicholas I* (London, 1854), pp. 24–25.

5. On the last days of Alexander, see Winkler, *Zarenlegende*, pp. 5–21, 156–70, Palmer, *Alexander I*, pp. 400–417, and Troubetzkoy, *Imperial Legend*, pp. 133–72.

6. Lee, *Last Days*, pp. 25, 30 and A. Castellani in *Proceedings of the Royal Society of Medicine (Section of Medicine)* 10(1917): 31–58.

7. It is curious that Diebitsch was himself something of a man of mystery; a number of people speculated that he was none other than the Lost Dauphin. See P. Delorme, *L'affaire Louis XVII* (Paris, 1995), p. 150.

8. The autopsy report was reproduced by Schilder, *Imperator Aleksandr*, 4:573–74, and translated by Troubetzkoy, *Imperial Legend*, pp. 271–73.

9. Lee, *Last Days*, p. 48.

10. See *Times*, Dec. 26, 1825, p. 2c, Jan. 2, 1826, p. 2d, Jan. 4, 1826, p. 2b, and Jan. 9, 1826, p. 3b, also MSS Bodleian 40200, which appears to be a partial translation of an anonymous pamphlet entitled *Die letzten Tage des Kaiser Alexander* (St. Petersburg, 1827).

11. Full accounts of the various traditions concerning Feodor Kuzmich are given by Winkler, *Zarenlegende*, pp. 201–25, and Troubetzkoy, *Imperial Legend*, pp. 189–203.

12. Hessen in *Finsk Tidskrift* 117(1934): 300–301.

13. On the secret of Feodor Kuzmich, see ibid., pp. 394–96, Winkler, *Zarenlegende*, pp. 232–33, and Troubetzkoy, *Imperial Legend*, pp. 202–3.

14. It is notable that this is denied by Grand Duke Nicholas Mikhailovitch, in *Beiträge zur russischen Geschichte*, p. 2.

15. Troubetzkoy, *Imperial Legend*, p. 11. For Soviet contributions, see Nikolaev, *Aleksandr I*, also the later article by A. Archangelskij in *Novij Mir* 11(1995): 183–210.

16. The letters of the empress are exhaustively quoted by Grand Duke Nicholas Mikhailovitch, *L'Impératrice Elizabeth*, 3 vols. (St. Petersburg, 1908–09). Volkonsky's memoranda are quoted by Mikhailovitch, *L'empereur Alexandre*. The notes of Tarasov and Wylie are in the *Russkaya Starina* 6(1872): 100–42, and 73(1897): 69–78. Finally, the "Histoire de la maladie . . ." is reproduced by Schilder, *Imperator Aleksandr*, 4:568–72.

17. Wellcome MSS 5098.

18. See the article by N. H. Schuster in *Proceedings of the Royal Society of Medicine* 61(1968): 185–90.

19. See the article by H. Müller-Dietz in *Sydsvenska Medicinhistoriska Sällskapets Årsskrift* 24(1987): 99–115, quoting a mysterious letter that may or may not be related to an obscure Russian book by N. Danilovsky, *Taganrog* (Moscow, 1828); see also the *Journal of the Friends Historical Society* 26(1929): 17–19. The pamphlet *Die letzten Tage des Kaiser Alexander* (St. Petersburg, 1827) also quotes various letters from people who were at the tsar's deathbed in Taganrog.

20. Quoted in the article by A. Törngren in *Finsk Tidskrift* 124(1938) 185.

21. The best-known version of Balinsky's whimsical researches was published in a Russian newspaper in Paris in April 1926 by a certain Madame Dubasov; it was translated by Strakhovsky, *Alexander I of Russia*, pp. 257–60. See also Troubetzkoy, *Imperial Legend*, pp. 251–53.

22. Arguments for and against these alternatives are discussed by A. Törngren in *Finsk Tidskrift* 124(1938): 191, and by Count Albert Ehrensvärd in *Göteborgs Handels-och Sjöfartstidning*, Sept. 27 (pp. 3, 5), 28 (pp. 3, 9), and 29 (p. 3), 1937. Information in E. F. Malcolm-Smith, *The Life of Stratford Canning* (London, 1933), pp. 93, 96–97, excludes the possibility that he was in Taganrog in late 1825. On Lansdowne's activities, see *Times*, Feb. 3, 1826, p. 4a.

23. See Paleologue, *Alexandre I*, pp. 300–303, and A. Törngren in *Finsk Tid-skrift* 124(1938): 190.

24. Palmer, *Alexander I*, p. 415.

25. Winkler, *Zarenlegende*, pp. 227–30.

26. Hessen in *Finsk Tidskrift* 117(1934): 300–301. Some other characteris-tics noted in the police documents, particularly that Kuzmich was illit-erate, also are at variance with the observations of Kuzmich in the 1850s.

27. Hessen in *Finsk Tidskrift* 117(1934): 394.

28. Hessen in *Finsk Tidskrift* 117(1934): 316–17, describes Khromov's chapel on Kuzmich's grave. What happened to it is unknown, since Trou-betzkoy, *Imperial Legend*, p. 8, describes a newly erected chapel in 1902, containing a marble slab that replaced the old cross.

29. A. Törngren in *Finsk Tidskrift* 124(1938): 197.

30. Troubetzkoy, *Imperial Legend*, p. 210.

31. A. A. Kulomzin in *Slavonic Review* (1923): 381–87.

32. This story is recounted by Strakhovsky, *Alexander I of Russia*, p. 273.

33. See A. Törngren in *Finsk Tidskrift* 124(1938): 197, and Winkler, *Zaren-legende*, p. 238.

34. The story of the disinterment in 1921 has been believed by almost every later writer on the subject; the interesting criticism is in Winkler, *Zaren-legende*, pp. 237–40. Hessen in *Finsk Tidskrift* (1934): 393, adds that a young Soviet historian issued an official denial of these rumors in the foreign press.

35. See *Times*, May 29, 1929, pp. 19f. Several people, including a relation of Sir James Wylie, objected to this falsification already at the time: see *Times*, May 31, 1929, p. 14d, June 14, 1929, p. 12d, and June 18, 1929, p. 12c. J. G. Lockhart, *Here Are Mysteries* (London, 1927), pp. 129–58.

36. *Times*, Nov. 15, 1965, pp. 8c–d.

37. Strakhovsky, *Alexander I of Russia*, pp. 257–60.

38. A. Törngren in *Finsk Tidskrift* 124(1938): 196–97, recounts all three

versions, with references to the sources involved.

39. Palmer, *Alexander I*, p. 416.

40. Quoted by Troubetzkoy, *Imperial Legend*, pp. 209–10.

41. The homepage www.dergava.tomsk.ru reproduces icons of Saint Feodor.

42. On Veliki, see Winkler, *Zarenlegende*, pp. 232–33, Hessen in *Finsk Tidskrift* 117(1934): 400–401, and Troubetzkoy, *Imperial Legend*, pp. 246–47.

43. On Uvarov, see Hessen in *Finsk Tidskrift* 117(1934): 401–2.

CHAPTER 4: PRINCESS OLIVE, HANNAH LIGHTFOOT, AND GEORGE REX

1. A. Bennett, *The Madness of King George: The Complete and Unabridged Screenplay* (New York, 1995). The film's original title, *The Madness of King George III*, was changed for its U.S. release, since it was feared that many Americans would think they had missed *The Madness of King George I* and *The Madness of King George II* and not bother to see the second sequel.

2. On George III, see J. Brooke, *George III* (London, 1972), and G. Hibbert, *George III* (London, 1999), among other biographies.

3. The British Library has several satirical works about the duke and his affairs. Most of them concern the Grosvenor trial, like the anonymous *The Trial of His R. H. the D . . . of C . . . July 5ᵗʰ 1770 for criminal conversation with Lady Harriet G. . . . r* (London, 1770), and *Free Thoughts on Seduction, Adultery and Divorce* (London, 1771).

4. On Anne Horton, see F. Gerard, *Some Celebrated Irish Beauties of the Last Century* (London, 1895).

5. There is no biography of this wicked prince; his antics were well described by the contemporary satirical press, and are briefly summarized by M. L. Pendered and J. Mallett, *Princess or Pretender?* (London, 1939), pp. 41–49.

6. See R. Fulford, *Royal Dukes* (London, 1948), and, more recently, J. van der Kiste, *George III's Children* (London, 1999).

7. The most detailed books on Princess Olive are Pendered and Mallett, *Princess or Pretender?*, and M. Shepard, *Princess Olive* (Shipston-on-Stour, 1984).

8. Anon., *Memoir of John Thomas Serres* (London, 1826), pp. 21–36.

9. Shepard, *Princess Olive*, pp. 15–16.

10. Kept in the British Library are *Flights of Fancy; consisting of Miscellaneous Poems. With the Castle of Avola, an Opera, in Three Acts* (London, 1805) and *St. Athanasius's Creed Explained for the Advantage of Youth* (London, 1814), but the princess certainly published several other books. See Pendered and Mallett, *Princess or Pretender?*, pp. 234–41.

11. O. Serres, *The Life of the Author of the Letters of Junius, the Revd. J. Wilmot, D.D.* (London, 1813). See also her later work *Junius. Sir Philip Francis Denied. A Letter Addressed to the British Nation* (London, 1817).

12. O. Serres, *Begin. Documents to Prove Mrs. O. Serres to Be the Legitimate Daughter of Henry Frederick, the Late Duke of Cumberland* (London, 1820).

13. On Olive's connection with this obscure and penniless aristocrat, see Pendered and Mallett, *Princess or Pretender?*, pp. 92–98.

14. Anon., *The Princess of Cumberland's Statement to the English Nation, as to Her Application to Ministers, with Letters Addressed to the Duke of York,* . . . (London, 1822).

15. See HO 44/1, ff. 139, 148, in the Public Record Office.

16. See HO 44/1, f. 149 for duke of York; ff. 139, 148, 164 for Serres, f. 131 for Thomas Wilmot, ff. 152–53 for Poniatowski. Deuley's evidence is in HO 44/16, f. 126. Parkins also wrote to the newspapers, see *Times*, Oct. 11, 1821, p. 3b, and Jan. 1, 1825, pp. 2e–3a.

17. See HO 44/1, ff. 149–51. The parliamentary inquiry is reviewed in *Times*, June 13, 1823, p. 2c, and June 19, 1823, pp. 2b–c.

18. On the wrongdoings of this pathetic Charles Wilmot, see *Times*, Oct. 3, 1826, pp. 3e–f, Oct. 16, 1826, p. 3f, May 6, 1830, p. 5d, and Sept. 3, 1831, p. 4e. Shepard, *Princess Olive*, p. 56, adds that he ended up in South Africa in 1867.

19. The British Library has two examples of her later pamphlets: *The Princess Olive of Cumberland to the English Nation* (London, 1829) and *The First Part of the Authenticated Proofs of the Legitimacy of . . . Olive, Princess of Cumberland* (London, 1830?). See also E. W. Macauley, *The Wrongs of Her Royal Highness the Princess Olive of Cumberland; Being a Plain, Unvarnished Statement of the Unparalleled Oppressions Inflicted upon That Distinguished Lady* (London, 1833).

20. On the biography of Mrs. Ryves, see Pendered and Mallett, *Princess or Pretender?*, pp. 172–225.

21. L. J. Ryves, *An Appeal for Royalty* (London, 1858). See also L. Praed, *A Suppressed Princess* (London, 1863).

22. On the trial, see Pendered and Mallett, *Princess or Pretender?*, pp. 190–225, and H. Wyndham, *Feminine Frailty* (London, 1929), pp. 259–90.

23. L. J. Ryves, *Ryves versus the Attorney-General: Was Justice Done?* (London, 1868).

24. W. J. Thoms, *Hannah Lightfoot. Queen Charlotte and the Chevalier d'Eon. Dr. Wilmot's Polish Princess* (London, 1867).

25. There is a large collection of material in the Public Record Office at Kew, in HO 44 and elsewhere.

26. As described in "The Real King and Queen," a documentary aired by the Discovery Channel UK, June 2, 2002.

27. See P. Storrar, *George Rex: Death of a Legend* (Johannesburg, 1974), plate opposite p. 33.

28. See C. E. Cary, *Memoirs* (London, 1825), and Pendered and Mallett, *Princess or Pretender?*, pp. 146–47, 262. A letter from FitzClarence is in HO 44/1, f. 138, and shows his calligraphic talents.

29. Pendered and Mallett, *Princess or Pretender?*, pp. 226–33.

30. For these stories, see ibid., pp. 86, 97–98, 139–40.

31. These spicy tales are in HO 44/1, f. 148.

32. The story of Hannah Lightfoot has been told by many authors. Early accounts are those by Thoms, *Hannah Lightfoot*, H. Bleackley in *Notes and Queries*, 10th ser., 8(1907): 321–23, 350, 402–4, and 10th ser., 9(1908): 24–25, 122–23, and W. B. Boulton, *In the Days of the Georges* (London, 1909), 87–138. The first full-length book was M. L. Pendered, *The Fair Quaker* (London, 1910); the same author published some valuable additions in Pendered and Mallett, *Princess or Pretender?*, pp. 149–71. J. Lindsay, *The Lovely Quaker* (London, 1939), is credulous but contains some new information; Storrar, *George Rex*, is erudite and critical; M. Kreps, *Hannah Regina* (London, 2002), contains nothing new or interesting.

33. Thoms, *Hannah Lightfoot*, and W. H. Jesse, *Memoirs of the Life and Reign of King George the Third* (London, 1867).

34. On Isaac Axford and his family, see the article by B. Wood-Holt in *Notes and Queries* 229(1984): 397–401, and the further note by S. Mitchell and W. I. Axford, ibid., 241(1996): 304–5.

35. See the various notes in the *Journal of the Friends Historical Society* 4(1907): 159 and 5(1907): 54, 93–94.

36. On Pearne, see Pendered, *Fair Quaker*, pp. 247–55, and Lindsay, *Lovely Quaker*, pp. 177–91.

37. Pendered, *Fair Quaker,* pp. xvii–xviii.

38. On the Reynolds portrait, see ibid., pp. 152–53, and Lindsay, *Lovely Quaker*, pp. 157–60. It is interesting that there was more than one "Fair Quaker" at this time. A discussion of a mezzotint portrait of a "Fair Quaker" by Houston suggested to be of Hannah Lightfoot showed that at least two other ladies shared the same attribute; a writer in the *Notes and Queries* 56(1929): 138–39, ruled out that this was a portrait of Hannah Lightfoot.

39. See the article by S. Mitchell in *Family Tree Magazine* no. 11 (1996): 4–5.

40. R. Sedgwick, ed., *Letters from George III to Lord Bute* (London, 1937), pp. 37–39.

41. Storrar, *George Rex*, p. 27, quoting from a manuscript in the British Museum.

42. For a discussion of these three early references, see Pendered, *Fair Quaker*, pp. 142–45.

43. *Monthly Magazine* 51(1821): 532 and 52(1821): 109, 110, 197–98.

44. Anon., *Authentic Records of the Court of England* (London, 1831). On Princess Olive's involvement, see Shepard, *Princess Olive*, pp. 47–49. Sheriff Parkins was well aware of Olive's trying to capitalize on the story of the "Quaker woman" already in 1824; see HO 44/1, f. 148.

45. See S. Ayling, *George the Third* (London, 1972), p. 36, and Brooke: *George III*, p. 389; see also the article by I. R. Christie in *Notes and Queries* 220(1975): 18–22.

46. Among them Pendered, *Fair Quaker*, and Pendered and Mallett, *Princess or Pretender?*

47. Among them Lindsay, *Lovely Quaker*, and Kreps, *Hannah Regina*.

48. See the article by P. D. Mundy in *Notes and Queries* 190(1949): 272–73.

49. Sheila Mitchell, a Swindon magistrate who is preparing a longer work on this subject, has been investigating the mystery for twenty years, but her search for Hannah Lightfoot's grave is as yet unsuccessful.

50. Of the books on George Rex, S. Metelerkamp, *George Rex of Knysna* (Cape Town, 1955), is credulous but C. H. Price, *George Rex: King or Esquire?* (Cape Town, 1971), is more critical of the old tradition. Storrar, *George Rex*, is the standard work on him.

51. I. R. Christie in *Notes and Queries* 220(1975): 18–22; see also Storrar, *George Rex*, pp. 165–90. I have discovered that there were actually two sons of the distiller John and his wife, Sarah, named George Rex. There is good evidence from John Rex's will and the correspondence with his sister Sarah that the George Rex who went to South Africa and made his fortune there was the older of these two, born in September 1765 in the parish of St. Mary's Whitechapel. The Rexes then had a son named John and a daughter named Sarah as well as two daughters who died young. Their youngest child, born in August 1777 in the parish of St. Dunstan in the

East, was another George, who was dead by the time his father wrote his will 1788. John Rex's widow, Sarah, took over the distillery business but went bankrupt in 1800, according to the *Times* of August 6 of that year.

52. According to Sheila Mitchell, there is actually a third, much more obscure George Rex, born in Yorkshire many years after Hannah Lightfoot disappeared but still alleged to be her son.

53. E. Bower, ed., *George Rex Genealogy* (Bowie, Md., 1998). This is an updated version of Leda Farrell Rex's work.

54. Pendered and Mallett, *Princess or Pretender?*, pp. 257–58.

55. On the Ritso family, see Pendered, *Fair Quaker*, pp. 286–98.

56. See *British Archeology*, no. 50, Dec. 2000, and the church web page under www.netministries.org/see/churches.

57. On Mackelcan and his family, see Lindsay, *Lovely Quaker*, pp. 285–93.

58. On the Parks connection, see Pendered, *Fair Quaker*, pp. 272–75.

59. H. Bleackley in *Notes and Queries* 10th ser., 9(1908): 24–25.

60. "The Real King and Queen," a documentary aired by the Discovery Channel UK, June 2, 2002. It should be noted that, unlike analysis of mitochondrial DNA, the method used in this investigation is sensitive to adulterous relations. Had any of the countesses of Munster encountered a milkman with a twinkle in his eye, this individual would have substituted his Y chromosome for that of the earl. And according to a recent Swedish investigation (*Aftonbladet*, March 7, 2003) one child out of five has a father other than the man believing he has sired it.

CHAPTER 5: THE TICHBORNE CLAIMANT

1. The vast majority of poetry quotations in this chapter are from handbills reproduced in H. Anderson, ed., *Baronet or Butcher?* (Hotham Hill, Victoria, 1999).

2. An almost encyclopedic work on the Tichbornes and the Claimant is D. Woodruff, *The Tichborne Claimant* (London and New York, 1957). Other books on the case include J. B. Atlay, *The Tichborne Case* (London, 1899),

Lord Maugham, *The Tichborne Case* (London, 1936), M. Gilbert, *The Claimant* (London, 1957), and G. MacGregor, *The Tichborne Impostor* (New York, 1957).

3. On Lady Tichborne and her family, see B. Falk, *The Naughty Seymours* (London, 1940).

4. Woodruff, *Tichborne Claimant*, pp. 99–117, 153–62.

5. Ibid., pp. 141–52.

6. On Ballantine, see his autobiography, *Some Experiences of a Barrister's Life* (London, 1898); pp. 311–27 concern the Tichborne case.

7. Woodruff, *Tichborne Claimant*, p. 213.

8. The standard work on Kenealy is M. Roe, *Kenealy and the Tichborne Cause* (Carlton, Victoria, 1974). See also his daughter's biography of him, A. Kenealy, *Memoirs of Edward Vaughan Kenealy LL.D.* (London, 1908); pp. 225–85 concern the Tichborne case.

9. Roe, *Kenealy*, pp. 15–16.

10. On Sir Henry Hawkins, see his *Reminiscences* (London, 1904), 1: 307–31, concerning the Tichborne case.

11. From "Jolly Old Sir Roger," in Anderson, *Baronet or Butcher?*, p. 106.

12. See the anonymous pamphlet *Tichborne in Prison* (London, 1874).

13. On Cresswell, see Woodruff, *Tichborne Claimant*, pp. 428–35, and Roe, *Kenealy*, pp. 148–62.

14. The later days of the Claimant are well described by Woodruff, *Tichborne Claimant*, pp. 436–46.

15. This confession was reprinted by Anderson, *Baronet or Butcher?*, pp. 7–38, and commented on by W. A. Frost, *The Orton Confession of the Tichborne Claimant* (London, 1913), and more critically by M. Roe in the *Tasmanian Historical Research Association, Papers and Proceedings* 18(1971): 115–48.

16. Woodruff, *Tichborne Claimant*. Douglas Woodruff's friend Evelyn Waugh shared his belief that the case remained a mystery; see the *Spectator* of June 21, 1957.

17. Woodruff, *Tichborne Claimant*, pp. 46–47, and Gilbert, *Claimant*, pp. 51, 54.

18. MacGregor, *Tichborne Impostor*, p. 58.

19. See the article by M. Roe in the *Tasmanian Historical Research Association, Papers and Proceedings* 18(1971): 115–48.

20. This is actually based on a quotation from a popular novel of the time, M. E. Braddon's *Aurora Floyd*.

21. See the editorial articles in *British Medical Journal*, 1873, vol. 2:64, 1874; vol. 1:654, and *Lancet*, 1873, vol. 2:54, 1874, vol. 1:345; see also *Medical Times and Gazette*, 1872, vol. 1:314–15.

22. W. Mathews, *From Chili to Piccadilly with Sir Roger Tichborne* (London, 1876). See also E. V. Kenealy, *Introduction to the Trial of Sir Roger C.T. Tichborne, Bart.* (London, 1874), pp. 312–18.

23. Kenealy, *Introduction*, p. 312. On the debate about the Claimant's ears, see also the *Medical Times and Gazette* 1872, vol. 1:320.

24. The physical marks of Tichborne and Orton have been described by Maugham, *Tichborne Case*, and Woodruff, *Tichborne Claimant*.

25. *British Medical Journal*, 1873, vol. 2:64, and *Lancet*, 1873, vol. 2:54.

26. Woodruff, *Tichborne Claimant*, pp. 48–49.

27. Kenealy, *Introduction*, pp. 113–14, and M. Kenealy, *Tichborne Tragedy* (London, 1913), pp. 232–34.

28. *Lancet*, 1874, vol. 1:345.

29. On the tattooing, see Maugham, *Tichborne Case*, pp. 301–4, and Woodruff, *Tichborne Claimant*, pp. 213, 276, 333, 362. See also the article by A. S. Taylor in *Guy's Hospital Report* 19(1873–74): 441–65, and J. Glaister, *A Text-book of Medical Jurisprudence and Toxicology* (Edinburgh, 1931), pp. 101–2.

30. See the articles by D. J. Lim et al. in *Journal of Urology* 153(1995): 1668–70, E. Lipszyc et al. in *European Journal of Pediatric Surgery* 7(1997): 292–95, and Y. Kojima et al. in *Journal of Pediatric Surgery* 34(1999): 1524–26.

31. On the Tichborne malformation, see Kenealy, *Tichborne Tragedy*, pp. 234–43, and Woodruff, *Tichborne Claimant*, pp. 138–40, also anon., *The Tichborne Malformation* (London, 1878), and R. M. Gunnell, *What Did Dr. David Wilson Say?* (London, 1878).

32. Woodruff, *Tichborne Claimant*, p. 434.

33. See the articles by S. E. Swedo et al. in *Pediatrics* 91(1993): 706–13, D. P. Moore in *Journal of Clinical Psychiatry* 57(1996): 407–14, and M. T. Mercadante et al. in *American Journal of Psychiatry* 157(2000): 2036–38.

34. See Lord Cockburn, *The Tichborne Trial* (London, 1874), p. 162, Kenealy, *Introduction*, p. 211, and Maugham, *Tichborne Case*, pp. 52–53. The Claimant himself writes about his "spasms" in a letter to Lady Tichborne reproduced by Gilbert, *Claimant*, p. 100.

35. C. Beavan, *Fingerprints* (London, 2001), pp. 56–60.

36. See J. Brown, *The Tichborne Case Compared with Previous Impostures of the Same Kind* (London, 1874), and Gilbert, *Claimant*, pp. 217–21.

37. G. Lenôtre, *The Woman without a Name* (London, 1923).

38. See the valuable article by H. Ellis in *Applied Cognitive Psychology* 2(1988): 257–64.

39. This case was reported by N. Davies in *Guardian Weekend*, Oct. 17, 1998, pp. 12–15.

40. This theory was first brought forward by an anonymous writer in the *Cornhill Magazine* of July 1929 and later elaborated on by H. T. Wilkins, *Mysteries Solved and Unsolved* (London, 1959), pp. 11–35. Wilkins's case is not helped by his audacious claim that the real Roger Tichborne was alive in Australia during both trials and that the family was aware of this.

41. Both versions are discussed by Roe, *Kenealy*, pp. 160–62.

42. Woodruff, *Tichborne Claimant*, p. 56.

43. Ibid., pp. 51–52.

44. H. Chance Newton, *Crime and the Drama* (London, 1927), pp. 111–16.

45. C. Reade, *The Wandering Heir* (London, 1873). H. af Trolle, *Östersjöns*

*Konung* (Stockholm, 1878), has the eighteenth-century Swedish pirate Georg Drake usurp the identity of the English baronet Sir Allan Fereford and claim his family seat and fiancée. Four novels inspired by the Tichborne case are J. Symons, *The Belting Inheritance* (London, 1965), R. Maugham, *The Link* (London, 1969), M. Schulz, *The Claim* (Sydney, 1996), and B. Alexander, *Death of a Colonial* (New York, 2000). The film is *The Tichborne Claimant*.

CHAPTER 6: THE DUKE OF BAKER STREET

1. For natural reasons, there is no biography of the fifth duke of Portland. What is known about him is summarized by T. Besterman, *The Druce-Portland Case* (London, 1935), pp. 12–17, by D. J. Bradbury, *Welbeck and the Fifth Duke of Portland* (Mansfield, 1989), pp. 31–34, and on the Internet (mss.nottingham.ac.uk/5thbiog.html). More scurrilous accounts appeared in *Modern Detective*, March 30 and April 6, 1898, and in A. M. Druce, *The Great Druce-Portland Mystery* (London, 1898), pp. 2–9. Three novels have been based on the Druce-Portland case: *When Rogues Fall Out*, by the popular crime novelist R. Austin Freeman (London, 1934), was the first, *The Underground Man*, by M. Jackson (London, 1997), is by far the best, and *The Disappearing Duke*, by A. Crofts and T. Freeman-Keel (New York, 2003), is a recent whimsical take on the story.

2. The building works at Welbeck have been well described by D. J. Bradbury, *Welbeck Abbey* (Mansfield, 1986) and *Welbeck and the Fifth Duke*.

3. See the duke's autobiography, *Men, Women and Things* (London, 1937), pp. 30–37.

4. The article in *World* magazine is quoted by Bradbury, *Welbeck and the Fifth Duke*, p. 31.

5. The story of the coffin on the roof is in *Modern Detective*, April 13, 1898. The fear of being buried alive was common in these days; see J. Bondeson, *Buried Alive* (New York, 2001).

6. Walter Thomas Druce had three elder brothers and an elder sister, all illegitimate, as they were born before their parents' marriage in 1851.

7. *Times*, June 23, 1894, p. 18f.

8. *Times*, Sept. 14, 1894, p. 2e, and Sept. 18, 1894, p. 2f.

9. Druce, *Great Druce-Portland Mystery*, gives a succinct summary of her arguments, as does *Modern Detective*, March 30, 1898, pp. 11–13.

10. Forbes Winslow was something of a busybody, not averse to appearing in the newspapers; he shamefacedly tried to explain his erroneous testimony concerning the homeopathist dancing bear in a letter to the *Times*, March 17, 1898, p. 12a. He was already well known for his meddling in the Jack the Ripper case.

11. The Portland (London) Collection, Department of Manuscripts and Special Collections, University of Nottingham Library (PLC) P1/L1/12/1/11, has press clippings from the *Daily Chronicle*, Aug. 9, 1898, *Morning*, Aug. 10, 1898, and *Standard*, Aug. 11, 1898, containing interviews with Mrs. Druce.

12. PLC P1/L1/12/1/12 has several clippings from the *Daily Mail*, from Aug. and Sept. 1898. PLC P1/L1/1/1/32 also lists the *Daily Chronicle* and *Lloyd's Weekly* as overtly pro-Druce newspapers.

13. Druce, *Great Druce-Portland Mystery*, pp. 2–9.

14. The duke's sneering comment is in his autobiography, *Men, Women and Things*, p. 31. The real story of his concerns and those of his solicitors is in PLC P1/L1/1/1–12, P1/L1/9/1/1–6, and P1/L1/11/1/1–16.

15. On Littlechild's career, see S. Evans and P. Gainey, *The Lodger* (London, 1995), pp. 183–87. This book is about a Ripper suspect, the American quack Francis Tumblety, who was originally suggested by Littlechild in a letter written in 1913.

16. PLC P1/L1/11/6/115–55.

17. Various suggestions are in PLC P1/L1/11/5/1–47.

18. PLC P1/L1//9/1/1.

19. PLC P1/L1/1/3/3.

20. See PLC P1/L1/9/1/2, P1/L19/4/38, and P1/L19/4/57. If Thomas

Charles Druce was twenty-one when he married, he should have been born in 1795. The International Genealogical Index does not provide a hit, but there is a Thomas Drew, son of Jon Drew, born in Eardley, Hereford, in 1795, and a Thomas Druce, son of Thomas Druce, born in Winkfield, Berkshire, in 1798.

21. PLC P1/L1/9/1/2.

22. PLC P1/L1/9/2/1.

23. The Mussibini correspondence is in PLC P1/L1/9/2; the letter about his success in persuading Mrs. Hamilton is P1/L1/9/2/34.

24. These depositions are given verbatim in PLC P1/L1/1/2/1.

25. A transcript of the trial is in PLC P1/L1/1/2/2–3.

26. This letter, which Mrs. Druce is unlikely to have herself donated to the ducal archives, is in PLC P1/L1/1/3/2.

27. Anon., *The Druce-Portland Case* (London, 1905), and anon., *Claim to the Portland Millions, Was Druce the Duke?* (London, 1905). In addition to producing these pamphlets, the *Idler* magazine printed much pro-Druce propaganda in vols. 29–31, 1906–7.

28. PLC P1/L1/9/4/127,129

29. Besterman, *Druce-Portland Case*, pp. 46–47.

30. PLC P1/L1/9/4/9,18–20.

31. The arguments presented during the second trial are given by Besterman, *Druce-Portland Case*, pp. 53–269.

32. The Littlechild papers give no hint whether this was the handiwork of one of his detectives, but it may well have been. See the MEPO 3/174 file in the Public Record Office, Kew, for further details.

33. PLC P1/L1/11/6/990 and the file DPP 1/11 in the Public Record Office.

34. PLC P1/L1/6/2–4 and P1/L1/9/4/79,83,86, and also MEPO 3/174 in the Public Record Office.

35. The story of the absconding Caldwell is uncritically reviewed by Bester-

man, *Druce-Portland Case*, pp. 271–73, but the original sources (PLC P1/L1/7, mainly PLC P1/L1/7/5/1–26) make it clear that it was strongly suspected that Caldwell was bluffing about his physical and mental disability. That he also faked his own death to get out of the asylum was a possibility insufficiently pursued at the time.

36. See PLC P1/L1/1/3/2–3. PLC P1/L1/3/5 gives details on her views on world Jewry, and her claim that the sixth duke of Portland had secretly married in Australia.

37. *Times*, June 28, 1895, p. 3f.

38. Not less than £60,000, according to *Modern Detective*, March 30, 1898, pp. 11–13.

39. On Littlechild's counterclaim, see PLC P1/L1/9/4/61. On Mrs. Druce's death, see PLC P1/L1/12/1/232–9.

40. Coburn's letter is in PLC P1/L1/11/6/1202.

41. This confession is abstracted by Besterman, *Druce-Portland Case*, pp. 273–84.

42. See PLC P1/L1/9/4/146,153,155–60 for Druce and P1/L1/9/4/161–206 for Coburn.

43. PLC P1/L1/12/1/232–9.

44. P. Howarth, *Intelligence Chief Extraordinaire: The Life of the 9th Duke of Portland* (London, 1986).

45. G. Headley and W. Meulenkamp, *Follies* (London, 1999), pp. 402–4.

CHAPTER 7: A WORLD OF MYSTERIES

1. On Anna Anderson, see P. Kurth, *Anastasia* (Boston, 1986), and J. Blair Lovell, *Anastasia: The Lost Princess* (London, 1992).

2. See the articles by P. Gill et al. in *Nature Genetics* 6(1994): 130–35, and P. Ivanov et al., ibid., 12(1996): 417–20. A complete history of Anna Anderson and her claim is given by J. Klier and H. Mingay, *The Search*

*for Anastasia* (London, 1995). An opposing analysis is that of L. A. Zhivotovsky in *Annals of Human Biology* 26(1999): 569–77.

3. It is notable that the missing bones were announced to have been found in 2002, according to BBC News online, May 25, 2002.

4. See the article by M. Stoneking et al. in *Nature Genetics* 9(1995): 9–10.

5. Eugenia Smith's book was *Anastasia* (New York, 1963). Pretended children of the last tsar have been critically reviewed by W. Clarke, *The Lost Fortune of the Tsar* (London, 1994), pp. 118–47. For a credulous view, claiming that the entire imperial family was rescued, see G. Richards, *The Rescue of the Romanovs* (Old Greenwich, Conn., 1975). Further mystifications are discussed by M. Occleshaw, *The Romanov Conspiracies* (London, 1993).

6. V. Retrov et al., *The Escape of Alexis* (New York, 1998), and M. Gray, *Blood Relative* (London, 1998).

7. On the Princes in the Tower, see S.B.-R. Poole, *Royal Mysteries and Pretenders* (London, 1969), pp. 1–22, A. Williamson, *The Mystery of the Princes* (Gloucester, 1981), and J. Potter, *Pretenders* (London 1986), pp. 80–112.

8. See P. L. Barbour, *Dimitry, Tsar and Great Prince of All Russia, 1605–06* (London, 1967), and M. Perrie, *Pretenders and Popular Monarchism in Early Modern Russia* (Cambridge, 1995).

9. See T. Wright, *In Search of the Lindbergh Baby* (New York, 1981), and P. L. Rife, *Premature Burials* (Lincoln, Neb., 2001), pp. 68–72; see also a story on Kerwin in *Cisco Bay Weekly*, Sept. 5, 2002, and an article by R. Kiriluk-Hill on www.lindberghtrial.com.

10. E. Aspegren, *Riksspöket* (Stockholm, 1979).

11. On the Sickert legend, see S. Knight, *Jack the Ripper: The Final Solution* (London, 1976), pp. 15–40, M. Fairclough, *The Ripper and the Royals* (London, 1992), pp. 73–115, and P. Begg et al., *The Jack the Ripper A–Z* (London, 1996), pp. 408–9. Joseph Sickert died in 2003.

12. On Charles XII, see the article by S. E. Bring in *Karolinska Förbundets Årsbok*, 1917.

13. On Prince Gustaf, see P. Hallström, *Händelser* (Stockholm, 1927), p. 260.

14. On John Orth, see J. G. Lockhart, *Here Are Mysteries* (London, 1927), pp. 33–64, and Poole, *Royal Mysteries*, pp. 156–66.

15. See J. A. Weston, *Historical Doubts as to the Execution of Ney* (New York, 1895), L. Blythe, *Marshal Ney: A Dual Life* (London, 1934), and R. Furneaux, *Fact, Fake or Fable* (London, 1954), pp. 96–107.

16. On the immortal Booth, see F. L. Bates, *The Escape and Suicide of John Wilkes Booth* (New York, 1908), I. Forrester, *This One Mad Act* (New York ,1937), and Furneaux, *Fact, Fake or Fable*, pp. 12–28. The story of the mummy is in *Dallas Morning News*, of April 10, 1998. A good recent book on the Lincoln assassination, E. Steers Jr., *Blood on the Moon* (New York, 2001), gives the stories of Booth's escape little credence.

17. Many of these stories are reviewed by Rife, *Premature Burials*, a credulous and lighthearted survey of famous people presumed to have faked their deaths; history is well and truly killed in this book, although the protagonists are said to have survived.

18. *Houston Chronicle*, June 14, 2001.

19. See APBnews of April 8, 2000, and the article by A. C. Stone et al. in *Journal of Forensic Sciences* 46(2001): 173–76.

20. On Kitchener, see Lockhart, *Here Are Mysteries*, pp. 227–51, and D. McCormick, *The Mystery of Lord Kitchener's Death* (London, 1959). On Amelia Earhart, see J. Klass, *Amelia Earhart Lives* (New York, 1970), and Rife, *Premature Burials*, pp. 78–89.

21. G. Brewer-Giogio, *Is Elvis Alive?* (New York, 1988), and Rife, *Premature Burials*, pp. 129–33.

22. G. H. Wilson, *Eccentric Mirror* 3, no. 2(1807): 1–36.

23. Anon., *Caraboo* (Bristol, 1817), and S. Burton, *Impostors* (London, 2000), pp. 219–31.

24. R. D. Altick, *Victorian Studies in Scarlet* (New York, 1970).

25. On Demara, see R. Crichton, *The Great Impostor* (New York, 1959); on

Weyman, see G. Sparrow, *The Great Impostors* (London, 1962), pp. 13–23, and Burton, *Impostors*, pp. 36–43. On bogus doctors and modern impostors in general, see the articles by J. Bondeson in *TIKA Information* 5(1991): 12–15, and 6(1991): 22–25, J. Hartland in *Health Services Journal*, Feb. 22, 1996, pp. 26–29, and P. Vallely in *Independent*, Sept. 9, 1996, pp. 4–5.

26. *Guardian*, Dec. 16, 2002.

27. J. A. Jeffreys in *Forensic Science International* 56(1992): 65–76.

28. See the articles by T. Gejrot in *Läkartidningen* 98(2001): 4601, and U. Clason, ibid., p. 5928.

29. P. Cornwell, *Portrait of a Killer: Jack the Ripper—Case Closed* (New York, 2002). Critical reviews of this book include those by A. Daniels in *Daily Telegraph*, Nov. 17, 2002, C. George in *Ripperologist* 43(2002): 20–22, P. Begg and A. Wood, ibid., 44(2002): 1–4, and S. P. Ryder in www.casebook.org.

30. "Sphinx: Mordfall Kaspar Hauser" on www.zdf.de.